OSAG

OSAGE WOMEN AND EMPIRE

Gender and Power

Tai S. Edwards

University Press of Kansas

Published by the University Press of Kansas (Lawrence, Kansas 66045), which was organized by the Kansas Board of Regents and is operated and funded by Emporia State University, Fort Hays State University, Kansas State University, Pittsburg State University, the University of Kansas, and Wichita State University.

© 2018 by the University Press of Kansas

Library of Congress Cataloging-in-Publication Data
Names: Edwards, Tai S., author.
Title: Osage women and empire : gender and power / Tai S. Edwards.
Description: Lawrence, Kansas : University Press of Kansas, [2018] | Includes bibliographical references and index.
Identifiers: LCCN 2018004555| ISBN 9780700626090 (cloth : alk. paper) | ISBN 9780700626106 (pbk. : alk. paper) | ISBN 9780700626113 (ebook)
Subjects: LCSH: Osage women—Social conditions—18th century. | Osage women—Social conditions—19th century. | Sex role.
Classification: LCC E99.O8 E39 2018 | DDC 978.004/975254—dc23.
LC record available at https://lccn.loc.gov/2018004555.

British Library Cataloguing-in-Publication Data is available.

Printed in the United States of America

10 9 8 7 6 5 4 3 2 1

The paper used in this publication is recycled and contains 30 percent postconsumer waste. It is acid free and meets the minimum requirements of the American National Standard for Permanence of Paper for Printed Library Materials Z39.48-1992.

CONTENTS

ILLUSTRATIONS

FIGURES

MAPS

ACKNOWLEDGMENTS

This book is part of my ongoing education on colonialism. Predictably, this all started with a great teacher, Rita Napier at the University of Kansas. Up until my enrollment in her "History of the Plains Indians" course, I thought I was a relatively well-educated person. Rita's teaching, and that of assisting Indigenous graduate students, disproved everything I thought I knew. Now I know that the denial of colonization and genocide have been central to American history and identity from the founding to the present. For settler colonizers (like the United States) in particular, this conquest continues to structure society—for Natives and non-Natives alike. Hence, this text is an inquiry into the logics of settler colonialism, how it was experienced, and how it was resisted in the context of gender.[1]

I am exceedingly grateful to the librarians, archivists, scholars, and museum staff who kindly shared their time and expertise. Enormous thanks to the Osage Nation Museum's former director Kathryn Red Corn, as well as Rhonda Kohnle and Lou Brock, for all of their insight and assistance. Thanks to the University of Kansas and Johnson County Community College (JCCC) libraries, with special appreciation for Jan Brooks at JCCC interlibrary loan. Thanks to David Miros and the Midwest Jesuit Archives; Faye Hubbard and John Waide of the Pius XII Memorial Library at St. Louis University; Dennis Northcott and the Missouri History Museum Library and Research Center; Bob Knecht, Nancy Sherbert, Teresa Coble, and the Kansas State Historical Society; Jacquelyn Slater Reese and the University of Oklahoma Libraries; Riche Sorensen and the Smithsonian American Art Museum; the Kenneth Spencer Research Library; and the Denver Public Library. Thanks also to J. Frederick Fausz, Tanis Thorne, Theda Perdue, Rose Stremlau, and Alessandra Tamulevich. A big, big thanks to everyone at *Kansas History: A Journal of the Central Plains*, especially Virgil Dean. And Bill Nelson makes incredible maps!

Thank you to my mentors and colleagues. George Mason University's (GMU) legendary Robert T. Hawkes Jr. and the University of Kansas's (KU) Rita Napier were both transformative to my education and career. Perhaps more importantly, I am grateful for their friendship, and I miss them both.

Paul Kelton is perhaps the best PhD adviser ever! His *sustained* commitment to his graduate students' education, research, and career is really astonishing and directly aided the completion of this book. Thank you to all of the other faculty members who contributed to my education and research at the following: KU—Kim Warren, Don Worster, Greg Cushman, Ann Schofield, Jennifer Weber, Jonathan Earle, and Leslie Tuttle; GMU—Paula Petrik, T. Mills Kelly, Jane Turner Censer, and Zach Schrag. Thanks as well to the Hall Center for the Humanities. Thank you to my graduate student colleagues Stephanie Russell, Lon Strauss, Eric Anderson, Brady DeSanti, Kyle and Becca Anthony, Shelly Cline, Mary McMurray, Chikako Mochizuki, Amanda Schlumpberger, James Quinn, Karl Rubis, Jeremy Byers, John Rosenberg, and Jason Emerson. At my PhD graduation, I walked the hill with Kristen Epps, and we have metaphorically continued walking together as professional historians; I am so fortunate to have her as a friend and colleague. And a special thanks to Ethan Schmidt for his mentoring and collaboration; losing him has been deeply felt by many. I am fortunate to work with some of the most supportive colleagues at JCCC, especially in the history department, specifically, James Leiker (who has worked tirelessly to mentor me as a teacher and scholar), Sarah Boyle, Jay Antle, Jim Lane, Sean Daley, Ed Smith, Sam Bell, Farrell Jenab, Andrea Broomfield, Vince Miller, and Allison Smith. Thank you to the University Press of Kansas and especially Kim Hogeland, Kelly Chrisman Jacques, and Michael Kehoe for all of their work in seeing this through to publication.

I am also fortunate to have a uniquely supportive group of friends and neighbors. I am particularly grateful to the network of women who are central to my life in every way.

Finally, I want to thank my family for their constant encouragement and interest in my work. To my husband, Ryan; my parents, Bruce and Denise Gerhart; my sister Laci Gerhart-Barley; and my sons Rockwell and Wiley: I love you.

The American Board of Commissioners for Foreign Missions (ABCFM) throughout the nineteenth century spent considerable time, energy, and funds to "civilize" supposedly "savage" people, both at home and abroad. The ABCFM distributed numerous publications to educate sympathetic Christians on the challenges facing missionaries, in hopes of spurring charitable donations to support the missions. Accounts of Indigenous gender roles proved a favored topic to these ends. Independent women, engaged in manual labor and often sexually free, were labeled "primitive" and thus in need of reform and even rescue.[1] Reflecting these themes, in 1827 the ABCFM published correspondence from Reverend William F. Vaill, a missionary to the Osage.[2]

> And [the women's] condition is truly degraded; for while the men are reclining at their ease in their camps, smoking, or telling stories, or engaged in the sport of war, or of hunting; the females have to build their houses, plant their corn, dress the skins, transport the baggage, and wood and water, and bear many a heavy burden. Instead of one day of rest in seven, they have not one from their marriage until death. It is one unceasing round of servitude and drudgery. And shall it be always thus? Shall their daughters be trained to servitude only? No—is the response of every female breast. Let us send them the Gospel, that they too may become respected, and useful, and happy.[3]

Such accounts prompt many questions. Were Osage women truly exploited and subjugated in their society? Can we trust Vaill's conclusions about men or women? Depending on how far back you want to go, female subordination had a long tradition in European (and later, American) history. Ancient philosophers and medieval theologians, referencing the biblical story of Eve's creation from Adam's rib in Genesis, helped entrench European patriarchy. Under this hierarchical organization, men wielded power over dependent women and children. Correspondingly, the work of men conducted outside the home in the "public sphere" held greater importance than that of women

Osage Woman and Child (detail, used with permission of the Denver Public Library, Western History Collection, call number X-32588). This photograph, believed to have been taken sometime after 1880, shows an Osage woman with her child in a cradleboard. Though less richly dressed than Wáh-chee-te in George Catlin's famous portrait from 1834, this woman's dress is nearly identical to her kinswoman's from at least half a century earlier. (George Catlin, *Letters and Notes on the Manners, Customs, and Condition of the North American Indians*, vol. 2, 3rd ed. [New York: Wiley and Putnam, 1844], 40–44; Denver Public Library, Digital Collections, accessed July 19, 2017, http://digital.denverlibrary.org/cdm/singleitem/collection /p15330coi122/id/35253/rec/112.)

conducted inside the home in the "private sphere." In other words, as historian Carol Devens has argued, European colonizers came from "political and socio-economic systems shaped by an earlier feudal patriarchy, a social order rooted in a tradition of masculine authority and activity that presupposed feminine passivity and domesticity." By the nineteenth century, a respectable Euro-American woman was considered "naturally" frail and weak, requiring protection from a laborious, lower-class, less evolved life. This social construction biased Europeans and Americans in their interactions with Indigenous people, producing misunderstandings. Women's labor was just one piece of evidence, not only of their alleged degraded condition, but also of an entire Indigenous society's lack of civilization.[4]

Unfortunately, for some time, many scholars shared this gendered bias and took sources like Vaill's at face value, believing Native women endured an existence scarcely better than slaves. Theories of universal female subjugation seemed to reinforce this view. Scholars today read sources like Vaill's with a much more critical eye. Gunlög Fur argued that a scholar's awareness of source-material bias can be "a useful and fruitful methodological tool" because one must critically examine what is both present and absent in a particular source in order to draw historical conclusions. To understand cultural systems like gender and the significance of behaviors in that context, ethnohistorians (including me) employ an interdisciplinary approach—involving archaeology, anthropology, ethnography, linguistics, and oral history—combined with a judicious use of documentary evidence. Certainly Vaill illuminated his own patriarchal, missionizing bias; yet even so, information can be gleaned from such material to learn about the lives of women and their roles in Indigenous societies. Studying women adds their story to the overarching history, while placing gender construction at the center of historical inquiry, complicating our existing historical knowledge and potentially creating an entirely new history.[5]

Gender is a useful method of analyzing Native life during colonization because gender served as a dominant feature of Native North American cultures. Through gender roles, every society constructs what behaviors are appropriate for each sex, while simultaneously defining relative status and power.[6] Unlike Euro-American society, many Indigenous societies, including the Osage, operated under a system of gender complementarity, where men and women performed typically separate but equally valued tasks. Individual autonomy, rather than a gender hierarchy and dependency, served as the basis for social relationships. Clan or extended family kinship and reciprocity bound people together in communities. Men and women both held status and power in their societies, which manifested in various forms for each gender, all sanctioned and reiterated by ritual. Though seemingly rigid, gender roles involved flexibility and variability, so men and women could help one another and make choices addressing material or spiritual circumstances. Accordingly, Osage society included more than two genders, which was the norm across Native North America.[7]

European and American colonization impacted gender in different ways over time in every community. Native women and men creatively confronted change by incorporating new technologies, political systems, and religious forms into established belief systems. Eventually Europeans, and later, Americans, colonized the entire continent, assaulting every aspect of Native life. Social constructions, including gender, being primarily housed and transmitted through ritual, were especially vulnerable to colonization. When a community, for a variety of reasons, abandoned all or part of a ceremony, the values such ritual supported likewise waned. Disturbance to the economy also rapidly altered gender systems. Yet numerous examples indicate across centuries that Native people, especially women, sought alternatives to marginality, recreating their social roles in new contexts. Gender then functioned to maintain societal order and served as a central site for experiencing, adapting to, and resisting the monumental change brought on by colonization.[8]

Even with several decades of scholarship on Native North American women and gender complementarity, significant gaps remain in the literature.[9] The Osage historiography emphasizes—for good reason—their hegemony in the western Mississippi valley in the late eighteenth and early nineteenth centuries. Once the French built trading posts along the periphery of Osage territory in the 1720s, they became middlemen in the exchanges between the French and more western and southern Indigenous communities. French traders attempted to initiate trade relations with western and southern Native groups; however, the Osage prevented, violently if necessary, any threats (both Native and European) to their position as middlemen. Taking advantage of their large population (estimates range from 10,000 to 18,000) and resource-rich location between the Mississippi River and the prairie plains, the Osage became the primary economic and military power in western Louisiana. As historian Kathleen DuVal put it, the Osage "proved far more successful than either France or Spain at building a mid-continental empire."[10]

Scholars agree the Osage held preeminent regional power during the eighteenth and early nineteenth centuries, but not everyone uses the term "empire."[11] Because all North American Indigenous people eventually experienced European or neo-European imperial marginalization, exploitation, and repeated efforts to exterminate culture and people that continue in many ways to the present, it is important to define and differentiate Indigenous imperialism. For Osage historian Louis Burns, his ancestors' dominance is empowering. During French and Spanish colonization, Burns stated that the "Osages conquered an area about the same size as that conquered by Bonaparte in roughly the same amount of time . . . [and through] blockade of the Missouri and Arkansas Rivers [they] denied Europeans any significant access to the heart of North America for one hundred fifty years," creating "the Osage empire." Based on Burns's analysis, the primary differences between the Osage and European or American empires were land claims and subjugation. Europeans and Americans often "claimed" Indigenous land over which they had no real authority. In contrast, the Osage actually used their land—for settlements, farming, or hunting—and patrolled all of their territory. Most notably, though, the Osage did not rule over subjugated Native groups in their empire.[12]

Pekka Hämäläinen made similar arguments in The Comanche Empire. The Comanches "never attempted to build a European-style imperial system" with a single central authority, settlement colonies, or direct rule over subject peoples. Instead, they built an empire using a more fluid, "creative blending of violence, diplomacy, extortion, trade, and kinship politics." Even so, Comanchería certainly resembled European empires in various ways: they conquered neighboring peoples, and exploited resources—creating a Comanche-dominated society tied together through a vast trade and alliance network. According to Hämäläinen, "Comanches exercised power on an imperial scale, but they did so without adopting an imperial ideology and without building a rigid, European-style empire." Though the Comanche would not have identified themselves as an "imperial power" at the time, Hämäläinen said, "It does not mean that we should not recognize them as one."[13]

The same could be said of the Osage: they used violence (and sometimes creative diplomacy) to control territory and people; they raided rivals for valuable goods; and they exploited natural resources. The decentralizing nature of Osage communities and politics meant power did not radiate out from a unified center in their territory or even among their own people. They too lacked an imperial ideology—nothing like the "savagery" and "civilization" dichotomy employed by Europeans and Americans ever informed Osage actions or justified their conquest. They expanded because they had the desire and ability to do so. Even though Europeans and Americans complained about (and even envied) Osage power, no one called them an empire at the time.[14] Though scholars might not agree on calling this dominance an Osage "empire" even today, the general consensus that imperial domination derived from some combination of political, economic, or military control certainly applied to the Osage in the eighteenth and early nineteenth centuries. At the same time, the lack of ideological and internal subjugation presented a marked difference from European and American imperial ventures in North America. As the Osage established their empire, other people definitely lost their lives, their property, and sometimes their family members. But cultural sovereignty was never under attack.

Studies of the Osage empire's rise and fall have almost entirely emphasized the lives of men as hunters, warriors, traders, and political leaders.[15] This is a common bias in the historiography of war, diplomacy, and politics—topics often associated with the masculine "sphere" in Euro-American and Native societies. Scholarship examining the adaptability, creativity, and skill with which Indigenous people built such empires has typically also concentrated on men, implying that women had little to do with men or tribal hegemony—especially if expanded power resulted from increased war or trade.[16] Kathleen DuVal argued that in Osage society, "Valued men were successful warriors and plains hunters . . . [so] expanding their hunting and trading and violently excluding other Indian hunters from French trade increased Osage men's opportunities to prove their manhood." Through warfare in particular, she stated, men could gain "influence and prestige." Historian Willard Rollings likewise contended the Osage culture "had always placed great value on economic and military success . . . [and] Osage men acquired status as a result of their hunting prowess and their courage in battle . . . [so] increased hunting and raiding fit well within the older social framework," resulting in their regional hegemony. Unfortunately, without more in-depth knowledge of the Osage gender construction, one could misinterpret their imperial growth as elevating men's status and correspondingly reducing that of women. As DuVal concluded, "Men's valor had changed Osage history. While women's economic importance remained strong . . . their place probably became less central than in the past." In sum, the Osage empire ostensibly resulted from men's hunting and warrior success, undermining gender complementarity.[17]

Certainly, hunting and war prowess directly related to a man's status but, in this society, hunting and war success, like everything else, involved women and men. Cosmology defined Osage men and women as necessary pairs; consequently, to understand either gender, or the power of the group as a whole, they must be studied together.[18] In order to provide for and protect their communities, men had to kill animals and enemies. Conversely, women, as creators and life channels, did not physically associate with death. This lack of physical association has obscured women's direct spiritual and economic relationship with hunting. While men hunted—a coordinated physical and ritual endeavor—women simultaneously prayed to Wa-kon'-da (Mysterious Power) for animal reproduction, hunter success, and community perpetuation through the birth of children. And when men returned with animal products, women commenced the laborious meat preservation and hide manufacturing that facilitated the entire community's subsistence and trade wealth. Processing the proceeds of the hunt into something useful (food, clothing, trade goods, etc.) was considered a creative act, under the purview of women. Scholars often passingly, like DuVal above, acknowledge the economic significance of women's work in the Osage empire.[19] But women's central economic role reflected their equal status with men.

The US settler empire eventually destroyed the Osage empire. All levels of government and settlers intended to eliminate Indigenous people so that Americans in particular, and the nation in general, could benefit from the wealth of Native land. By the early nineteenth century, the United States "claimed" the Louisiana Purchase (including the Osage homeland), which was intended to be the new residence of eastern Native groups who were pressured, and eventually forced, to leave and thus open their land for American development. These eastern Native nations, serving as "proxy invaders" for the United States, increasingly encroached on Osage territory, competing for land and game. Then, Euro-American settlers invaded, further compromising Osage dominance. Americans justified acquisitioning Native land by claiming that the "savage" Native lifestyle was unsustainable in the modern world, and it was the duty of "civilized" people—supposedly Americans— to remake Natives into Christian yeoman farmers and save them from what Americans asserted was inevitable extinction. Assimilation programs then served as the final elimination effort to rid the United States of the rightful owners of the land.[20]

With their lives under siege, Osage leaders had little choice when, in 1825, federal officials demanded land cessions to expel the Osage from Missouri and Arkansas.[21] Now confined to a small fraction of their western territories in present-day Kansas, variable weather, repeated disease outbreaks, and settler invasion further challenged Osage survival.[22] They adapted to these changing circumstances, becoming increasingly mobile while depending more and more on hunting and trade for subsistence. While missionaries unsuccessfully tried to convert them to Christianity and Euro-American culture, American settlers built houses, began farming, stole Osage crops, and allowed their livestock to graze in Osage fields.[23] Finally, in July 1870, Congress simply added provisions to an Indian appropriation bill to buy Osage land, eliminate their presence in Kansas, and provide for their final confinement in Indian Territory where they settled in 1872.[24]

Colonization brought significant change, but it did not fundamentally alter the Osage economy or spiritual practices until the late nineteenth century. This study examines that period of continuity. Osage complementary gender roles manifested in virtually every aspect of their lives. Women and men who had long collaborated in subsistence and Native trade expanded these roles to incorporate new people, technologies, and exchange networks after European contact. The scale and location of Osage hunting and warfare notably increased during the French and Spanish colonial period, which some have viewed as bolstering male status, leading to declensionist assumptions about the role of Osage women.[25] However, the Osage viewed warrior success as the product of both men's physical and spiritual, and women's spiritual efforts. And a man's hunting success only became valuable when the women in his family processed those hides into desirable goods, making women as vital as men to the hide trade. At the same time, Osage women did not abandon their role as producers, and continued farming, with particularly large bounties while they remained in self-selected town sites. Once confined to Kansas, where climate and settler invasion made subsistence more difficult, Osage men and women increasingly focused on hunting and trade as the best way to reduce disease virulence and avoid those who wanted to change their culture. While they continued to practice their combination agriculture-hunting-trading economy— a system that predated European contact—the social structures that underlay this economy, including gender construction, endured.

By focusing on gender, this study argues that men *and* women were the critical actors in the period when the Osage rose to power in the western Mississippi valley and when that power later declined on their Kansas reservation. Clearly, colonization changed Osage life, especially in terms of regional power structures, but they repeatedly adapted to this in ways that guaranteed their survival in both the spiritual and physical realms, which required men and women working together. Gender, in addition to other factors, contributed to Osage resistance to colonization.

The following chapters examine how the first century and a half of colonization impacted the Osage gender construction. It is not the intention of this book to serve as a definitive guide to the Osage ceremonial complex or their imperial and political history—that has been done with great skill by other scholars. Instead this book brings gender construction to the fore in the context of Osage history through the nineteenth century. In terms of sources, this study utilizes many traditional archival materials, including ethnographies, government documents, missionary records, and traveler narratives. As noted earlier, the creators of these sources harbored significant biases; hence, critical analysis was essential to using such material. Some of the most significant sources for this project, though, came directly from Osage scholars. Osage men and women—John Joseph Mathews, Louis Burns, George Tinker, Robert Warrior, Andrea Hunter, Jean Dennison, and Alice Anne Callahan, among many others—have produced decolonizing scholarship that "removes colonial interests from central positions in the narrative and shifts the focus to Indigenous people."[26] As Warrior has demonstrated, this scholarship is part of an often overlooked, centuries-long intellectual tradition that has asserted Indigenous sovereignty, and resisted colonization and assimilation.[27] These powerful sources are referenced throughout this text and prove invaluable to studying Osage gender.

Chapter 1 explores the cosmological foundation of Osage gender complementarity. A significant amount of Osage spiritual, ritual, and historical knowledge was recorded in early twentieth-century ethnographies compiled by Francis La Flesche, an Omaha man and Bureau of American Ethnology (BAE) employee. As two Dhegian-Siouan nations, the Omaha and Osage had a shared history—mutually intelligible languages—in addition to ritual and organizational similarity. Justifiably, scholars often criticize ethnographies as biased sources in documenting gender constructions because men were often excluded from women's ceremonial or even daily activities; however,

La Flesche interviewed several women and added their insights to his work. Female informant Mon'-ci-tse-xi (Julia Lookout, whom La Flesche referred to as "Mrs. Fred Lookout") provided information used throughout La Flesche's Osage dictionary, including the traditional uses of corn. Another, Hon-be'-do-ka (called Wakon'dahionbe in another La Flesche text) dictated chants and songs associated with her role as a ceremonial weaver. And Mrs. Btho'-ga-ih-ge provided a ceremonial loom. With his cultural knowledge, language skills, and diverse informants, including women, La Flesche produced important cosmological resources.[28]

These ethnographies and other primary sources are used as the basis for understanding gender roles in earlier times. This methodology, known as upstreaming, allows ethnohistorians to specifically explore continuity within a culture and relies on the assumption that "major patterns of culture remain stable over long periods of time, producing repeated uniformities." Thus, scholars can follow cultural constructions from the known ethnological present, such as the Osage rituals La Flesche recorded in the early twentieth century, to the less well-known past, in this case, the eighteenth and nineteenth centuries. Upstreaming demonstrates cultural continuity when source material from the earlier centuries (discussed in subsequent chapters) bears out the findings La Flesche recorded much later.[29]

The Non'-hon-zhin-ga (Osage priesthood) organized Osage life based on the dual masculine and feminine forces they observed in celestial and seasonal cycles. Rituals required both male and female participation and defined a sexual division of labor without hierarchical difference. Spiritually, two things were necessary for continued national existence: (1) women creating, and (2) men protecting and providing. This meant women created future citizens (bearing children), food (cultivating crops, gathering wild foods, curing meat), trade goods (tanned hides, food), and all the domestic items (clothing, lodges, utensils, etc.). Men killed game animals (providing raw materials for food and trade), and enemies in warfare (to protect homes and families). Therefore, men and women worked together to guarantee the nation's future. Because of their different roles, each gender achieved status and power in distinct ways: women were born with it and men had to earn it. But life was not as strictly divided as one might think. In order for hunting to produce anything, men had to kill, and women had to process. Warfare required male valor, but women ritually combined their courage with men's, and both were credited in victories. Men held political leadership positions as chiefs, but their authority was subordinate to the priesthood, which incorporated women in a variety of ways. In other words, men and women collaborated in virtually everything, and very little could be strictly divided into "separate spheres."[30]

Chapter 2 examines how the advent of European colonization impacted gender construction, as the Osage built an empire through expanded hunting and trade while using violence toward Europeans and Natives to maintain their hegemony. This chapter disputes that the era of expanded hunting, warfare, and exchange disrupted gender complementarity or diminished female status, because all of these things, physically or spiritually, required women and men. In the eighteenth century, the Osage incorporated Europeans into Native systems of dominance and exchange while preserving their cosmology. Once the Osage claimed exclusive French trade, they altered their social organization to facilitate commercial hunting, while maintaining significant agricultural production.[31] Women continued to play a central spiritual role in Osage warfare and corresponding military victories. In the hide trade, both men's and women's work in procuring and processing hides gained additional economic importance. The Osage responded to frequent male absence and mortality in their empire by adopting matrilocality and polygyny. Women's sexual freedom and availability for divorce precluded female subjugation in this context. With greater trade competition and the end of New France in the late eighteenth century, the Osage, especially prominent clans, eventually embraced intermarriage with European and American traders, where women served as an economic tie between two communities that relied on each other for power and wealth. Osage dominance during this period resulted from the combined physical and spiritual roles of men and women.[32]

Chapter 3 describes life in the early nineteenth century, when the Osage empire declined as the US settler empire expelled eastern Indigenous groups into Louisiana territory, closely followed by Euro-American missionaries and settlers. Warfare with these "proxy invaders," particularly the Cherokee, severely disrupted Osage exchange and subsistence. Of course that was the point, and federal officials leveraged it to force Osage land cessions. Missionization had long served as the ideological justification for imperial manipulation, exploitation, and even genocide. Indigenous people's alleged "savagery" negated their right to their resources, which "civilized" people—Europeans and Americans—could rightfully acquisition while working to convert Natives into "civilized" people.[33] The Osage resisted any efforts to change their spiritual beliefs and instead used Protestant missionaries as mediators in confronting the mounting American presence in the region. Federal Indian policy's contradictions also undermined the civilization program. US trade relations with the Osage encouraged commercial hunting, which facilitated a mobile lifestyle that kept the Osage away from missionary influence during much of the year. Throughout the 1820s the Osage continued much of their established subsistence, trade, and ritual activities. However, the US settler empire intended to eliminate Indigenous people, and when it came to the Osage in Missouri and Arkansas, this mission was unfortunately accomplished.

Chapter 4 discusses the Osage experience on their Kansas reservation. This is a period somewhat marginalized in the historiography because it was after their imperial hegemony and before their shrewd and profitable use of land sales and ranching, farming, and oil drilling leases in Oklahoma.[34] Life in Kansas presented considerable challenges for the Osage in virtually every sense. Though they had long hunted in the region, they now had to build their towns and agricultural fields in a new landscape that placed significant pressure on gendered work. Weather, insects, and colonizing settlers hindered agriculture and thus undermined the associated ritual practices and their reiteration of complementarity. Nevertheless, women kept planting as the entire nation tried to maintain their spiritual and physical survival. In Kansas, the Osage preserved other aspects of gendered work as they focused on hunting and trade (a product of men's and women's labor) as the primary method of subsistence. Hunting and trading were successful early on in Kansas, but dwindling game and settler horse theft made acquiring bison increasingly difficult over time, limiting survival in both the physical and spiritual contexts. And as the primary Osage enemy became Americans, they abstained from warfare, preferring to preserve lives rather than fight the invading population, meaning the war rituals that reaffirmed women's and men's roles in perpetuating the nation correspondingly declined.

Also in Kansas, federal officials funded the Catholic Osage Mission, and these missionaries hoped to succeed where their Protestant predecessors failed. Difficulty in farming—for Americans and Natives—hindered these "civilizing" efforts, and the Osage reliance on hunting produced a mobile lifestyle that again kept them away from the missionaries and federal agents. Yet the Osage were hospitable toward missionaries, using them as diplomatic allies in relations with the federal government and as sources of education needed to survive in the American empire. From the 1830s into the 1850s, the Osage supplemented their economy with federal annuity payments and trade with the Comanche on the western plains. This additional income ended at the same time American settlers arrived. Settler depredations, variable climate, and disease prompted prolonged use of mobility as a survival strategy. The rising power of the American population culminated in the final Osage confinement in present-day Oklahoma, where their lives changed in unprecedented ways: their agriculture-hunting-trading economy was destroyed, the rituals that defined this economy no longer seemed relevant, and their population was significantly diminished.

However, their time in Kansas was important because they effectively used their religious and economic structure, built on gender complementarity, to control and direct change. With all of their struggles in Kansas, this should have been the period when the Osage people became culturally or literally extinct. As Patrick Wolfe has argued, "Settler colonialism destroys to replace." The United States needed the "elimination of the natives in order to establish itself on their territory."[35] The pressure just to survive was intended to make the Osage and all Indigenous people acquiesce to demands by federal agents and missionaries to change everything. Osage women should have been subjugated as men became farmers and everyone adopted Christianity. Or the destruction and despair of it all should have killed them. But that did not happen. Maintaining gendered work and the corresponding religious practices in still-relevant ways preserved their social structure that had long used self-directed adaptations to persist and even thrive in a changing world. In Kansas they made some changes to their economic and ritual practices in light of new circumstances. However, many of the "old ways" —though severely challenged—were the best methods of survival. In Oklahoma, things were different, and that was where they made more significant changes. Nevertheless, the longevity and solidarity the Osage nation has today would never have happened if they had become assimilated, sedentary, Christian farmers in Kansas. And that is why aspects of gender complementarity still connect the modern Osage with their imperial ancestors.

The conclusion briefly discusses the importance of "recovering the feminine" in the Osage empire and connects this study's main arguments with Osage history after the nineteenth century. As US colonization continued, Osage economics and spirituality changed, but again, the Osage directed these changes in whatever ways they could to maintain Osage sovereignty. And most notably, gender complementarity remains prominent.[36]

The Osage belong to the Dhegian-Siouan language family, which also includes the Kansa, Omaha, Ponca, and Quapaw. Similar language, oral history, and religious and social organization indicate that these five nations previously lived as one group east of the Mississippi River. All Dhegian oral traditions describe a westward migration, across the Mississippi River, after which the five groups eventually separated from one another. Scholars disagree, however, on Dhegian history prior to French colonization. Some argue Dhegian peoples were once Chesapeake Piedmont residents who eventually migrated to the lower Ohio River until sometime in the seventeenth century, when they moved westward in search of game. Other scholars contend that aggressive eastern groups, possibly the Iroquois, forced this westward migration. Still others, using comparisons of Osage and Omaha rituals with Cahokia Mounds archeological data, suggested that Dhegian peoples may have lived at Cahokia. The Osage Nation Museum also states the Osage "are believed to be descendants" of Cahokia residents.[1]

Regardless of the starting point, the Osage eventually built their towns where the Little Osage, Marmaton, and Marais des Cygnes Rivers came together forming the Osage River, in present-day western Missouri. The Osage utilized the diverse prairie plains environment and subsisted on agriculture, gathering, and hunting. This semisedentary life involved spending part of the year in large settlements, each with over 100 lodges and 1,000 residents. Their annual cycle began in April when women planted their corn in the fertile flood plains along the rivers near their homes. In late May or early June the entire community traveled to the plains, where men hunted bison and women cured the meat—most of the year's supply—and tanned the hides. By late July they returned to their towns so women could harvest some of the "green" corn (also called roasting ears) and store it for winter. Women then planted squash (often called pumpkins) and beans (often called peas) between the remaining cornstalks; and once all reached maturity, they were harvested, dried, and also stored. In the late summer, women gathered many wild plant foods, likewise storing the surplus for winter. In late September or early October the townsfolk again traveled to the plains to hunt and process bison products, acquiring the thicker and more valuable hides until cold weather set in, and then they separated into small family groups, following game animals to sheltered parts of the prairies or forests. Much smaller hunts conducted by individuals or a few men, often acquiring deer or fur-bearing animals, continued throughout the winter to augment the stored foods. Bear hunts for meat and oil notably provided winter nourishment as well. And once weather warmed enough for planting, everyone gathered in the home communities to begin the cycle anew.[2]

For the Osage, and Indigenous Americans in general, this cycle took place in a spiritual context. According to various Osage traditions, differing by clan, the people once existed in the invisible upper worlds where they acquired souls, intellect, and communication. Desiring to descend to the earth below, they requested and received blessings from Day (sun, grandfather), Night (moon, grandmother), Male Star (morning star), and Female Star (evening star). A golden eagle then led the people down through the "four heavens," and they "alighted" on the "tops of seven trees"—some say seven rocks—finally acquiring physical bodies as they emerged into the visible world (earth). Because the Wa-zha'-zhe (water people) were the first to reach the earth, they were deemed the "mother group," and thus these "Children of the Middle Waters" or "Little Ones" would henceforth refer to themselves as Wa-zha'-zhe (pronounced "Wah-zhah-zhay" and later corrupted by the French into "Osage"). Unfortunately, water covered the ground beneath the trees. Various animals tried and failed to part the waters for the Little Ones, until finally, Great Elk "threw himself [four times] violently upon the earth . . . and he made the land of the earth to appear, to become dry and habitable." Then Great Elk made the winds of the four cardinal directions, giving each the "breath of life," and instructed "the little ones [to] call to the winds when in distress . . . and their voice shall always be heard by Wa-kon-da . . . [and] they shall . . . live to see old age as they travel the path of life." Great Elk threw himself on the ground again, creating various geological features—including plains, hills, mountains, valleys, streams, and rivers. Lastly, different animals—depending on the clan—provided various items necessary for the Little Ones' survival and success, such as food plants, game animals, and sacred objects.[3]

In the early days of their existence, the people united for protection with little formal organization. At some point, an exclusive group of "seers," known as the Non'-hon-zhin-ga (translated as Little Old Men), assembled in an attempt to formulate national governance. Osage rituals repeatedly referenced the people's "move to a new country." This phrase denoted instances where the Non'-hon-zhin-ga (which eventually became a priesthood) changed the religious, social, or political organization in order to accommodate new realities facing the nation. Various circumstances (both before and after colonization) prompted such changes, including environmental events, incorporating new people and clans, creating civil government through dual hereditary chieftains, defining war and peace ceremonies, and arranging war expeditions.[4] The Non'-hon-zhin-ga's power within Osage society stemmed in part from their willingness to accept and direct cultural change by incorporating new elements into the older cosmological framework; as historian Willard Rollings argued, such flexibility proved central to the nation's rise to power after colonization.[5]

Over time, the Non'-hon-zhin-ga, pondering the source of life, observed a connection between celestial cycles and seasonal vegetation changes on earth. They concluded that procreative relationships between the sky and earth, sun and moon, and the morning and evening stars provided the continuity of life. The ancient Non'-hon-zhin-ga believed celestial bodies moved under the guidance of a governing power, called Wa-kon'-da (Mysterious Power), "which gives life to all things and whose abode is believed to be within everything and in every place, both celestial and terrestrial." Wa-kon'-da's silent, invisible, and creative power gave life to the sun, moon, stars, and earth, maintaining eternal cycles in perfect order. As the source of life, wherever Wa-kon'-da moved, there was life. The mysterious presence of Wa-kon'-da made the sun, moon, stars, earth, humans, insects, animals, grasses, trees, and water indivisibly one.[6]

Humans bore responsibility for their survival, but they could not sustain life without Wa-kon'-da's aid.[7] Their integrated spirituality manifested in religious ceremonies that sought Wa-kon'-da's assistance while reminding everyone of the universe's interconnectedness and the Osage role in it. Accomplishing anything—fruitful harvests, hunting game, and war victories—required spiritual and physical action. And success in any of these pursuits necessitated celebratory ritual as well. A person's life cycle, from infant naming, to marriage, to healing the sick, to interring the dead, involved requisite ceremony.[8] Even on a daily basis, through prayer vigils (public rituals), each Osage person appealed to *Wa-kon'-da* for a long, healthy life and preservation of the nation. *Wa-kon'-da*'s mysterious creative power embodied in the night brought forth the day—"two mystic powers that forever follow each other." Therefore, night was the "mother of day." Sunrise symbolized the merging of masculine and feminine forces and life's beginning and end. At dawn, men, women, and children touched the earth—viewed as "one of the abiding places of Wa-kon-da"—and placed soil on their foreheads and then stood in the open air, or in doorways of their homes and cried, lamented, and wailed for *Wa-kon'-da*'s life-giving aid and to mourn the deceased. Their cries mimicked the "natal cries" of babies— because when children were born, they were considered "little stars from the Spiritland," coming from the sky where they had learned "prayer-crying to *Wah'Kon-Tah* . . . before they came to earth." With the sun also considered "one of the abiding places of Wa-kon-da," the Osage repeated these prayers at midday and at dusk, following the sun's "path of life" across the horizon.[9]

Based on their observations, the ancient *Non'-hon-zhin-ga* gradually formulated a social organization that, in its entirety, symbolized the universe's duality, and thus *Wa-kon'-da*, in all visible aspects. The *Non'-hon-zhin-ga* recognized masculine and feminine forces throughout nature and characterized this complementarity in all Osage rituals. They concluded that all life resulted from the union of the two greatest physical forces, the masculine sky and the feminine earth, which combined to give life to all things. They divided the people into two moieties—*Tsi'-zhu*, representing the sky, and *Hon'-ga*, representing the earth—that united to ensure the Osage future.[10] *Tsi'-zhu* men married *Hon'-ga* women and vice versa, binding together both divisions as inseparably as *Wa-kon'-da* bound the sky and earth. The *Tsi'-zhu* and *Hon'-ga* people were further subdivided into clans.[11] Each clan, represented in every town, had a unique creation story, life symbol, sacerdotal function, and *wa-xo'-be* (sacred bundle). Thus, performing ceremonies required every clan's participation, further reinforcing national solidarity.[12]

Osage cosmology defined women as "the channel through whom all human life must proceed and continue."[13] The Osage revered and adored women because *Wa-kon'-da* favored them with the mystic power of creating human life and performing the sacred duty of motherhood.[14] *Wa-kon'-da*'s greatest demonstration of divine favor manifested in women through their perpetual fertility and birth of children, indicating *Wa-kon'-da*'s enduring desire for "a never-ending line of descendants," and thus the nation's future existence.[15] In the Osage language, "*Wa-kon*" means "mysterious," and "*da*" means "great"; therefore, "*Wa-kon'-da*" means "great mysterious." The term "*wa-ko*" meaning "woman" also refers to women's mysterious creative power.[16] Men basically provided "raw materials"—such as sperm or game animals—that women "reproduced" into something useful. Women's work demonstrated their reproductive and creative role: bearing and rearing children, raising crops, gathering edible plants, processing meat and hides, constructing lodges, and manufacturing all of the clothing and utensils of their household.[17]

Men then protected "woman" and everything she created: "the children she bears, the home she builds for their shelter and comfort, [and] the fields she cultivates." Likewise, "the land upon which the tribe depends for plant and animal food must be held against invasion."[18] The ancient *Non'-hon-zhin-ga* regarded war as a "necessary evil." Consequently, men's heroic deeds defending homes and fields counted as more prestigious *o'don* (war honors) than aggressive acts against an enemy. In fact, when a warrior ceremonially recounted his war honors, he had to recount one *o'don* for protecting homes and fields for every *o'don* he earned in attacking an enemy.[19] As the providers and protectors of their communities, men hunted, conducted diplomatic and war expeditions, and manufactured the tools necessary for all of their work.[20]

All people held power in Osage society, and neither domination nor submission defined relationships between men and women. Rituals reaffirmed the necessity and interdependence of both genders to ensure group survival, without giving their separate and autonomous duties comparative significance over one another.[21] Osage boys spent their entire childhood and adolescence learning successful hunting techniques and war strategies in order to excel at these pursuits during adulthood. Certainly, farming, tanning, food preparation, lodge building, and all the other aspects of women's material work required similar training and practice. However, the root of Osage women's power came from their innate power after puberty to create human life. They did not need training or education to reproduce. Therefore, Osage women and men accessed power in different forms: women were born with it and men had to earn it.[22]

Though polarized by male and female, Osage gender construction included a range of gender identities. If Europeans and Americans struggled to understand gender complementarity, a multiple gender paradigm was almost beyond comprehension. Yet, an abundance of evidence indicates, as

Will Roscoe has argued, that "alternative gender roles were among the most widely shared features of [Indigenous] North American societies," and the Osage were no exception.[23]

A few nineteenth-century missionaries and travelers noted Osage "men" wearing women's attire and performing women's work.[24] In the 1890s, Black Dog (Shon-ton-ca-be), a one-time Osage principal leader, described in greater detail several instances of Osage "men who become as women," known as mixu'ga (instructed by the moon). The stories began the same way: "A young man went to fast, and was gone many days" seeking dreams or visions to give him strength and success in war or hunting. In each instance, the man envisioned himself as a woman, or holding women's tools, or speaking in the women's dialect. From then on he would dress, behave, speak, and work as a woman. These dreams provided spiritual instruction or sanction for a person to occupy an alternative gender role. In another story, Black Dog described a young male war leader who had also often fasted and received dreams "that would make him a man of valor." After a battle victory, he was dancing with his followers when everyone heard an owl repeatedly saying: "The leader is a mixu'ga!" Initially the man seemed to resist this: "I have done that which a mixu'ga could never do! However, on reaching his home the young leader dressed as a woman and spoke as a woman." Meanwhile, this person also married, had children, and continued as a successful warrior—donning men's clothes in battle. This constituted a "gender role split" rather than a gender role change because this individual lived out both roles in parallel.[25] All of these complexities have led many Native people, and subsequently scholars, to refer to such individuals as Two-Spirit to more accurately convey the overlapping gender, sexual, spiritual, and social roles that made up Indigenous gender construction past and present.[26]

Evidence of Osage women in alternative gender roles was scanty and inconclusive. Francis La Flesche recorded one folk story where a widow, lacking friends or relatives, led a successful mourning war party in order to "secure companions for her husband on his journey to the land of the spirits." This was considered "novel," and "no woman was ever known to have led a war party."[27] Perhaps women could take on male occupations when circumstances such as this made it necessary. In another war-related example, a combined force of Comanche and Osage warriors attacked a US Army battalion along the Arkansas River in 1848. The commanding officer, W. B. Royall, reported: "We saw about one hundred yards from us during the fight a female who seemed to be their Queen mounted on a horse decorated with silver ornaments on a scarlet dress, who rode about giving directions about the wounded." It is unclear, though, if he saw a Comanche or Osage woman.[28] Victor Tixier, a French traveler among the Osage in 1840, repeatedly referenced an Osage "Woman Chief" named Vitimé, the second wife of "Head Chief" Majakita (the son of White Hair/Pawhuska's sister). According to Osage historian Louis Burns, the title "Woman Chief" typically denoted a woman's marriage to a chief. And in this case, Vitimé generally engaged in typical female work. However, she was one of three women who followed her husband and other men on a war expedition. Tixier wrote that "Woman Chief did not want to leave her husband," perhaps, he concluded, because Majakita had a wounded leg, and the pain of riding a horse caused him to abandon the expedition the next day and return home, presumably with Vitimé.[29]

Perhaps Royall and Tixier's observations indicate some Osage women were physically involved in warfare. Or, their presence in these particular instances reflected healing work that related to women's role as life channel. Adding to the complexity, Tixier also wrote,

> In the Head Chief's lodge lived a warrior named la Bredache. This man, who a few years before was considered one of the most distinguished braves, suddenly gave up fighting and never left Majakita, except when the latter went to war. The extremely effeminate appearance of this man, and his name, which was that of an hermaphrodite animal, gave me food for thought. Baptiste accused him of being the lover of the Woman-Chief; but the Osage tell only half of what they think.[30]

Here is another example of a mixu'ga, but this time characterized as an alleged sexual partner of a "Woman Chief." Tixier also noted that Osage town chief Baptiste Mongrain "showed a violent hatred against the Head Chief and above all against the Woman-Chief." Tixier surmised Baptiste viewed Majakita as a rival in terms of influence over Osage people. Of course, if he hated Vitimé the most, that could indicate she held even more influence than her husband. As discussed later in this chapter, this could have resulted from a variety of typical leadership roles for women, or Vitimé could have inhabited a role indicative of a range of genders between those traditionally associated with men and women. Or Tixier's European cultural bias could have obscured more accurate descriptions.[31]

The lack of more concrete evidence of alternative gender "women as men" likely resulted from colonialism and observer bias, rather than an actual absence of such individuals. Research has shown that a variety of alternative gender "women's" roles historically existed in multiple plains tribes, but Euro-American observers often could not differentiate these individuals. By the nineteenth century, increased need for women's labor in the hide trade, and population demise due to US imperialism and disease may have also discouraged women from abandoning their material and biological reproductive capabilities that may have been part of some alternative gender roles.[32] Nevertheless, it is clear—as was common in Native North America—the Osage gender construction included a diversity of roles that valued individual autonomy, and embraced flexibility for all Osage people.

An exclusive group of initiated priests (who shared the name *Non'-hon-zhin-ga*) maintained all of the clan-specific ritual knowledge, divided into seven degrees. Different clans had different versions of Osage rituals typically related to their life symbols (manifestations of *Wa-kon'-da*), whose qualities each clan embodied. This is the ceremonial order of the degrees for the *In-gthon'-ga* (Puma) clan of the *Hon'-ga* (Earth/dry land) moiety:

1. Wa-zhin'-ga-o, The Rite of the Shooting of a Bird
2. Non'-zhin-zhon Wa-thon, The Songs of the Vigil Rite
3. Wa-xo'-be A-wa-thon, The Singing of the Wa-xo'-be Songs
4. Ca Tha-dse Ga-xe, The Making of the Rush Mat Shrine
5. Mon'-sha'kon Ga-xe, The Making of the Sacred Burden-Strap
6. Wa-do'-ka We-ko, The Call to the Ceremonial Distribution of Scalps
7. Ni'-ki Non-k'-on, The Hearing of the Sayings of the Ancient Men

The different versions also seemed to document different parts of Osage history. For example, the Puma clan creation story discussed the primacy of gatherable foods and deer hunting. The Sky Peacemaker (*Tsi'-zhu Wa-shta-ge*) version focused on the seemingly later emergence of buffalo hunting and corn cultivation. Francis La Flesche transcribed the second, third, and seventh rituals from this list.[33]

Initiation into any one degree constituted priestly status, but initiation was costly. Initiates spent seven years collecting various items, such as seven different animal skins (mottled lynx, gray wolf, male puma, male black bear, male buffalo, elk, and deer), used in the ceremony and as gifts for those conducting the initiation. Even with familial aid, procuring these items, especially the skins, proved difficult; and even after the introduction of horses and guns, this often took three years. Therefore, few people joined the priesthood, and even fewer obtained more than one degree. Beyond wealth, personal character also determined who joined the priesthood. Potential initiates "manifested a proper spirit of reverence for things sacred" and were "mentally and ethically superior persons" evidenced by strict adherence to social customs, obtaining war honors (o'don), and lifelong generosity—"normally, this meant that [a priest] had given away everything [they] owned at least three times." Such rigorous standards ensured that Non'-hon-zhin-ga members could understand, maintain, and pass on Osage spiritual beliefs, history, and social organization—a paramount responsibility for the entire community's survival.[34]

Just as all rituals reiterated the union of the masculine (sky) and feminine (earth) forces, they also required female and male participation. Osage marriages mirrored this union, and "a husband and wife were considered to be a single entity," so only married men could join the priesthood. All three initiation rituals La Flesche recorded contained roles for a priest's wife and any female relatives she chose to accompany her, all of whom paid fees for their instruction, much like the man undergoing initiation. For example, the "Rite of Wa-xo'-be" instructed women on the specific ceremonial aspects of corn cultivation. In the "Sayings of the Ancient Men" ritual, the wife learned ceremonial body painting and hide dressing to ensure a long life and consistent food supply for her children.[35]

The "Rite of Vigil" priesthood degree actually initiated female members, specifically widows, who were considered the surviving part of the "single entity" created through marriage, filling the position vacated after her husband's death. The widow paid the same fee as a male initiate and recited the wi'-gi-e (ritual chant) used by her husband's clan. The widow omitted all references to the destruction of life because as a woman her ability to bear children—and thus create life—still required an avoidance of such topics and activities. In 1910, La Flesche attended parts of a "Rite of the Wa-xo'-be" ceremony where the male initiate wailed while he touched the heads of the Non'-hon-zhin-ga with the ceremonial pipe and the symbolic bird-hawk, during which La Flesche noted "the women members of the order also wail."[36]

It was also possible that official wa-xo'-be weavers were considered members of the priesthood in some way. One of La Flesche's female informants,

Hon-be'-do-ka, referenced "the horses, blankets and other valuable articles she and her husband paid as fees for her initiation" seemingly into the priesthood. And when another (male) Non'-hon-zhin-ga "harangued her in a vigorous manner" to not share her ritual knowledge with La Flesche because Wa'-xpe-gthe (supernatural punishments) befell all priests who irreverently transferred sacred knowledge, "the old woman retorted" that she had "faithfully fulfilled" all of her obligations, again seemingly as a priest, and "consequently she had nothing to fear." Hon-be'-do-ka was an official wa-xo'-be weaver, and this constituted some kind of membership in the Non'-hon-zhin-ga.[37]

Although Non'-hon-zhin-ga translated as "Little Old Men," in the "Rite of Chiefs," La Flesche initially called the ancient priests "the Seers," without gendered reference. Missionary and ethnographer James Owen Dorsey, based on his work among the Osage in the 1880s, described how "when a woman is initiated into the secret society of the Osage, the officiating man of her gens gives her four sips of water, symbolizing, so they say, the river flowing by the tree of life, and then he rubs her from head to foot with cedar needles." Cedar was also considered a source of life akin to women's fertility because the tree was "evergreen." Hence, women as spouses, substitutes for men, or possibly as full members, participated in exclusive, sacred rituals and the priesthood. At least two unrecorded priesthood rituals ("The Making of the Rush Mat Shrine" and "The Making of the Sacred Burden-Strap") primarily involved women, and it is probable women played an even more prominent role in these ceremonies. Therefore, access to sacred knowledge was not reserved for men. In fact, wealth served as the major barrier to priesthood initiation, not gender.[38]

At some point in Osage history, the Non'-hon-zhin-ga—in a "move to a new country"—established a governance system where each town, as separate and independent political units, had two "chiefs" (Ga-hi'-ge), one from each moiety. Men holding these positions came from specific lineages and clans. The two chiefs selected ten accomplished warriors (A'ki-da, soldier) —also from specific clans—who served as an advisory council, and selected new chiefs when required. Both hunts and battles (or raids) required communal cooperation, and constituted the only times an Osage chief wielded direct influence over other people. The rest of the time, the chiefs primarily mediated conflicts between community members, especially preventing revenge killings, and decided whether captives obtained in war were adopted. The Non'-hon-zhin-ga held more authority than the Ga-hi'-ge or A'ki-da because the priests ensured the community's spiritual well being, determined by appropriate supplication to and veneration of *Wa-kon'-da*. Priests also organized war parties and negotiated peace with enemies. Furthermore, the *Non'-hon-zhin-ga* established social organization and made cultural adaptations, such as a "move to a new country," including creating the dual chiefs. One scholar argued *Non'-hon-zhin-ga* supremacy resulted from representing the "entire tribe," because "all clans were represented in the *Non-hon-zhin-ga*." We could add that the *Non'-hon-zhin-ga* represented the "entire tribe" by correspondingly including women. Chiefly authority thus rested in the hands of men. But the superior *Non'-hon-zhin-ga* incorporated women in a variety of ways, meaning even official leadership roles were not the exclusive domain of men.[39]

Food, in many ways, embodied the Osage gender construction. In Osage tradition, the male and female buffalo came from the "mysterious invisible world to the material and visible world" and into "the light of day" with "full procreative powers" illustrated by the simultaneous emergence of their calf. Buffalo, sometimes described as an earlier food source, then gave corn— yellow, red, blue, and speckled—and squash to the Osage. Alternatively, some clan histories described the use of bison and corn as so old, "the origin of the two was placed, mythically, by the ancient [*Non'-hon-zhin-ga*], at the beginning of the earthly career of the tribe." Buffalo was considered the primary food animal, hunted by men; corn was the primary food plant, cultivated by women. Both were "direct gifts to the people from the Mysterious Power (*Wa-kon'-da*)," and reverent ritual was involved in acquiring all of this sustenance.[40]

Buffalo's spiritual preeminence paralleled its economic significance in providing the "principal supply of meat and pelts"; hence, buffalo hunting required "solemn rites, always with recognition of the Great Creative Power (*Wa-kon'-da*) that brought this sacred animal to man." Virtually the same ceremonies prepared men for battle and for the two annual buffalo hunts. Osage scholar Louis Burns concluded, "Welfare of the people depended on the grand hunts; it was a war for survival as was warfare against humans." Each community's two chiefs (*Ga-hi'-ge*) alternated leading the buffalo hunts, where they, with the help of ten soldiers (*A'ki-da*), maintained strict discipline to ensure communal cooperation and a triumphant hunt.[41]

For the two annual buffalo hunts, all the townsfolk traveled west onto the plains. Chiefs strategically chose temporary camp sites based on proximity to the bison herd, access to water, and protection from enemy attack. While traveling between the camp and the herd, hunters stopped four times to smoke a ceremonial pipe that signified life—like the human body—and was the "medium through which they approach [Wa-kon'-da]" for aid from the spiritual force "who causest the four winds to reach a place, help ye me!" In the time before horses, Osage hunters approached the herd from downwind and typically drove them into a canyon—sometimes with yelling and dancing, other times by setting small brush fires—where many bison would fall to their death. Surviving animals were then beaten with clubs made from the sacred "willow tree, a tree that never dies" or shot with arrows. To ensure the stampede went in the proper direction, sometimes a hunter, disguised in a hide, complete with the head, would "grunt like a contented buffalo would do," leading the "main herd into thinking safety lay in that direction." Hunters sometimes donned this disguise in order to "graze" downwind from a cluster of bison and then shoot them again with arrows from close range. Needless to say, this was very dangerous work that required significant training and preparation, and justified chiefly direct authority during the hunt. Men, using the sacred round-handled knife, commenced butchering, while everyone, including women and children, assisted in carrying the carcasses back to camp for processing and feasting.[42]

Women, as life channels and creators, could not associate with death, and did not physically participate in hunting or warfare.[43] Through singing specific songs though, a woman who "remains at home follows [the hunter] with expectant wish that [an animal] might approach the spot where her brother stands and be shot by him." Ritual singing articulated her anxiety for the hunter's safety and hope for his success. While singing, she visualized the wounded animal, its skin being cut "in such a manner as to make it convenient to shaping into clothing." In addition, the song was a prayer for "the continual reproduction of this animal," and because this was "made by a woman, this [prayer] is not only for the continued life of the animal but is a prayer for the continuity and the perpetuation of the people of the tribe."[44] After men killed the animals, women commenced the work of "creating" something useful out of the carcasses—meat and hides.

> It is all bustle and labour with the Indian women . . . [they are] engaged in cutting up and drying [the meat] for future use. Their method is . . . to cut the meat into long strips, and plait them together with bark about twelve inches wide and four or five feet long. When the process of plaiting is finished, they place the meat on poles over the fire, till it becomes well

heated through; throw it upon the ground, and tread it back and forth
. . . with the view of making it more tender; and then keep it near the fire
until it is thoroughly cooked and dried.[45]

This tenderizing method involved women placing the meat between two buffalo robes and dancing on it. When drying the buffalo meat, "the brains were carefully saved for the tanning, the hooves for glue, the horns for spoons and other utensils, and the sinews along the backbone became cord and thread and bowstrings when many of them were twisted together." Bones were also "roasted and cracked for the marrow." Then, the hides: first, soaking removed stains, then they were stretched on the ground, held tight with pegs, and with a "chisel-like scraper," a woman removed any remaining flesh or fat from the skin and "planed the surface to an even thickness." This process could take several hours with scraping and drying repeated as needed. Women fleshed the hides while out on the hunt, but tanned them after returning to their hometowns. To tan, women oiled the hide with a mixture of fat, brains, or liver, then soaked it for several days, typically "in a stream, weighted down by rocks," followed by rapidly pulling it through a small loop of sinew or rubbing it with a piece of bone or pumice stone to ensure uniform smoothness and softness. Now softened, women fashioned hides into all manner of leather goods including clothing, lodge covers, and carrying cases or straps.[46]

In Osage communities, archaeological evidence seemed to indicate "hunting supplied the mainstay of their diet," possibly even before European contact. This hunting likewise supplied vital hides and leather, which only became more valuable as trade goods after colonization. But this should not be viewed as demonstrating male dominance in the economy generally or in food provision specifically. Transitioning an animal from the wild to meals and leather required cooperative—and complementary—effort from men who killed, and women who processed and manufactured.[47]

In rituals, the ancient Non'-hon-zhin-ga emphasized women's mystic power as the life channel, mirrored in plant form by corn (ha'-ba). As the bearer of children, "no one [was] better fitted than she to perform the sacred symbolic act of preparing the soil, planting therein the seed of the maize, and helping it come to the light of day."[48] Corn needed to bear food, which the children had to eat, and women knew the plant required the same kind of motherly care to bring it to fruition.[49] A man could assist in clearing fields, but "he must work under the direction of the woman who is the owner of the field."[50] Later, American observers frequently misinterpreted Osage men working in the fields as evidence of assimilation. In reality, they witnessed longstanding gender complementarity in action.

The priesthood rituals La Flesche recorded included specific instructions for women concerning corn cultivation and gathering, some of which he obtained specifically from a female informant—Mon'-ci-tse-xi (Julia Lookout whom La Flesche referred to as "Mrs. Fred Lookout")—experienced in the ritual task. Prior to European contact, the Osage used a "wapiti" (elk) shoulder blade hoe in cultivation. When clearing and planting, a woman ceremonially painted the parting of her hair red to represent the path of the sun, the path of life, and the paths of all living things converging toward the woman and her children, providing them with food, shelter, and clothing. This painting appealed to *Wa-kon'-da* for aid in food procurement and as a request for strength and health in maintaining their population through reproduction. During planting, a woman also sang requests to *Wa-kon'-da* for fruitful harvests and for male success in hunting and warfare—highlighting the complementary role of both genders in community survival. Sowing ceremonially commenced when each woman created seven hills "facing" the sun, placing the first grain of corn in the first hill, two grains in the second hill, and so on through the seventh, covering each hill with a footprint. After the seven sacred mounds, the woman sowed the remainder of the corn without ceremony. In Osage history, they had existed as spiritual beings in the upper world, but it was not until they descended to earth that they became physical beings. The Non'-hon-zhin-ga considered planting corn a sacred and powerful act, reenacting their own creation as the grain awakened to active life (became a physical being) when it forced its way through the woman's footprint, the mark of *Wa-kon'-da*'s presence, into life-giving sunlight flourishing to abundance.[51]

The harvest ceremony most clearly demonstrated the value of Osage women's creative role in society. During what observers called the "corn feast," or the "Green-Corn Dance," women exercised "almost unlimited authority."

> The oldest and most respectable mother in the tribe prepares for, and conducts the ceremony: she also claims and exercises the privilege of informing her children as she calls her tribe, when they may commence eating the green corn. . . . She frequents the fields, daily examines the silks of the young spikes, and when they become dry, plucks and prepares

some of them in different ways, and then presents them to her friends. Afterwards she decorates the door-way leading to her lodge, with the husks of the recently gathered corn, which are regarded as signals for the approaching feast.[52]

Then the entire community, with the festive air of skipping, dancing, singing, and shouting, proceeded to the fields, where women (owners of the fields) harvested, or directed others to harvest, enough corn for the feast. For several days thereafter, the remaining corn—a gift from *Wa-kon'-da*—was harvested and either eaten or stored.[53] This celebration embodied the themes from the corresponding planting ritual: women had achieved creating life; in this context, their motherly care successfully produced corn, a central food source.[54]

In addition to cultivation, Osage women gathered wild plants to feed their families. In fact, La Flesche noted while documenting different clan creation stories that the first food "to be protected by force . . . against intrusion by unfriendly tribes were the [gathered] food plants." Later, after the Osage acquired the bow and arrow, men began hunting deer, possibly a food source that predated buffalo. So, in their earliest history, Osage women potentially supplied virtually all the community's food via gathering. The ancient *Non'-hon-zhin-ga* deemed one of these original gathered foods, the *tse'-wa-the* root (water chinquapin, American lotus, or *Nelumbo lutea*), a sacred life symbol, which women ceremonially gathered and dried for winter use.[55] A woman painted the parting of her hair as a sign of gratitude to *Wa-kon'-da* for the sun passing over her, and the water chinquapin and shedding life-giving power. After arriving at the body of water where she gathered the root, the woman cut a willow pole to use as a staff for support and aid in digging. She used willow because the Osage believed this tree never died and also represented life. Before gathering, a woman touched a bit of mud to her head and body as an act of reverence to the earth, wherein lay *Wa-kon'-da*'s life-giving power. When she found the first root, she rubbed her arms and body with it in order to receive the "blessing of life" and then threw that root back as a wish for the plant's continued growth. Then she gathered the remaining roots without ceremony.[56] An array of other foods women gathered also contributed to the incredibly varied and well-balanced Osage diet of walnuts, hazelnuts, acorns, pecans, grapes, plums, pawpaws, persimmons, hog potatoes, hickory nuts, chestnuts, wild liquorice, sweet myrrh, anise, sweet potatoes, wild onions, crab and may apples, Osage oranges, strawberries, gooseberries, whortleber-ries, blackberries, and dew-berries.[57]

Acquiring food involved both genders, but provisioning it into meals pri-marily involved women; "she it is who prepares food for the 'little ones' to strengthen them for their life's journey." Again, "little ones" referred to the entire community, not just the children. To do so, women cooked fresh meat, often venison or turkey, by roasting it over the fire or wrapping it in leaves on a bed of coals. Dried meat, often buffalo, and dried vegetables were boiled or mixed with oil or tallow and served as a stew. Some gathered foods could be eaten raw, but many more required some kind of labor such as roasting and boiling nuts; separating seeds from persimmon pulp, which then re-quired drying and baking; and cutting and drying lotus roots. Women also prepared cakes or bread from pounded corn, persimmon, or acorns. Though children could eat whenever they were hungry, adults ate three meals on the long summer days and two meals on the shorter winter days. However, cer-tain aspects of men's work involved spending significant time away from women—especially on war expeditions—when men temporarily engaged in meal preparation and other domestic tasks because circumstances war-ranted. Also, when women were occupied processing meat and hides on the bison hunts, men cooked the buffalo ribs for immediate consumption.[58]

Cooking meals took on greater significance though when it was part of hospitality and ceremonial feasting. Europeans and Americans frequently noted how, upon entering an Osage town, they were welcomed and fed in one home after another, sometimes "invited to fifteen or twenty in the same evening." Women then played at least an indirect diplomatic role by feeding these visitors, which led one Frenchman to admit that "this genuinely noble way of showing hospitality would make one forgive these so-called barbarians many a fault." Likely that was the point, especially in dealings with coloniz-ers. Generosity characterized interactions within the community too, where frequent, sometimes daily, visiting allowed people to socialize and spread the wealth, manifested predominantly in meals produced by women, to the less-prosperous households.[59] Women's labor also produced feasts that cor-responded with male-dominated activities, such as diplomatic negotiations and ceremonial or social dancing. Such events then reiterated gender comple-mentarity because the actions of both genders were necessary to accomplish the celebration.[60]

Much like hunting involved cooperative effort by Osage men and women to produce food and goods, war success also required both genders. Through ceremonial and ritual actions, the Osage continually sought *Wa-kon'-da*'s favor to accomplish the two aspects essential to Osage existence: 1) women's continued fertility and 2) men's valor as warriors in protecting women, children, and homes.[61] As Osage scholar John Joseph Mathews explained, the ancient *Non'-hon-zhin-ga* observed these two characteristics in the falcon.

> After a long season of observation, they became convinced, as have
> many others, that, of all the animals and birds, the falcon is the most
> admirable, in savage courage, with a swiftness so great that one had not
> time in which to defend himself against its attack, and with a ruthlessness
> that is fascinating in its silence and cleanliness. To the ancient Little Old
> Men . . . the falcon seemed to have a very long life, since . . . they had
> never seen a falcon defeated or destroyed by his enemies. . . . They noted
> too that the prairie falcon came back year after year to the same nesting
> spot . . . a double-edged symbol for the two most important necessities
> of their existence: military adequacy and the longevity of the individual
> and the tribe.[62]

La Flesche's sources similarly confirmed that the "sacred bird-hawk" symbolized courage and aggressiveness because "he is gifted with swiftness of wing and makes his attack with unerring precision, striking his prey so that it is unable to flee." As Mathews elaborated, the sacred bird also symbolized the dual masculine and feminine forces in Osage life.

> The Little Old Men said [the bird] must be born of heaven, the child of
> Grandfather the Sun and the Moon Woman, and they straightway made
> him so, and they gave him a shrine of three coverings. They said the
> valor of the falcon must be the valor of the men of the tribe, so that the
> tribe could not be overcome by their enemies, and it must be this valor,
> speed, ruthlessness, alertness, and freedom from the bonds that bind
> the little ones of the earth that would keep intact to the Little Ones their
> remaining days. The hawk became a being somewhere between the
> Sacred One (Earth) and the Sky Lodge, favored of both and a son
> of both.[63]

The bird-hawk represented life for the Osage—embodied in women—and death for all their enemies—accomplished by men. Rituals stated that "the quality most essential to the man, the warrior, for the performance of his duty was courage." Men appealed to *Wa-kon'-da* for the "gift" of courage by carrying the sacred bird-hawk *wa-xo'-be* into battle. Part of the female creative role involved a priest's wife serving as the *wa-xo'-be* weaver and reverent caretaker. La Flesche obtained two *i'cagthe dapa*—the collective name for the loom stand made of stakes and slats, and the batten made of a deer's antler—from Osage women. Mrs. Btho'ga-hi-ge provided the first loom; however, La Flesche was unable to gather any of the ritual chants or songs from her. And her husband "declined to recite it himself because it belonged to the woman's part of the rite." As discussed earlier, one ceremonially initiated weaver, Hon-be'-do-ka, recited the *wi'-gi-e* and sang the lamentation song for La Flesche, providing the ritual context for this sacred role.[64]

The *wa-xo'-be* consisted of three ceremonially woven envelopes protecting the preserved remains of a sacred bird-hawk (falcon), the central figure in war rituals and priesthood ceremonies. The ancient *Non'-hon-zhin-ga* determined the *wa-xo'-be* woven envelopes held "equal dignity and sanctity with the object to be enclosed therein," demonstrating the role of women in warfare.

> The part they [Non'-hon-zhin-ga] gave the woman to perform at this particular stage of the ceremony has reference, not only to her sacerdotal office as weaver of the shrine proper that symbolizes life in all its forms, celestial and terrestrial, but to the reverent care she bestows upon the shrine when it passes into her keeping, because of the initiation of her husband into the mysteries of the tribal war rites. The part also has reference to woman's position as representative of the potential power of the tribe through its warriors who are born of woman, therefore, in the warlike achievements of the tribe her part is regarded as no less important than that of the men who face death upon the fields of conflict.[65]

Men fought battles, but women, as warrior mothers, were viewed as equally important in war success. The entire *wa-xo'-be* shrine manifested life in all its forms; the upper portion of the woven rush case represented the sky (masculine), the lower portion the earth (feminine), and the inner part where the bird-hawk lay represented the space between the sky and the earth (ho'-e-ga), where human life existed until death. Many ceremonies, not just those related to war, involved ritually opening the wa-xo'-be and identifying its sacred contents, allowing for its significance, including reference to gender roles, to be reiterated and transmitted to ceremonial participants. One could argue that the wa-xo'-be's woven rush cases also embodied gender diversity by including a space between the masculine sky and feminine earth, which could denote alternative gender individuals.[66]

Specific women, ceremonially chosen and trained through initiation into "The Making of the Rush Mat Shrine" ritual, wove new wa-xo'-be envelopes when needed. Typically the weaver required four days to complete the task. She partitioned off her home to seclude herself during this ceremonial work. The weaver's process constituted a ritual materialization of spiritual powers, and her seclusion prevented anyone from improperly or irreverently employing her methods. On all four mornings, the weaver continually sought Wa-kon'-da's aid in her work and displayed her vigil by smearing one piece of dirt on the right of her forehead, associated with Hon'-ga moiety, and another on the left side, associated with Tsi'-zhu moiety, unifying nature's dual forces. Next she sang a song of longing and sorrow, known as the "Weaver's Lamentation," for her deceased relatives. Finally, before beginning her work, the weaver recited the wi'-gi-e of the rushes, which figuratively described the sun, moon, sky, and phases of night and day because, upon completion, the woven rush mat embodied the visible universe's power. A woman served as weaver because, as a woman, she was a life channel and a creator.[67]

Prior to war expeditions, women sang and danced in the "Songs of Triumph," during which a priest's wife and wa-xo'-be weaver hung the sacred bird-hawk from her back as commanders wore it during battle. Other women accompanied her, dancing and carrying the other wa-xo'-be items. This ritual singing honored the woman's specific role as sacred weaver and caretaker of the shrine. When dancing and singing, the women struck the ground with their loom poles, used as an upright of a loom frame, beating time to the music. At the end of the song, the women violently threw down their poles so they lay pointing toward the west, the direction of destruction, indicating the women's appeal to Wa-kon'-da for the defeat of their enemies and the maintenance of the Osage.[68]

When a warrior needed the wa-xo'-be for a war expedition, he appealed to its female caretaker for her "good wishes for success" in this endeavor. After she provided the *wa-xo'-be*, and the warrior left on his journey, this woman spent several days ceremonially painting and rubbing soil on her face by which she sent sympathy, courage, and her wishes for his success. Every night when she washed off the paint and soil, she recited, "I remove from my head the soil of the earth and wipe my hands upon the body of the chief of our enemies, that he may come to his death at the hands of our warriors." In this way, the ancient *Non'-hon-zhin-ga* determined the woman sent her aid to the warrior and all his comrades carrying her *wa-xo'-be*.[69] Women other than *wa-xo'-be* caretakers also took part in ceremonies to send their good will on behalf of warriors. By particular face painting, women invoked *Wa-kon'-da*'s aid in destroying their foe. In the "Symbol of the Sending of the Will" ceremony, over the course of four days a woman painted the parting of her hair red every day, and then on the left cheek painted an upright blue line on day one, then added an upright red line next to the blue on day two, continuing the alternation through day four when there were four lines on the left cheek. The red line on the parting of the hair symbolized the sun's daily path. The blue and red lines referenced death to the enemy "young man," and "maiden," respectively. Primarily, though, these rituals ensured that "[women's] courage shall be added to that of the warriors when they battle with the enemy."[70]

After successful warriors returned home, women and men often participated in the scalp dance. Women whose husbands or male relatives returned with scalps served as the principal actors in this dance.

> The women . . . strip to the waist. . . . They pretend to be men, decorating themselves with feathers, paint, etc. They are led by one who carries the scalp on its pole. She is chosen for that purpose by one of the captains. Some women carry bows, others take arrows, some have war pipes, and some carry peace pipes. The drummers sit in a small circle around the pole. A great warrior arises and tells of his exploits. Then the drum beats, and the women dance. All start together, the women of the [Tsi'-zhu] gentes moving in one direction, and those of the [Hon'-ga] gentes in the other, around the pole. The successful warriors . . . come in their war dress, and [dance] around the pole, close to the women, telling of their deeds.[71]

This dance was demonstration of both women and men's courageous victory.[72]

Sacred objects existed solely for women as well. John Joseph Mathews contended, "What the *wah-hopeh* (sacred bird-hawk) was to the warrior, the *mo'n-sha-ko'n*, the burden strap was to the woman." La Flesche also briefly described the sacred burden strap as "the wa-xo'-be of the woman," considered "the emblem of her duty as a homebuilder." A burden strap included a broad buffalo hide band worn across the chest and long thongs that typically tied a firewood bundle on a woman's back. A sacred burden strap, however, served a ceremonial rather than functional purpose and "was hung by the side of the entrance to the lodge; on the left if her father was *Tzi-Sho*, and right if *Hunkah*."[73] "The Making of the Sacred Burden-Strap" was one of the seven ceremonial degrees into which priests were initiated, and some of La Flesche's informants contended the sacred burden strap held greater sanctity than the sacred bird-hawk. Returning to the dual characteristics necessary for Osage existence, certainly without women's spiritual, physical, and creative work, men would have nothing to protect.[74]

Both Osage men and women had ritually applied tattoos that depicted their complementary role in society and relationship to one another. Tattooing required an expensive tattoo ceremony, performed by a man specially trained in this art and ritual. A specific *wa-xo'-be* dedicated to this ritual contained large pelican wing quills used in marking the skin. This bird, representing long life and old age, revealed the mysteries of tattooing to the Osage and supplied the required implements. Tattooing "ink" was made from charcoal of the "sacred redbud," and the artist pricked the skin "and thus the charcoal was pushed into the epidermis." This was the same charcoal used in blackening the face in war ceremonies.[75] La Flesche wrote in 1914 that one of the most difficult parts of his Osage research involved gathering information on this ceremony. Prior to the twentieth century, he said, "only the warrior who had won war honors was entitled to have the ceremony performed and have the war symbols tattooed upon his body."

These were: The sacred ceremonial knife. The outline of this implement runs from under his chin down the middle of his chest to his abdomen; the sacred pipe which he used for offering smoke to Wa-kon'-da when appealing to him for success, and which he carried throughout the war expedition. The outline of this pipe runs from either side of the middle of the knife design and terminates beyond his shoulders; the thirteen rays of the sun which symbolize the number of o-don' (military honors) every

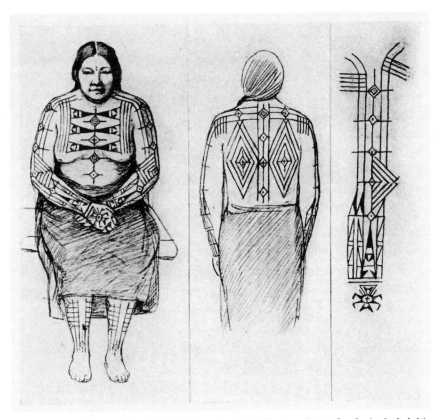

Osage Woman with Conventional Symbols Pictured on Her Body. Francis La Flesche included this drawing of female tattoos in his work on Osage ceremonies and history. The designs were indicative of women's creative power and also served as a supplication to *Wa-kon'-da* for "an endless line of descendants." (Francis La Flesche, "Researches Among the Osage," *Smithsonian Miscellaneous Collections* 70, 2 [1919], 113; and La Flesche, "The Osage Tribe: Rite of the Wa-Xo'-Be," *Forty-Fifth Annual Report of the Bureau of American Ethnology* [1927–1928] [1930], 531–532.)

warrior must strive to win. These conventional rays run upward from either side of the knife between its point and the pipe design, terminating behind the shoulders.[76]

If a man could afford it, he would also have the tattoo ceremony performed for his wives and daughters.

The woman, upon whom depends the continual existence of the tribe, was no less honored than the warrior who risks his life for the people.

Upon her forehead, chest, back, arms, hands, and the lower part of her legs are pictured, in conventional designs, the sun, stars, the earth, the powers from whose united force proceed life in all its manifold forms. The lines running down from her shoulder to her wrist symbolize the "paths of animals," in reality, life descending from the sun and the stars to the earth, represented in the conventional design of a spider pictured on the hand.[77]

These tattooed women served as the "holy guardians of the lodges and symbols of protective motherhood," creating warriors and maintaining the entire community into old age. In total, a person's tattoos represented their "endless line of descendants," and "the symbolic marks ceremonially put upon the body [stood] as a supplication to a higher power to bestow these blessings upon the person tattooed." In other words, tattoos embodied everything, including Wa-kon'-da's power and people's spiritual relationship to that power demonstrated by women's production and men's protection.[78]

Osage cosmology embodied the union of masculine and feminine forces in the universe, which translated into a system of gender complementarity that dominated their lives. Women had innate power as the creators of human life, while men earned power through protecting and providing for women and children. The ability to dominate others did not determine gender status or power. Both genders constituted necessary pairs, and all of their work ensured, with Wa-kon'-da's aid, Osage perpetuation and prosperity.

The gender construction seemed to clearly separate men's and women's tasks, but in reality, activities typically in some way involved men and women. Alternative gender roles perhaps best demonstrated the breadth of fluidity in Osage society. Yet even ostensibly gendered pursuits such as hunting required cooperation: men killed game animals and women made the dead carcasses into food and goods. Though sometimes men cooked during the great bison hunts when women were employed elsewhere, processing hides and meat. Women controlled agriculture, but men, under the direction of women, assisted in clearing fields. Men killed enemies, but women were credited with assisting because they created these warriors and spiritually combined their courage with men's in battle. Men served as political leaders (chiefs)—an outgrowth of their roles as protectors—but women contributed diplomatically through hospitality. More importantly, the priesthood, which was preeminent in spiritual and political matters, included men and women. In other words, from the Osage perspective, men and women relied on each other to mirror *Wa-kon'-da*'s construction of the universe and to achieve any kind of success, evidenced by their nation's existence into the future.

After European contact, Osage hunting and war prowess eventually led to the growth of their empire. The historiography has primarily and erroneously attributed this to the work of men, while simultaneously claiming that this regrettably produced a decline in the status of women. But, in Osage society, hunting and war success required men and women. In the remaining chapters, evidence of gender complementarity demonstrates how men and women were both central to Osage domination and survival.

CHAPTER 2 "GENERAL HAPPINESS":
GENDER AND THE OSAGE EMPIRE

In August 1811, Fort Osage factor George C. Sibley observed over 1,000 people in an Osage hunting camp "in the full and free indulgence of all the luxuries of their rude condition." He noted an absence of illness and an abundance of supplies, including "buffalo, elk, deer, marrow bones, tongues, hominy, beans, dried pumpkin, plums and other dainties." Men's hunting and women's meat production, cultivation, and gathering produced this bounty. Vigilant elder warriors maintained camp security, while elder women "were busily employed jerking and curing on scaffolds, the flesh of the fat buffalo." Young men and women "adorned in the highest style of fashion" mingled in small groups. Older boys tended the horses, many girls aided their mothers, and "swarms of children" swam in the creek or frolicked on the prairie. Sibley concluded, "Mirth and hearty merriment prevailed. Never had I witnessed such general happiness in any community as prevailed here." These observations demonstrate how, even after a century of colonization, in many ways Osage life continued to follow a familiar, and clearly flourishing, cycle. Not surprisingly, some aspects of their society changed to facilitate this. Nevertheless, gender complementarity remained a central aspect in both material and ritual life as men and women cooperated to build an Osage empire.[1]

European colonization of the Americas theoretically rested on the doctrine of discovery. From the 1490s on, the doctrine became an international legal principle that legitimized European, and later, American dominion over "newly discovered" land and people based on the presumed superiority of European culture and religion. In other words, Christian European property rights and sovereignty superseded those of non-Christian Indigenous Americans. European colonizers then framed imperialism as a "civilizing mission" that would exert paternalistic control over Natives until their "savage" ways were replaced with European religious and cultural norms. European empires could then claim that their possession and exploitation of Indigenous people and resources was really a benevolent enterprise.[2]

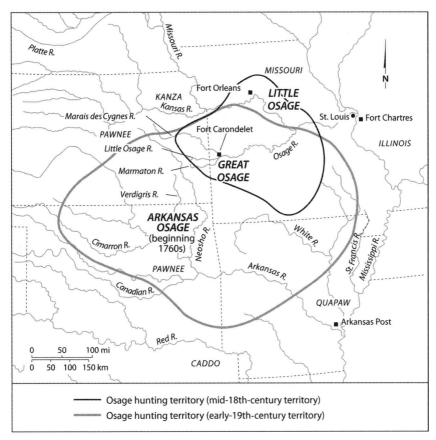

Osage Homeland, 1720s–1800s. (Map by Bill Nelson.)

In this context, King Louis XIV "founded" the French colony of "Louisiana" in 1701 to deny his English rivals the opportunity of obtaining the region's wealth and power. The colony included the entire Mississippi valley region from the Plains to the Appalachians. However, Louisiana was France's most remote, least profitable, and sparsely settled colony. Indigenous people not only outnumbered the small European population, but also they controlled the region throughout the eighteenth century. French missionization in this period suffered from factional infighting and poor or often absent administration. Hence, to preserve the colony, the French needed alliances with the true powers in the region—Native peoples. And these alliances were secured through trade. Long before colonization, the region's Native peoples had been part of continent-wide exchange systems, and the arrival of Europeans and their goods was another vehicle for improving a Native group's power relative to their Native rivals. Therefore, especially in the region west of the Mississippi River, the "successful expansionists" in the eighteenth century were Native, and for much of this time those people were Osage.[3]

The Osage solidified their power by blockading or raiding rival Indigenous communities and attacking or killing European traders bound for their enemies. Nearby Native people either had to ally with the Osage or concentrate in towns outside of Osage-controlled territory for protection. The small French military presence in the region only aggravated their need to accommodate Osage trade and alliance in order to sustain the colony's existence. Osage hegemony continued to grow during the Seven Years' War when they exploited the French-British conflict by trading with both sides and monopolizing the few European goods that made it to western Louisiana. In 1763 the war ended in French defeat, and Spain "acquired" the Louisiana colony west of the Mississippi River. The Spanish hoped to manage this colony more strictly and efficiently than their French predecessors. Nevertheless, Spanish Louisiana also remained isolated, understaffed, full of rogue French traders, and, most importantly, Osage-dominated.[4]

Spanish officials hoped to use traders and Indigenous peoples to transform Louisiana into a strong barrier between the British colonies and New Spain. Attempts by the Spanish colonial state to organize and manage trade undermined this goal. They angered Native traders by implementing price controls on imports and exports, altering the French system that often paid higher than market value for hides and furs simply to maintain Native alliances. The Spanish also attempted to regulate exchange by licensing traders and directing Osage exchange specifically through St. Louis. This benefited one of the city's founding families: the Chouteaus, whose intermarriage with the Osage solidified their access to valuable goods, expanding the power and wealth of this merchant family, the city of St. Louis, and the Osage.[5] In an attempt to stabilize relations between Native groups and end raiding, Spanish officials outlawed trade in Native slaves.[6] The Spanish also discontinued the livestock trade, hoping to prevent Native raids on western and southern Spanish communities where most of the livestock originated.

These sanctions seemed to outlaw a significant portion of Osage exports.[7] Osage raiding continued, though, eventually prompting Spanish Louisiana governor general Francisco Louis Hector, Baron de Carondelet in 1792 to prohibit all Osage trade, and he instructed "any subject of His Majesty, or individual of the other nations, white or red, may overrun the Great and Little Osages, kill them and destroy their families, as they are disturbers of the prosperity of all the nations."[8] Regardless of Spanish restriction, the lucrative Osage trade continued to attract French and British traders, and illicit exchange plagued the region, including at the isolated and poorly manned Arkansas Post.[9] As Zenon Trudeau, lieutenant governor of Spanish Illinois and the commandant at St. Louis noted in 1798, "On many occasions they [the Osage] compel the traders to an unequal and unjust exchange, maltreating them if they resist. But these vexations do not prevent the traders from returning next year to seek others like them." It was, as many scholars have declared, an Osage empire.[10]

Using the term "empire" can obscure the differences between Osage and European imperialism. As Osage historian Louis Burns has argued, Europeans "claimed" Osage-controlled lands, even though colonizers could not enforce their "claims" on the ground. In contrast, "Osage land title was held by occupation, conquest, and the ability to enforce one's own claim." Most notably, when the Osage expanded their territory in the eighteenth century, they did not employ an ideology reminiscent of the "civilizing mission." Again, Burns explained that "having an alien people subject to their rule, by force or otherwise, was unknown to the Osages. Their practice was to adopt alien individuals and to either merge with whole groups or to force them to move out of the desired area. Failing in these measures, the conquest was either abandoned, or a total war was undertaken. But the idea of subjugation was never used."[11]

To increase access to game and enhance trade, the Osage separated into three divisions, each made up of several towns, in the eighteenth century. The "Great Osage" remained in their precolonial settlement area, where the Little Osage, Marmaton, and Marais des Cygnes Rivers merged to form the Osage River. The "Little Osage" moved north to the Missouri River sometime between 1714 and 1719 to take advantage of rich hunting grounds and trade traffic on this river where they remained until many started to rejoin the Great Osage, beginning around 1794. In the 1760s, the "Arkansas Osage" moved south to the Three Forks region, where the Verdigris and the Neosho Rivers joined the Arkansas River, to exploit Caddoan horses, furs, and slaves, often trading at the Arkansas Post.[12]

Prior to the appearance of Europeans in Osage-controlled territory, the Osage initially obtained foreign goods through Indigenous exchange systems.

The horse, one of the earliest and arguably most important new trade items, reached the Osage at least by the 1680s. The Osage word for the horse, *ka-wa*, has questionable origin. Some scholars argue *ka-wa* roughly translated as "mystery dog," while others contend the term referenced *Kaw-Thu-Wah*, or the Kiowa, believed to have first traded horses to the Osage. Francis La Flesche's Osage dictionary said the term was "a corruption of the Spanish word for horse, caballo."[13] For other European goods, notably firearms, the Osage primarily depended on their Illinois and Missouri neighbors to the north.[14] Diplomatic relations with these groups provided European trade goods and the weapons and ammunition necessary for protection from expanding and powerful eastern groups, who frequently raided Osage towns.[15] As early as 1680, Osage envoys traveled up the Illinois River to trade with the French.[16] By 1694, unlicensed French traders (*coureurs de bois*) exchanged goods in Osage communities, yet the Osage remained at an arms disadvantage without sustained and direct contact with French trading posts.[17]

Initial dependence on Illinois and Missouri middlemen for European goods made women's food products—both meat and crops—some of the Osage's most accessible and desirable early trade items. Many Louisiana colonists relied on trade with groups like the Osage for practically all of their sustenance. In the "Illinois Country" (named for the local eponymous Native group, but including other peoples), the Osage supplied corn, buffalo meat, and other foodstuffs consumed at isolated colonial settlements, like the Arkansas Post. In 1751 French officials lamented their colonists' disinterest in cultivation, and without enough African slaves in the region's settlements, food production remained in Native hands. Those hands made the Illinois country into one of the most reliable food sources for French colonists through the Seven Years' War. Osage women contributed to this agricultural trade by growing corn, beans, and squash in their hometowns, traded to posts throughout the region. From there, food flowed south along the Mississippi River to New Orleans and north to outposts, including Fort Ouiatenon, Fort Duquesne, and Fort Detroit, providing thousands of pounds of food annually.[18]

Women's agricultural production remained sizable, successful, and spiritually important throughout this period. During Zebulon Pike's journeys through Osage towns during 1806 and 1807, he noted they "raise large quantities of corn, beans, and pumpkins, which they manage with the greatest economy, in order to make them last from year to year. All the agricultural labor is done by women."[19] Louis Bringier, who spent time among all three major divisions in 1812 noted, "They all cultivate Indian corn and pumpkins, in one field common to all and not fenced in; none but the women work in these fields, which are about half an acre for each woman. All their tools consist in one hoe, and a large tomahawk."[20] John D. Hunter, an American captive adopted by the Osage, wrote, "The squaws raise for the consumption of their families, corn, tobacco, pumpkins, squashes, melons, gourds, beans, peas, and within a few years past, potatoes in small quantities."[21]

Though scholars have emphasized this as a time when the Osage focused on commercial hide trade, women's agriculture continued to produce a surplus through the 1820s, resulting in caching, to provide foodstuffs through the winter. The Osage built caches in well-drained areas, dug in the "shape of a jug," meaning a narrow neck led to a widened hole, lined with sticks, then filled with foodstuffs. After filling the hole with dirt, they drove horses over the cache or used a fire to disguise the soil disruption.[22] Various visitors made note of caches in spite of efforts to keep the locations secret. In 1815, Jules de Mun, on a trip through the Great Osage towns along the Osage River, described that "whenever the inhabitants of the village go off on a hunt they put their corn in some place removed from the woods where they think there is less risk of its being discovered by their enemies." De Mun noted that elderly Osage men and women unable to travel on hunts guarded these caches.[23]

Ceremonial celebrations continued when women began harvesting the "green" corn (roasting ears)—acknowledging women's food production, creative power, and Wa-kon'-da's (Mysterious Power) favor. During this jubilant time, children cheered,

"Corn is ripe!" . . . scores of Osages repeated the cry, and ran on to the cornfields, for now all Osages could gather roasting ears—as many as they could eat. In the village, fires were soon burning, and corn was being roasted by every family. All day long the feast continued . . . they danced the green corn dance . . . and sang of the goodness of the Great Spirit and the faithfulness of the Osages.

According to John Hunter, only the annual first appearance of the bison accorded the same community-wide level of excitement, illustrating how the complementarity of food sources (bison and corn) remained emblematic of their cosmological understanding and gender construction.[24]

French trading posts built close to Osage communities in the 1720s facilitated direct access to European goods and an end to Osage dependence on other Native middlemen.[25] Archaeological excavations of mid-eighteenth-century Osage towns indicated European traders supplied guns, beads, kettles, knives, square nails, awls, hoes, and axes.[26] Becoming middlemen themselves, the Osage then traded similar goods to more western and southern Indigenous communities, acquiring horses, slaves, skins, and meat in the process to trade with the French or utilize internally. Scholars credit the large Osage population, an estimated 10,000–18,000, as enabling significant and rapid expansion across the region during this period. For the Osage, this population was a product of Wa-kon'-da's favor and women's fertility (a creative power). They literally had the "manpower" to expand their hunting and raiding range while preventing Native rivals and French traders from having contact. By the 1750s, Osage-French trade expanded at the expense of their former Illinois trading partners, who complained that French traders saved all of their best goods for exchange with the Osage.[27]

A significant part of Osage power involved the fur and hide trade. To supply French traders, and obtain valuable goods in return, the Osage expanded their hunting territory over three ecological zones internal to or bordering their homeland: plains, prairies, and the Ozark Mountains. This territory produced a wide variety of peltry and hides from deer, elk, bison, bears, wolves, raccoons, foxes, wildcats, weasels, and muskrats. Osage hunting lands covered an estimated 100,000 square miles, encompassing the present-day state of Missouri, half of Arkansas, and portions of Oklahoma and Kansas.[28] Though the Osage hunted beaver, the mild winters in this region prevented local beavers from producing the thick pelts of their Canadian counterparts, lowering the exchange rate.[29] In the eighteenth century, the most lucrative hide trade derived from deerskins, which required more extensive female labor in tanning and trimming than beaver peltry.[30]

Without a doubt, the laborious and time consuming hide processing and corresponding meat production added to an Osage woman's workload. Excavations of an eighteenth-century Little Osage town identified large flint scrapers used in tanning hides as the most abundant Native-made artifacts in the entire site, and iron awls as one of the most prolific European-made objects.[31] As their processing work grew, to save time and labor, women increasingly consumed European goods, such as iron awls, kettles, and cloth, and then utilized these items in the rest of their still voluminous domestic production.

Nevertheless, women did not full-scale abandon Native-made goods, such as stone hide scrapers or skin-clothing, which remained commonplace well into the nineteenth century. One Euro-American observer noted after visiting an Osage community, "It is to their [women's] industry and ingenuity, that the men owe every manufactured article of their dress, as well as every utensil in their huts."[32]

The vast majority of artifacts recovered from an excavated Great Osage town site inhabited during European colonization pertained to women's cultivation, food preparation, skin work, and weaving. Osage anthropologist Andrea Hunter has argued that "from a cultural materialist viewpoint, the behaviors that harness more energy are more important to a culture and can be expected to have the most profound affect [sic] on the overall state of the system." With the large quantity of female artifacts, she concluded, "The women's role can be considered the dominating influence on the techno-economic system at Osage village sites." Women's power was spiritually derived from their fertility, which manifested materially in creative work that had always made them vital to the economy. After colonization, this continued.[33]

Likewise, the expansion of commercial trade did not signify a decline in female status as women's roles in processing hides gained additional economic importance. By the late 1700s, Osage men likely doubled or tripled the amount of time they spent hunting.[34] Hunters procured enough hides and meat to occupy multiple women for days or weeks at a time. An Osage man's hunting prowess mattered little, though, without female labor because traders demanded expertly tanned hides that would survive the trip back to Europe. Indigenous women in the hide trade generally, and among the Osage specifically, monopolized the skills needed to produce these finished goods, placing a high value on their labor. From the Osage perspective, hunting had always been a collaborative effort, but in the eighteenth and early nineteenth century, this cooperation led to imperial domination.[35]

But there were larger spiritual implications for the nation. The Osage homeland was a place of abundance, where Wa-kon'-da had provided many blessings, especially in plant and animal resources, that the Osage utilized to support themselves. Both Osage historians Louis Burns and John Joseph Mathews refer to animals in particular as "brothers." Wa-kon'-da had given animals "protection against the elements" that had not been given to humans. Through prayer and ritual the Osage sought permission to acquire things like skin, hides, and tallow from animals. Animals also had spiritual skills the Osage lacked. "Thus did they pray through the panther, the buffalo, the turtle, the beaver, the otter, and the eel, as well as through the hawk and the eagle, and even the lowly spider, for arts and abilities which *Wah'Kon-Tah* had not seen fit to give them." The Osage "considered themselves to be caretakers appointed by the Mysterious Being to protect these gifts." How did commercial trade impact this relationship? Burns stated, "Possibly the most difficult [spiritual] adjustment was the necessary apology to the 'little brothers' for killing them and trading their pelts for the new 'necessities.'" Even with apologies, the Osage ultimately "hunted the 'little brothers' nearly to extinction," and Burns concluded, "We doubt that a full justification [for this] was ever reached in Osage minds." Hence, it was not entirely clear how the Osage perceived their increased hunting in terms of spiritual relationships and responsibilities to animals.[36]

What was clear: Osage men and women produced hides on a staggering scale. Prices varied, based on animal, size of the skin, quality of the processing, and European market rates. Historian J. Frederick Fausz called the Osage the "'true bankers of this region,' since they produced the largest quantity of the best-quality deer leather, and their chamois-like 'bucks' served as the main currency in Upper Louisiana." Typically, twenty medium-sized hides could buy a musket, and one medium hide could buy a horn full of powder or two pounds of bullets. A dressed deerskin typically weighed one to two pounds, depending on the size of the animal. Packs, or bales, of these skins weighed approximately 100 pounds. From 1764 to 1803, the Osage produced more than half of the hides in Spanish Illinois, amounting to roughly 600 packs of skins per year, or over 20,000 packs in total. As a result, they became "the best-armed Indians on the central prairies," furthering their military and hide trade dominance. US officials calculated the illegal Osage trade at the Arkansas Post for just the final four years of Spanish rule involved tens of thousands of skins valued at $20,000—nearly $400,000 today. During that same period, the Little and Great Osage produced $43,000 worth of furs (over $800,000 today), showing the enormous volume of their hunting and hide processing.[37]

With horses, Osage men could conduct hunts more independently, which they often did to acquire deerskins and other small game. In theory, horses and guns eliminated the need for the entire community to travel out onto the plains for the two buffalo hunts; however, they did not make this change. For a century, visitors witnessed how "they move from home in a body, men, women, and children, leaving none behind." These single-file processions, used to prevent enemies from knowing the number of people traveling together, could stretch from two to ten miles in length. The temporary hunting camps had "all the coverings to their houses, their cooking utensils, and provisions; and continue the same community of social interest, as in their villages." In 1811, US trading factor George Sibley described the Little Osage on their summer hunt as "a whole tribe, men, women, and children, horses and dogs, with all their movable effects, enjoying the summer buffalo hunt in the vast prairies of the West, for this great hunt is literally a season of enjoyment with all these roaming tribes." The hunts were not just a practical economic endeavor; they were a time of celebration and embodiment of their deeply rooted cosmological values, which conducted in the appropriate and reverent fashion (mirroring the universe's gendered duality), garnered Wa-kon'-da's favor, yielding Osage dominance.[38]

The addition of horses did change some things on the buffalo hunt. Women used horses instead of dogs to carry all the necessary provisions to the temporary camps, including skins for bedding and shelter, surplus meat, and corn. They also needed these horses to carry the monstrous loads of meat and hides they acquired in this period. Men utilized specially trained "buffalo horses"—selected for their speed, endurance, intelligence, and courage—to kill large numbers of bison. A hunter did not even ride this horse until the chase began. Mounted hunters no longer needed to drive the buffalo over a cliff. Instead, as Osage historian John Joseph Mathews described, "They milled them like cowboys mill cattle when cutting. They now rode around them in the tribal hunts and set them to milling, then shot the fat cows and young bulls, charging quickly on their hunting race horses to come up with the ones that broke away." Firearms at this time were both cumbersome and inaccurate, presenting danger to fellow hunters, so mounted men continued using bows (between three and six feet in length) and arrows. Even with the horses, the Osage still viewed the hunt as a communal effort; the two town chiefs (Ga-hi'-ge) maintained strict authority with the help of their assistants (A'ki-da). And as George Sibley conveyed in the quote that began this chapter, the general merriment was a testament to their success.[39]

Horses were more than assistants in hunting. When Charles Claude du Tisné made the first official French visit to Osage communities in 1719, he traded for their horses. In 1785 the Spanish governor-general Esteban Rodriguez Miró wrote that Osage wealth "consists in having many horses which they get from the Laytanes or Apaches and from the frequent raids that one nation makes on another." Even with sizable herds, they did not intentionally breed these horses. Miró criticized that the Osage "entirely prevent the raising of colts by loading the [mares] more than usual and making them run too much." Henry Marie Brackenridge, a Euro-American visitor in 1811, noted that "their stock of horses requires to be constantly renewed by thefts or purchases: from the severity of the climate and the little care taken of the foals, the animal would otherwise be in danger of becoming extinct." Remarkably, as Mathews observed, "There is little or nothing in the traditions of the Little Ones about their dramatic acquisition of the horse." For Indigenous peoples, incorporating livestock required an adaptation to spiritual and cosmological gender construction to determine if men or women should take on animal husbandry. By not breeding horses, the Osage prevented a reorganization of gender roles. Men obtained horses in traditional male occupations. They hunted the wild horses, especially between the Red and Canadian Rivers. Men also raided the neighboring (and enemy) Pawnee and other Caddoan nations for horse "captives," sometimes collecting hundreds at a time; they also served as middlemen, trading European goods with western Native peoples for horses. And, as Osage historian Louis Burns noted, "The Osages rarely used the horse in warfare. They preferred to fight on foot even on the Plains."[40]

The Osage also traded slaves. Without thick-pelted fur-bearing animals like the beaver in their homeland, the Osage embraced this "commodity" the French always wanted. French participation in ritualized kinship captive exchanges with Great Lakes and upper Mississippi valley peoples led many traders to turn Native slaves into profitable commodities exploited locally in French communities or trafficked as far away as Caribbean plantations. Historically, the Osage took primarily women and children as captives in war with other Natives. Warriors typically decided if they wanted to kill a captive they acquired in raids. If not killed, chiefs (Ga-hi'-ge) decided to trade the captive, or initiated adoption, with the captive becoming a full member the captor's clan, often replacing a deceased family member. Captive exchange played a significant part in Native diplomacy because captives symbolized life-giving rather than life-taking, and solidified kinship, sometimes initiating peace between enemies. Although men seemingly dominated determining a captive's fate, women often exercised influence in such matters, evidenced by John Hunter, a Euro-American boy adopted into an Osage family in the late eighteenth century.

I had not been long with the Osages, before I was received into the family of Shen-thweeh, a warrior distinguished among his people for his wisdom and bravery, at the instance of Hunk-hah, his wife, who had recently lost a son, in an engagement with some of the neighbouring tribes. . . . This good woman . . . [and] a daughter almost grown . . . took every opportunity, and used every means which kindness and benevolence could suggest, to engage my affections and esteem . . . so constant and persevering were their attentions, and so kind and affectionate their care of me, that not to have loved and esteemed them, would have argued a degree of ingratitude and apathy of feeling to which, if I know myself, I then was, and shall forever remain a stranger.[41]

As Hunter could attest, these adoptees received the same affection and attention, especially from women, as biological children and did not have permanent inferior status. Creating families was "women's work," and adoptive mothers embraced this role too.[42]

The slave trade seriously destabilized relations between Native groups as French allies, like the Osage, increasingly raided their neighbors, like the Caddoan peoples along the Arkansas and the Red Rivers, for slaves. Limited contact with French traders isolated the Caddoan peoples in this region, keeping them relatively unarmed and vulnerable to Osage attacks. Though many of the slaves came from a variety of Native nations, so many slaves came from Caddoan communities that French colonists generically termed Native slaves "pani" in reference to the Caddoan-speaking Pawnees, Panimahas (Skidi Pawnees), and Panis Noirs. Osage raiders primarily procured slaves from enemy nations and viewed slave trading as simply another way of defeating their enemies. Because captive exchange existed in Osage society prior to colonization, this aspect of European trade also did not require a reorganization of historic gender roles. Nonetheless, the colonial European slave trade proved massively destructive to Indigenous populations across the continent. Increased violence between Natives to obtain slaves caused deaths, while enslavement eventually resulted in incorporation into European society and erasure of Indigenous identity. Overall, this dramatically reduced North American Indigenous populations.[43]

The Non'-hon-zhin-ga's (priesthood) influence and the entire community's relationship with Wa-kon'-da also did not wane in this period. Visitors were often startled awake at dawn by "crying, mourning, lamentations, muttering, sobs, [and] hideous howlings," by every "man, woman, and child" observing daily prayer vigils, where each person appealed to *Wa-kon'-da* for an individual and collective long life, and mourned the loss of kin.[44] John Hunter reported that elderly women also educated their fellow citizens on Osage history and tradition, "of which they are by the consent of custom, the unerring and sacred depositories. . . . The memory of the squaws is the principal repository of their historical treasures." It was not clear if he was referring to women generally or women involved in the priesthood specifically. As the Osage experienced it, *Wa-kon'-da* continued to play a dominant role in their lives, which motivated the Osage to maintain a community organization that mirrored *Wa-kon'-da*'s duality-based universe.[45]

Before colonization, Osage leadership status primarily derived from heredity and wealth. Their social structure divided people into leader and commoner clans, with certain prestigious clans, subclans, and chieftainships fixed in ritual and tradition. The expense of *Non'-hon-zhin-ga* induction often meant only a few people from the prestigious clans and families could ever afford initiation. French trade changed this. As many families achieved status and wealth, they could afford to purchase things like expensive priesthood initiations. And do not forget, the priesthood incorporated women in a variety of ways. General prosperity actually served to expand the number of people who held sacred knowledge, which likely contributed to the strong commitment they retained toward their cosmology in this and later periods. Character, also a determining factor in priesthood membership, required generosity; and redistribution continued with more successful families "giving away" their wealth, further leveling the class structure, without accelerating individualism.[46]

Though many aspects of cosmology and gender roles remained intact, other aspects of Osage social organization changed during European colonization. Historian Willard Rollings has demonstrated that the *Non'-hon-zhin-ga*'s power in Osage society derived from their "willingness to accept and direct changes" that allowed them to accommodate challenges and changes without sacrificing core values. It could have been that the diversified and enlarged membership in the priesthood during this period provided motivation for expanding the entire leadership structure. Clan *wi'-gi-e* (ritual chant), maintained and passed on by priests, documented numerous "moves to a new country" in Osage history where communities separated, and new clans were created. Rollings argued that some of these separations happened in the eighteenth century, when horses, weapons, and prosperity facilitated people living in smaller groups. Every town had full clan representation, priests from every clan (Non'-hon-zhin-ga), a chief from each moiety (Ga-hi'-ge), and a warrior council (A'ki-da, soldier). More towns meant more leadership opportunities. Every clan had separate history, sacred objects, and was assigned a specific role in rituals, which required every clan's participation. So by creating new clans in this period (wi'-gi-e indicated the number increased from fourteen to twenty-four), the Non'-hon-zhin-ga found another way to accommodate widespread achievement, while maintaining Osage identity, cultural solidarity, and spiritual devotion.[47]

Various scholars have discussed how Osage dominance during this period resulted from their military prowess. Previously, the Non'-hon-zhin-ga conducted a two-week-long war ceremony that ensured Wa-kon'-da's support to achieve victory, while allowing time for priests to make an effective plan of attack; select a war leader; engage in ritual fasting and opening of the birdhawk wa-xo'-be (sacred bundle); and prepare sacred charcoal used to blacken warrior faces so they would embody the "relentlessness of fire in its attack of destruction." The war ceremony, conducted typically in summer, involved all twenty-four clans, included dancing and singing by women, and highlighted the need for communal cooperation to eliminate dangerous threats. But with an increasingly dispersed population and more frequent raiding, the Non'-hon-zhin-ga authorized smaller war parties often made up of men from one or a few clans that could respond to immediate threats. This made the Osage more militarily nimble, facilitating their empire's expansion. And they utilized a combination of the old (large, communal, lengthy, summer) and new (small, male-warrior, quick, year-round) war parties, depending on the circumstances.[48]

To many outsiders—Native, European, and later, American—the prominent height of Osage men symbolically reflected their national power.[49] For decades, many people noted, "The Osages may justly be said to be the tallest race of men in North America, either of red or white skins; there being very few indeed of the men . . . who are less than six feet in stature, and very many of them six and a half, and others seven feet."[50] In comparison, most Europeans in mid-eighteenth-century Louisiana and Illinois only stood a few inches above five feet.[51] Osage men shaved "their hair close to their heads, except a rim about half an inch wide around the crown of the head, which they wear about an inch long."[52] Further enhancing their height, men would often attach a five-inch-long roach, typically of porcupine quills or deer tails, to their strip of hair, sometimes topped off with a decorated eagle feather.[53] As the relatively tall six-foot-two-inch Thomas Jefferson wrote in 1804, "The Osages arrived yesterday . . . twelve men & two boys, and certainly the most gigantic men we have ever seen."[54] Osage men, carrying seven-foot-long lances, seemed to dwarf even their horses, and proved a fearsome and intimidating sight.[55]

Much has been made of Osage dominance in the eighteenth century resulting from the increased warfare, perceived as part of the male role in society, often directly or indirectly characterized as resulting in deteriorating female status.[56] Osage cosmology defined military victories as not only the result of male bravery but also as a product of women who, as mothers, literally created warriors and were thus honored as equally important in war achievement. John Hunter noted that a woman was "esteemed in proportion to the number of children she raise[d]," and her son's bravery or cowardice was deemed a direct consequence of her mothering. "In the cowardice or bad conduct of an Indian, his mother, sister, or daughter, suffers in a degree, and their chances of a respectable marriage are diminished; because . . . good and bad qualities may be both inherited and entailed . . . [and] a squaw who loves her country and reputation, and does her duty, can never be the mother of a bad Indian." Young boys were encouraged to roughhouse and quarrel with one another in order to develop courage. But if a mother observed her son's cowardly behavior in this context, she would employ "a very extraordinary discipline."

> She begins by placing a rod in his hand; assists him to beat and make flee the dog, or any thing else that may come in his way, and then encourages him to pursue. An adept in this, she teazes and vexes him, creates an irritable temper, submits to the rod, and flees before him with great apparent dread. When skilled in this branch, she strikes him with her hand, pulls his hair, &c. which her now hopeful boy retaliates in a spiteful and becoming manner. Some time having passed in this way, by which her pupil has learned to bear pain without dread, she takes him again [to play with other boys], and I have never known an instance of a second disappointment in these trials of courage.[57]

Osage historian Louis Burns reaffirmed, "If one were to pick a single factor that made the Osages outstanding physically, mentally, and spiritually it would have to be the Osage mothers."[58] Touché.

The ritual nature of war, for men and women, also endured, allowing women to combine their courage with that of men's in order to ensure military success. They still ritually opened and carried the sacred bird-hawk *wa-xo'-be* into battle, with its embodiment of the entire universe and gender duality, still woven and cared for by women. Women and men still appealed for *Wa-kon'-da*'s blessings and assistance in vanquishing their enemies through ceremonial dancing and singing.[59] Numerous witnesses described Osage men and women performing the scalp dance, an embodiment of men's and women's combined courage achieving success in battle.[60]

> In the performance of the scalp dance, the squaw usually attaches all the scalps that are in her family to a pole, which she bears on the occasion. As they dance round the council lodge or fire, they alternately sing and recount the exploits that were achieved on their acquisition. The one who sings is for the time the principal, and all the others obsequiously follow her. The men and children join in the whoops and rejoicings. During these festivities, marks of favour are lavished, particularly by the squaws, on all such as have distinguished themselves. The most worthy are seated by the old men and chiefs; the women dance round them, decorate their persons with dresses ornamented with feathers, and porcupine quills stained of various colours; and crown them with wreaths of oak leaves, fantastically interwoven with flowers, beads, and shells.[61]

From the Osage perspective, expanding violence and warfare to achieve their regional dominance involved actions—physical or ceremonial—of both men and women. So an Osage empire built on hunting and war success, was an empire built on Osage gender complementarity and the actions of men and women.

In another example of adaptation, during the eighteenth and nineteenth centuries, the Osage combined patrilineal descent with matrilocal residence, producing an unusual cultural construction in Native North America.[62] Other Dhegihan-Siouan-speaking nations used patrilineal descent and patrilocal residence, leading scholars to conclude the Osage once organized in the same way before this "move to a new country."[63] Several scholars argued that increased European trade demands for hides, horses, and slaves prompted the Osage to adopt matrilocality.[64] Even before colonization, members of one clan formed an Osage hunting or raiding party. In the eighteenth century, these men could travel up to 500 miles from their towns, amounting to months away from home.[65] Under a patrilocal system, an entire household would not have its male protection and production during every hunt or raid, and if disaster struck, the household could potentially lose all these men.[66] Matrilocal residence reorganized the household to include men from various clans, preventing total male absence at any one time. Anthropologist Robert Wieger argued that adopted Caddoan women captives may have proposed or aided in implementing the Osage transition to matrilocality, which was the established system in Caddoan culture.[67] In addition, matrilocal residence allowed successful hunters and warriors to marry women from the established hereditary leadership clans, thus providing kinship relations that melded the precolonial Osage leadership structure with the more mobile eighteenth-century lifestyle that accommodated individual male achievements while maintaining national unity.[68]

The hide trade, matrilocality, frequent male absence and sometimes death, fostered, or at least encouraged, plural marriages.[69] Sororal polygyny—one man marrying women of the same family—was the most common, and likely developed among the Osage as an adaptive strategy just like matrilocality, though the majority of marriages remained monogamous. Increased warfare and thus mortality likely decreased the number of available marriageable males, reinforcing polygyny to bolster the Osage population.[70] Polygynous Osage families in this period typically involved a man with two or three wives, although some prestigious or accomplished men had four or more wives. One could only gain multiple wives through excellence in hunting and other pursuits that allowed him to economically support multiple women and their offspring. Sometimes each wife had a separate lodge that she constructed and owned, and the husband moved between them based on the Osage custom of avoiding a pregnant or lactating wife's home (lactating mothers refrained from intercourse). John Hunter witnessed that co-wives often visited each other, "and generally live on the most friendly terms."[71] Some scholars view polygyny as evidence of female subordination, but it did not automatically imply male dominance in this context.[72] A polygynous Osage man married sisters or cousins who, in a matrilocal society, would have lived or worked together regardless of marital status.[73] Similar examinations of the Omaha and Pawnee indicated that in the hide trade, women welcomed and desired the communal assistance sororal polygyny provided in maintaining households and processing hides.[74]

Sexual freedom and the availability of divorce also precluded female subordination. European and American visitors, illuminating their bias, typically viewed Osage women's sexual relations—with other Osages and with outsiders—as immodest, adulterous, and "so brazenly licentious that it is quite disgusting."[75] John Bradbury, traveling up the Missouri River in 1811, stopped at a trading post near a Little Osage town where a local physician supposedly educated him on the customs and manners of the Osage people by "walk[ing] with me down to the boats, where we found several squaws assembled, as Dr. Murray assured me, for the same purpose as females of a certain class in the maritime towns of Europe crowd round vessels lately arrived from a long voyage, and it must be admitted with the same success."[76] It seems more likely these women were exercising sexual freedom. And as we shall see later in this chapter, these women engaging with traders could have been part of kinship creation.

Osage women and men seemed to exercise significant sexual freedom. Men, as John Hunter described, "have it in their power to, and do associate with the females" as long as the men were not "engaged in war, hunting, travelling excursions, etc." The men actually seemed to have a harder time garnering female attention because they needed to prove their ability as a hunter or warrior "since so many and important results are believed to depend on their success in [these occupations]: their happiness, their standing in society, and their sexual relations." And "females, both young and old, affect to despise the Indian who openly becomes the lover, without the authority of having acquired distinction either in the chase, or in fighting against the enemies of his country." Unlike Euro-American culture, Osage marriage was not considered the commencement of one's sexual relations, nor did marriage seem to require sexual exclusivity. As Osage historian Louis Burns put it, "Sex was not necessarily an object of the marriage." Various sources indicated that some Osage co-wives "cohabited" with other men, and having a child "out of wedlock" had nothing to do with perceived morality.[77]

Women and men were equally able to initiate divorce. Louisiana resident Louis Bringier in 1812 noted an Osage man "may have as many wives as he can obtain; these may leave their husband when they please, and the man, on his part, can repudiate his wife." In either case, the woman retained her property—the lodge and all of its household goods—as well as the children, except for boys of sufficient age to accompany their father in adult male occupations.

Though Hunter noted the rarity of divorce, especially after a couple had children, he also indicated that neither party experienced any stigma attached to the separation, and each could easily remarry should they so desire.[78]

Osage marriages conveyed respect for social values and consequently influenced an entire lineage's status and the possibility of later priesthood initiation. Families ensured respectable status by arranging their children's first marriage, called mi'-zhin. Young people did not publicly prefer a particular partner, even though attachments sometimes developed in childhood. Before a woman's family would accept a man's marriage offer, he had to demonstrate his value as a husband and potential father through proficiency in hunting and warfare. Women reached an eligible age for mi'-zhin marriages right after puberty, typically around age fifteen. Men, because of the achievement requirements, typically did not enter a first marriage until their twenties. This highlighted how, after menarche, women had innate creative power, while men needed training, practice, and time to earn status and become marriageable. Just in case young people forgot this, older women serving as "duennas" and armed with knives, chaperoned young women and intimidated young men.[79]

Once a man had proven himself, his relatives would contact a woman's family with a marriage proposal. If the woman and her family approved the match, the two families negotiated a sizable gift exchange, typically involving horses, food, and clothing. One marriage in 1854 involved the bridegroom and his family supplying all the provisions for the ceremony and fifty horses to the bride's family. John Joseph Mathews argued that Osage individuals could marry without horses, but so doing indicated that either party "had no pride." The exchange coincided with feasting, after which the man joined his wife's household. Divorced or widowed individuals, previously mi'-zhin married, could subsequently partner in an o-mi'-hon marriage. Individual men and women initiated o-mi'-hon marriages, but often they attempted to mirror the mi'-zhin process and involved extended family members to demonstrate a reputable social position. Those who did not follow these customs and simply cohabitated with a partner, entered into an illegitimate marriage, called gashon'th migthonge, which translated as "a union in the natural state or in disregard of tribal custom." Because these individuals deliberately disregarded social mores, they could not obtain formal positions of authority, and their children were not regarded as full members of the nation.[80]

Osage women also eventually married European men to create kinship ties that solidified trade relationships.[81] Early to mid-eighteenth-century trade relied on numerous French-Native communities along the Mississippi and the Missouri Rivers. The population in these communities derived from inter-marriage between French traders and Native female slaves, who did not serve as cultural mediators between the French and Native nations. The Osage, like the majority of Indigenous people in colonial Louisiana, initially established French trade without intermarriage. As historian Kathleen DuVal has demon-strated, shrewd Osage diplomacy and military might facilitated their domi-nance, violently if necessary, without requiring literal kinship with Europe-ans. However, the rise of the competing Comanche empire to the west and arrival of Spanish colonial authority in the late eighteenth century prompted the Osage to develop direct kinship connections with traders to ensure their economic hegemony.[82]

The French were more than willing to oblige. In the waning years of the French "claim" to Louisiana, the colonial governor authorized a new settle-ment, in hopes of expanding kinship and trade with the Osage. This plan finally came to fruition in 1764 when French traders Pierre Lacléde and his stepson Auguste Chouteau "founded St. Louis as the original gateway to the Osage West." Historian J. Frederick Fausz called the Osage "co-founders" of this "Indian capital" because they "gave the town its commercial prosperity," and thus Europeans were dependent on Osage goodwill. St. Louis developed into the most significant fur trading community in this region, serving as home to many French colonists who remained in North America after the Seven Years' War. The city was built on elevated ground to facilitate trade and discourage European-style farming, which would disrupt wildlife, Na-tive hunting, and the local economy. Fausz argued St. Louis was an "alter-native western frontier" resulting in a "successful multicultural commercial enterprise." Populations in surrounding Native communities outnumbered St. Louis for much of its early history, and less than 1,000 people lived in the city as late as 1803. French traders protected Indigenous "lands, liberties, and lifeways" in order to profit from Native men's hunting and women's hide processing. For the next forty years, Lacléde-Chouteau family members be-came St. Louis' leading merchant-traders because of kinship with the Osage, involving generous gift giving, respect for customs and language, and inter-marriage with women.[83]

In terms of intermarriage, the status of an Osage woman mirrored the status of the European man she married.[84] John Joseph Mathews explained how illegal traders (coureurs de bois), trappers, and men who simply abandoned

European settlements to "go native" entered into *gashon'th migthonge* marriages, and tended to attract "widows whose chances of remarriage were not too bright, or girls of the second class whose immediate ancestors had mated . . . without benefit of formality."[85] This could have been the case for the women John Bradbury and Dr. Murray witnessed greeting traders in 1811, discussed earlier.[86] Conversely, prominent late eighteenth-century French merchants, such as the Mongraine, Lambert, and Chouteau families, developed kinship ties through *mi'-zhin* or *o-mi'-hon* marriages to prominent women from prestigious or hereditary chieftain clans, requiring extended family member participation and considerable gift giving. For example, Noel Mongraine married "Marie" Pawhushan, the daughter of one of the Osage's most powerful turn-of-the-century chiefs, Pawhuska (White Hair). Osage clans then adopted these prominent traders to ensure their children's patrilineal clan affiliation. Such marriages between prominent individuals in both communities then led to continued material wealth for both.[87]

In the late eighteenth and early nineteenth centuries, Native women all along the Missouri River valley gained, or in the Osage case, perhaps maintained, status through marriages and liaisons that united Native nations and traders. In this way, Osage women, like other Indigenous women, served as cultural mediators, providing "sustained and enduring contact with new cultural ways" and advancing the economic goals of all involved.[88] Generally, Osage women reared their children during early childhood at trading posts or in Osage towns. Fluid residency in these communities corresponded with fluid marital ties (an Osage norm), exemplified by "Marie" Pawhushan, who married and lived with Noel Mongraine in St. Louis for years before moving back to her hometown and marrying an Osage man. European men, notably from the Chouteau family, also observed relatively fluid marital, sexual, and residency patterns, including polygyny, in Osage communities that maintained their access to this trade. Most of the offspring received some kind of Euro-American education, usually from missionaries. Sons often joined their father's profession, while still participating in Osage communal activities like the summer buffalo hunt. Sons typically married Osage women while daughters often married European or Osage men, perpetuating the enmeshed kinship relationships. Though intermarriage with Europeans was a new occurrence, the type of marriage and the status of those marrying still held to Osage traditions, with women again serving as creators, this time of relationships that ensured clan and community economic success in a changing world.[89]

MO-HON-GO.
OSAGE WOMAN.

Mo-Hon-Go. Osage Woman, from *History of the Indian Tribes of North America* (used with permission of the Smithsonian American Art Museum). Mo-Hon-Go (or Mi-Ho'n-Ga or Mi-hun-ga), translated as Sacred Sun, was believed to have been one of A. P. Chouteau's Osage wives. Their daughter, Amelia (among other so-called half-breeds), received a section of land in the 1825 removal treaty. In 1827, Sacred Sun was one of six Osage people swindled into traveling to France as part of a get-rich-quick scheme for their host, David Delauney, who used them as a tourist attraction. He eventually abandoned the group, leaving them starving and wandering Europe in search of a way home. Demonstrating the fluidity of Osage and Chouteau marital and sexual relations, one of the other Osage travelers, Black Bird (Washinka Sabe), was referred to as Sacred Sun's husband. On February 10, 1828, in Belgium, Sacred Sun gave birth to their twin daughters. One girl was adopted by a wealthy Belgian woman, but the baby died the following year. On their return trip to North America, Black Bird died of smallpox. Finally arriving in Washington, DC, in 1830, Charles Bird King painted this portrait of Sacred Sun and her surviving daughter before they returned to their Arkansas Osage home. In 1836, it was reported that Sacred Sun had also died of smallpox. (John Joseph Mathews, *The Osages: Children of the Middle Waters* [Norman: University of Oklahoma Press, 1961], 539–547; Charles J. Kappler, ed., *Indian Affairs: Laws and Treaties, vol. 2 Treaties* [Washington, DC: Government Printing Office, 1904], 218; and William Least Heat-Moon and James K. Wallace, ed., *An Osage Journey to Europe, 1827–1830: Three French Accounts* [Norman: University of Oklahoma Press, 2013], 9.)

During the eighteenth century, European colonization resulted in the rise of an Osage empire. The Osage markedly increased the volume of trade, while transitioning into a more mobile and dispersed society that altered marriage and residence patterns. Clearly, the Osage made changes that improved their lives and facilitated their dominance. But not everything needed to change in order to do this—certainly not gender complementarity. Women's food production of crops and meat provided many of the initial goods used in early French trade. Even after the expansion of commercial trading, women continued subsistence agricultural production with the associated ritual significance. Hunting and its products had always resulted from cooperative labor, which continued in the hide trade where a man's hunting prowess translated into wealth and status only when the women in his family expertly processed the hides. Sexual freedom and availability of divorce meant the polygynous relationships, even with Europeans, formed in this period did not decrease women's status. Horse and slave trading evolved from established raiding and captive exchange, preventing a reorganization of gender roles for men or women. Plus, the Osage viewed warfare success as a product of both male and female efforts; thus, their regional hegemony during this period resulted from the physical and spiritual cooperation of both genders. As colonial empires changed and rival Native nations gained power, Osage women used marriage to incorporate Europeans into kinship networks, ensuring sustained trade. Due to their complementary efforts, Osage men and women entered the nineteenth century with a flourishing economy and successful incorporation of colonizers and their goods. It was no wonder then that George Sibley witnessed such wealth and "general happiness" in the hunting camp he visited in 1811.[90] For the Osage, though, the United States would prove their most formidable foe to date.

CHAPTER 3 "A VERY UNFAVORABLE CHANGE IN THEIR CIRCUMSTANCES": THE OSAGE AND US IMPERIALISM

By the late eighteenth century, European empires had spent centuries competing over control of North American land and wealth, yet most of the continent remained—as Kathleen DuVal termed it—a "Native Ground." In Louisiana in particular, Indigenous life "was made more cosmopolitan for its [European] trade connections but not controlled by them." The arrival of the US empire changed everything. Whereas the French and Spanish needed Natives as allies and trading partners to maintain any semblance of a colonial "claim," settler colonizers, like Britain and the United States, needed to eliminate Indigenous peoples to replace them with the empire's settlers.[1] As a result, one Protestant missionary to the Osage noted in 1834: "From the commencement of [American] transactions with [the Osage], they date a very unfavorable change in their circumstances—a great increase of diseases, the destruction of their game, and in a word, almost all their troubles are ascribed to their connection with the white people. 'You have brought poverty to us,' was the expression used by one of them on this subject."[2] Even though US imperialism resulted in marginalization and suffering for the Osage, their cosmology, with its emphasis on complementarity, continued to inform their economy, spiritual practices, and gender roles.

In the years following the American Revolution, eastern Native nations initially bore the brunt of US colonization. For many British colonists, increased access to Native land was one of the preeminent reasons for declaring independence. In the United States, representative governments actually emboldened settler colonialism because "elected officials were accountable to the settlers, not to the Indians" and "wherever settlers went, they formed a concentrated political bloc in favor of obtaining Indian land as soon as possible." Having already faced decades of British settler invasion, many Native nations experienced the Revolutionary War as a war of conquest that culminated in the destruction of food, homes, towns, and ultimately lives, capped off with forced expulsion when many Native nations were deemed British allies and thus defeated enemies.[3] As a result, thousands of Native refugees moved west, with some encroaching on Osage lands. From the north, Osage towns increasingly faced attacks and competition from the Potawatomi, Iowa, Sac, Mesquakie, and Kickapoo. The same thing happened in the south with the Cherokee, Choctaw, Chickasaw, Shawnee, and Delaware.[4]

Clearly the US settler empire was already beginning to eliminate eastern Native populations, but elimination of Natives in the heart of the continent accelerated during Thomas Jefferson's presidency. Jefferson spent much of his professional life employing the doctrine of discovery to dispossess Indigenous people, and after 1776 this was part of his effort to build a continental US empire. Legal scholar Robert J. Miller described Jefferson as "one of the most aggressive and strategically expansionist presidents who ever held the office." This was on full display with the Louisiana Purchase in 1803. Though scholars have often called this "the greatest real estate deal in history," in reality Jefferson was fully aware that the United States had actually purchased discovery claims and preemption rights (sole right to buy land from Natives). Based on this centuries-old European legal tradition, the United States allegedly held ultimate dominion over this land—entailing political and commercial control—while Native nations retained a temporary "right of occupancy" until they "chose" to sell their land to the only legal buyer: the United States of America.[5]

Though George Washington proposed it in the 1780s, and Andrew Jackson infamously championed it in the 1830s, Thomas Jefferson was actually "the first person to formulate an official federal policy of removal, the first to set it in motion, and the first to start removing tribes west of the Mississippi." His intention for the Louisiana Purchase was to expand upon the Native migration already in progress by formally relocating all eastern Native nations into the "new" territory. Though "American historians have antiseptically labeled [this] the 'Removal Period,'" historian John Mack Faragher, among many others, has argued this was more accurately "the era of ethnic cleansing." In a settler empire, these "removed" peoples served as "proxy invaders," warring with locals, like the Osage, eventually decimating all. After eastern land was filled with American settlers, Jefferson expected the United States to establish additional states in the Louisiana territory. Evidently the plan was to eliminate all Natives in the entirety of the United States.[6]

Publicly, Jefferson emphasized a far more benevolent goal for the Louisiana Purchase: it would be the place where both emigrant and local Natives became "civilized." This culminated in the federal civilization program that sent missionaries into Native communities to gain Christian converts and to teach Euro-American cultural norms. As Osage scholar and theologian George Tinker has argued, this was cultural genocide. Receiving federal funding and serving in various official capacities, missionaries were part of the systemic and systematic effort to destroy, erode, and undermine the culture and values that oriented Native life. Missionaries attacked ceremonial practices, extended kinship relationships, economic and political systems, and gender complementarity, among other things, all while "belittling every aspect of native culture." Tinker and others have concluded this was a concerted effort to "destroy, in whole or in part, a national, ethnical, racial or religious group," as the United Nations defines genocide. Violent extermination and assimilation programs both intended to destroy a "group," and even though cultural genocide was more subtle, it should not be construed as a "lesser" genocide because "it is no less devastating to a people." The settler empire needed Native elimination in order to obtain their land, and the civilization program was one way of accomplishing this.[7]

Jefferson used the Lewis and Clark expedition (1804–1806) to exercise discovery rights over Native nations from the Mississippi River to the Columbia River. In their interactions with Indigenous peoples, Lewis and Clark constantly reiterated US sovereignty and Indigenous economic, military, and political subordination. To this end, the president instructed Lewis and Clark to send Native leaders to Washington, DC, in hopes of further intimidating them. Because of Osage power and their central location, Jefferson intended to direct the first eastern Native expulsions into Osage territory. Hence, an Osage contingent arrived in Washington in July 1804—the first Native representatives Lewis and Clark sent to visit the president.[8]

Another aspect of Lewis and Clark's expedition specifically, and Jefferson's policy generally, was establishing trade relations with Native nations. The federal factory system had been established by Congress during the Washington administration, but Jefferson transformed the trading factories into a method of gaining Native "consent" for land cessions. He instructed a variety of government and military officials, including William Henry Harrison who initially administered Upper Louisiana, which encompassed Osage land, that the way "to promote this disposition to exchange lands which they have to spare & we want" was to "push our trading houses, and be glad to see the good & influential individuals among them run in debt, because . . . when these debts get beyond what the individuals can pay, they become willing to lop them off by a cession of lands." The factories basically served as a tool of imperial coercion, where Natives allegedly accumulated such sizable trading debts that the only way they could repay the federal government was by selling land. In their first visit to Washington, Jefferson disingenuously promised Osage leaders continued trade and maintenance of their territory.[9]

Back home, Osage life and land was increasingly under attack. Facing raids from the rival Comanche empire to the west and migrant eastern Natives to the north, south, and east, the Osage responded in kind. Meanwhile, Euro-Americans invaded, establishing settlements west of St. Louis that during 1807 and 1808 experienced Osage retaliation as well. Jefferson had frequently framed such violent Native resistance to US colonization as "barbarities [that] justified extermination," and the Osage were no exception. As "punishment," Meriwether Lewis, now territorial governor of Upper Louisiana, proceeded to ban all trade with the Osage and encouraged other Native people, "proxy invaders," to attack them. William Clark, now general of militia and superintendent of Indian affairs in St. Louis, then leveraged all of this into a land cession treaty.[10] Treaties in general were a legacy of European colonization, when empires needed Native alliances to help maintain their colonial "claims" against rival Europeans. Likewise, Natives used "play-off diplomacy" to ally with the European empire that best served Native interests. In this context, treaties could function as diplomatic negotiations between at least relative sovereigns. Americans maintained the practice, structuring treaties as contracts that implicitly recognized Native sovereignty. But as the United States became the dominant empire on the continent, "play-off diplomacy" ended, and treaties became a tool of conquest.[11]

The Treaty of 1808 was a classic example of treaty coercion. As Jefferson had instructed, Clark abruptly demanded land cessions when Osage leaders thought they were meeting to discuss other matters—in this case, invasion by and retaliation against American settlers. Negotiations were only conducted with a few Great and Little Osage leaders, who did not have the authority to make land cessions, and the entire nation (Arkansas bands included) was expected to abide by the treaty's provisions. And finally, Clark flatly lied about what was in the treaty; he allegedly admitted to a friend that "it was the hardest bargain against the Indians he ever made, and that if he was to be damned hereafter it would be for making that treaty." The Osage leaders were led to believe that they had agreed to share some territory with Euro-American hunters in exchange for annuity payments, goods, blacksmith services, plows, a grain mill, a new trading factory (Fort Osage), and federal military protection against rival Natives. However, Clark, Lewis, and Jefferson claimed the Osage had ceded "their title to an extent of country nearly equal to the State of Virginia, and much more fertile," on which refugee Natives and Americans would settle. Osage leaders were already voicing their displeasure to Lewis about this fraudulent acquisition of 52 million acres before he had even mailed the treaty to the president. But it was to no avail. Osage historian Louis Burns concluded, "Considering that all forms of compensation for these lands totaled less than one-sixth of a cent per acre, it is reasonable to suspect that someone was cheated."[12]

Osage complaints were irrelevant because Jefferson had already set in motion a plan that by 1810 had settled over 1,000 Cherokee on Osage land. By 1820, the local Cherokee population reached at least 5,000. Of all the eastern Natives moving into the region, the large, well-armed Cherokee population posed the most serious threat to date to Osage access to game and the trade wealth it produced. The Cherokee also created alliances with Osage rivals, who cooperated to steal Osage horses, attacked hunting parties and communities, raided food storage caches, and burned agricultural fields. Though William Clark had promised federal protection for the Osage in the Treaty of 1808, it was not forthcoming. While Natives killed each other, US military protection was reserved for the tens of thousands of American settlers colonizing the region. As Jefferson had intended, Indian policy ultimately functioned to facilitate American access to land, continent-wide. Hence, Clark, now serving as territorial governor of Missouri, Secretary of War John C. Calhoun, and President James Monroe preferred to make arrangements "favorable to the Cherokees; as the President is anxious to hold out every inducement to the Cherokees, and the other Southern nations of Indians, to emigrate to the West of the Mississippi." Thus, the Osage were "punished" for warfare with the Cherokee, culminating in another land cession treaty in 1818 that was deliberately misleading, not negotiated with the necessary leaders, and its promises never fulfilled. By 1825, thousands of American settlers squatted on Osage lands, and, as had been the tradition for decades, Osage leaders were forced to accept whatever payment US officials offered before

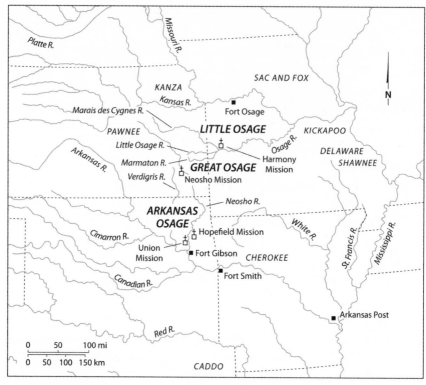

Osage Homeland, 1800s–1830s. (Map by Bill Nelson.)

they lost the land completely. The result was expulsion to Kansas, and the Osage presence in their eastern homeland was effectively eliminated.[13]

The Little Osage lived along the Missouri River until attacks from northern Native groups pushed them to rejoin the Great Osage, beginning in the 1790s. However, travelers continued to observe Little Osage homes and fields along the Missouri River at least until 1818. By the time Protestant missionaries arrived in the 1820s, the Great and Little Osage lived together where the Marais des Cygnes and the Marmaton (Little Osage) Rivers joined to form the Osage River. The Arkansas Osage remained along the Verdigris where they had established communities in the 1760s.[14]

Although generally separated into the northern (Missouri) and southern (Arkansas) bands of approximately equal population (up to an estimated 10,000–14,000 total), the community-based ritual and political structure further decentralized during this period. The dual moiety *Ga-hi'-ge* (chief) system was undermined by untimely deaths of Osage chiefs, Spanish alliances with men outside the traditional chiefly clans, particularly among the Arkansas Osage, and Chouteau influence in distinguishing nonhereditary leaders, which led to a large migration of some northern Osage to join the southern bands in protest. Anthropologist Garrick Alan Bailey argued the "traditional Osage political and war organization was unable to cope with the mass invasion of the eastern tribes" that basically fostered a situation of constant warfare.

Hence, influence of the dual chiefs declined as the Osage people separated into smaller towns, led by successful warriors, which were easier to protect and feed in a world of escalating violence. Community separation though was not new and had been sanctioned and directed by the Non'-hon-zhin-ga (priesthood) at various points in Osage history, including during the rise of their empire. In order to accommodate the fact that towns often did not have the dual chiefs or full clan representation necessary for conducting ceremonies, the Non'-hon-zhin-ga allowed individuals rather than clans to purchase a wa-xo'-be (sacred bundle) and the associated ritual knowledge and responsibilities. Historian Willard Rollings described this as "the democratization of Osage spirituality"; more people now had more access to their cosmology. As the offspring of sun (masculine) and moon (feminine), the sacred bird-hawk present in most wa-xo'-be was an embodiment of the universe's duality, while also imparting courage in battle through ceremonial use. A woman, of course, had to weave and care for the existing and new shrines, demonstrative of her role as warrior mother and considered just as important as male valor in war success. Most rituals involved a wa-xo'-be and "opening of the mat must be done by a warrior priest," allowing for repeated reinforcement of their spiritual values, including gender roles, that it encapsulated. Again, the Non'-hon-zhin-ga embraced changes that provided an alternative for individuals to achieve status in a modified political and community structure, while more broadly disseminating sacred knowledge, and maintaining ritual practices and cultural identity. This meant that many core values, such as gender complementarity, remained central to Osage life, while things like community leadership changed.[15]

The Osage were so devout in their commitments to their spiritual practices throughout this period that even outsiders begrudgingly admitted they had "a native religion of their own." Daily prayer vigils continued, where everyone—men, women, and children—appealed to Wa-kon'-da (Mysterious Power) for long individual and national life and mourned the dead by ritual actions at sunrise, when the dual feminine and masculine forces merged. They "rise in the morning before day dawns, black their faces with earth, look towards the rising sun, and, with an affected air, pray sometimes until the sun has risen." Josiah Gregg, like many visitors to an Osage community in the early 1800s, reported, "I was awakened at the dawn of the day by the most doleful, piteous, heart-rending howls and lamentations." Numerous missionaries even found Osage religious fervor a model for Christians to emulate: "Their early rising and their constancy in attending to their devotions of this kind make me sometimes inquire what is the power of my religion, and whether it ought not to make me and all Christians rise to pray, after the example of our Saviour, at least as early as these Indians." Osage imperial decline did not correspond with a religious or spiritual decline.[16]

An uptick in violence in this period obviously had negative consequences for lives and property, but it may have served to maintain cosmology because so many ritual actions that embodied the Osage worldview, including gender complementarity, were involved with warfare. As missionaries noted, "They can never attack an enemy with success, even in the most auspicious situation, without first performing such ceremonies and receiving favourable dreams." Warfare played a central role in Osage culture and identity; war practices involved appealing to Wa-kon'-da for the gift of courage men needed to defeat the enemy, and ritually acknowledging women's role as warrior mothers while combining their courage with men's. And failure in battle "they attribute to the omission of these religious duties." Organizationally, they appeared to still use a combination of the relatively new, small-scale raids as well as the older, large, communal war parties. Missionaries could never find an available audience for their sermons when they arrived in town during ceremonies related to warfare because "wars most literally affect all . . . chiefs, warriors, counselors, soldiers, men, women, and children and almost their horses and dogs are agreed to it." When missionaries visited a Little Osage community in 1832, they "found their whole village absorbed in a war dance, while the warriors and the youth, pursued the ceremony, day and night . . . every one seeming to be interested in the expedition, far more intently than in our preaching. . . . Now if the committee or some one from the missionary rooms were here they would witness our discouragement." Not only did war rituals reiterate Osage cosmology, they thwarted attempts by missionaries to make any changes to Osage spirituality.[17]

After valiant warriors returned home, "not a woman, but rejoices in, the victory . . . with what eagerness does the wife sit to hear the tale and details of her husband's exploits." In 1833, one missionary went on a preaching tour through several Great Osage towns, hoping to spread the gospel. Instead, "we were entertained, or rather annoyed, by their dance over the scalps." Apparently he found this annoying because no one would listen to his sermons. Hearing "drumming, dancing, yelling, [we] stepped out to see the dance."

It proves to be a female dance. Thirty or 40 of the relatives of the victors, arrange them selves [sic] in a row one side of the lodge, facing the other side. All appear well. Most of them young . . . and while there [sic] fine and fantastic dress, looks like dancing, their countenances betoken mourning or deep sobriety of tho't. . . . All arranged, the musick [sic] strikes, and they set themselves in motion taking a kind of side way step, keeping time with there hands and the bush of feathers they hold in each, and so encircle the musick who sit, pounding on their sort of drum in the centre. . . . This motion proves to be a ceremony. They run as token of rejoicing, to meet some of the warriors, who are equipped and coming to mingle in the dance. Now they all march back to the lodge, the scene changes. They dance round, the musick in progression, two and two. Here passes two modest, lovely females. And now passes a hideous looking warrior, jumping and pounding along. Here two more females gently moving along, and here another terrific form of a man. And so the men move round among the women. Some black, some red, holding their weapons on one hand and shield in the other performing wild . . . maneuvers as they pass round.[18]

The scalp dance continued to celebrate the combined courage of men and women that produced battle victories.[19]

In Osage cosmology, rituals sought *Wa-kon'-da*'s favor for the dual aspects of Osage survival: population growth via women's fecundity, and men's warrior courage that protected women, children, and homes. Consequently, men earned the most prestigious *o'don* (war honors) for defending homes and agricultural fields. But during this period, the Osage frequently experienced attacks and defeat; men were not always able to protect. Some of the most egregious examples were the 1817 and 1821 Cherokee attacks on Arkansas

Osage communities while men were away, leading in each case to the capture of approximately 100, the deaths of more than thirty inhabitants, and destruction of homes and food. For a society that exalted combat bravery resulting from the actions of men and women, this had to be a serious turn of events, and might explain their continued fervor in performing war-related rituals. They needed *Wa-kon'-da*'s favor now more than ever. Osage scholar John Joseph Mathews described how during this time the scalp dance was performed in victory and defeat,

> This dance would renew [the men's] spirits and, if need be, their courage. If they had brought no scalps this time, the dried scalps of another war movement waving above the dancing girls at the ends of poles would remind them that they were great warriors, and that their enemies were still riding over the plains. And this dance was good for the spirit especially in defeat, when the women who had lost their men could be heard keening from the hills around the camp or village. It was good to remember that the Little Ones were men pre-eminent.[20]

A decline in their military capability was clearly impacting masculinity; perhaps only magnified by the overwhelming success they had enjoyed during their imperial dominance only a generation before. The scalp dance then allowed women and men to seek divine favor, reinforce their combined role in warfare, and bolster everyone's confidence, especially men's.[21]

Due to violence with the Cherokees and other rivals, hide trading became somewhat more inconsistent during this period as refugee and local groups competed over the same herds. Some scholars have interpreted the presence of women and children on Osage buffalo hunts as compromising food production by leaving fields unattended and reducing the number of available hunters. Entire towns, including the children and elderly, had always traveled onto the plains for the two annual bison hunts, where women set up temporary camps to process meat and hides as the men brought in slaughtered game. The hunts had always been timed around the planting and harvesting schedule, so agriculture was not undermined by women's absence. Some men did start to stay behind in the camps to provide protection while their kinsmen hunted, but the numbers seem to indicate maybe a dozen men remained. These same communities could muster between 400 and 1,500 warriors when necessary, so it seems that the years when they were able to conduct hunts, the vast majority of men participated. Hunting failure was more often a product of coercive federal policy. Osage historian Louis Burns noted that failed or missed hunts preceded most of the Osage land cession treaties, sometimes (like in 1808) because US officials suspended trade during hunting season to force this exact outcome. Other times, like in 1825, federal officials demanded treaty negotiations during prime buffalo hunting months at eastern locations, like St. Louis, undermining the Osage economy and subsistence, which furthered the settler empire's ultimate goal of Indigenous elimination.[22]

At the same time, beyond all of the obvious cultural reasons, the Osage had little incentive to abandon commercial hunting when federal officials promoted and ensured Osage access to trade. Of course, federal trade relations were all part of settler colonialism. Native indebtedness was contrived in order to force land cessions. Similarly, as settlers trespassed and undermined Osage agriculture, the increasing reliance on hunting and trade rendered their lifestyle more "nomadic" by Euro-American standards and thus less "civilized." If "savage" Natives were not continually present to "occupy" their territories, then, in effect, this land was "open" for American settler "improvement." In other words, federal emphasis on trade ideologically and materially aided settler colonialism. At the same time, the mobile Osage hunting and trading economy undermined missionary efforts and actually protected, at least temporarily, some aspects of cultural sovereignty. On one hand, this showed the contradictions in federal policy, but on the other, it demonstrated priorities; the civilization program was far less important than land acquisition.[23]

Without dual chiefs in every town to lead the hunt, the Non'-hon-zhin-ga now shared planning duties with a council of warriors. Again the priesthood's willingness to adapt leadership structures helped maintain their own influence and many of the Osage spiritual beliefs. In preparation for the hunt, men continued to smoke the ceremonial pipe; "they want to have [Wa-kon'-da] take notice that they are about to smoke, and they desire him to grant their wish to find game."[24] In years when the Osage conducted their hunts—which was most years—they continued to produce a large volume of hides for trade. "Some of the most skillful hunters will kill nearly a hundred deer in five or six weeks." Though they continued to "eat more than four-fifths of the deer they kill," after acquiring the valuable skins, the remaining "bodies are left for the wolves to devour." The trade competition was so intense, and the

Osage were sometimes so desperate, they even abandoned meat. In 1806, the Osage (northern and southern bands) traded $63,000 worth of furs and hides, receiving 40 cents per pound of deerskins, their highest-volume hide. Fort Osage, a US trading factory on the Missouri River from 1808 to 1822, and the subfactory Marais des Cygnes, from 1820 to 1822, at the river of the same name's junction with the Osage River, consumed 20,000–30,000 Osage-produced skins in most years. After the end of the factory system in 1822, numerous traders, including Chouteau family members, opened private trading houses in the south near Arkansas Osage communities and in the north near the old Marais des Cygnes factory site, constituting tens of thousands of skins annually, most of which came from the Osage.[25]

This still sizable hide trading economy continued to rest on the complementary labor of both men and women. The entire town traveled together: "Hunters led the way, followed by the women and children; the pack-horses brought up the rear." Men continued killing the animals, while the women "not only have it to cure and pack, but to skin and dress." Plenty of outsiders commented on the still sizable female workload: "What little manufacturing is done among the Indians is also the work of the women . . . the most extensive article of their manufacture is the buffalo rug, which they not only prepare for their own use, but which constitutes the largest item of their traffic with the Indian traders." Increased hunting competition in their eastern lands and the eventual loss of this territory in the Treaty of 1808 permanently undermined their hide trade economy. Instead of abandoning commercial trade, the Osage increasingly focused on the western bison herds. Women processed buffalo hides that could each weigh eighty pounds and measure up to fifty-square-feet; the sheer number produced demonstrated that men's hunting and women's hide processing work remained substantial and significant, even though Osage hide trade primacy and wealth declined overall.[26]

Though the civilization program had long served as a justification for US colonization of Native land, it received little official attention until 1819, when Congress finally allotted $10,000 annually for missionary work among Natives. Osage scholar George Tinker called this "an attempt to co-opt the churches and their missionaries to serve the government's political ends." In return, missionaries and their parent societies and denominations received economic benefits, including federal land grants and funding for mission schools. As a result, Tinker concluded missionaries "were partners in genocide." Certainly that was not the missionaries' expressed intention. The problem resulted from missionaries' conflation of Christian faith with Euro-American culture—a social norm in the nineteenth century. They failed to question their society's implicit belief in European/American cultural superiority and thus were "unwittingly . . . guilty of complicity in the devastating impoverishment and death of the people to whom they preached." They were tools of the colonial state, and their work helped to achieve political ends, namely the elimination of Indigenous people, both culturally and literally.[27]

Following Congress's creation of the Civilization Fund in 1819, missionary groups could seek federal funding to establish missions to and schools for Natives. One such partner was the United Foreign Missionary Society (UFMS) that in 1821 established two Protestant missions to the Osage: (1) Union, built along the Neosho River, near the Arkansas communities; and (2) Harmony, built along the Marais des Cygnes River just above its junction with the Osage River, near the Great and Little Osage communities. The UFMS accumulated sizable debt in maintaining these missions, and after the Treaty of 1825, the Osage eventually moved over 100 miles from the mission sites, increasing costs and limiting their impact. Therefore, in May 1826, management of these missions transferred to the larger and more financially stable American Board of Commissioners for Foreign Missions (ABCFM). Facing the same challenges, though, the ABCFM closed the Union Mission in 1833, and Harmony Mission followed suit in 1835.[28]

In their efforts to encourage acculturation, missionaries frequently commented on and, due to their ethnocentric bias, lamented the perpetuation of Osage gender roles. Reverend Benton Pixley, missionary to both the Great and Little Osage, wrote in 1827,

> The women plant the corn, fetch the wood, cook the food, dress the
> deer-skins, dry their meat, make their moccasins, do all the business of
> moving, pack and unpack their horses, and even saddle and unsaddle the
> beast on which their husbands and other male kindred ride; while the
> men only hunt and war, and when in their towns, go from lodge to lodge
> to eat, and drink, and smoke, and talk, and play at cards, and sleep.[29]

Misunderstanding the spiritual significance and complementarity of Osage gender roles, missionaries continually characterized female labor as "drudgery." The Union Mission journal stated, "In their hunting parties, the women take care of the horses, and prepare their encampments, and do all the drudgery."[30] William C. Requa, an assistant missionary, farmer, and teacher at Union Mission, wrote, "Indeed, all drudgery is imposed upon the female sex." Cornelia Pelham, who taught at the Harmony, Union, and Neosho Missions, repeatedly discussed Osage women's degradation: "They are trained up to drudgery from infancy; indeed, their whole lives are one course of servitude and debasement."[31] Reverend William F. Vaill, superintendent of Union Mission, described the life of an Osage woman as "one unceasing round of servitude and drudgery," and through conversion he and the other missionaries believed Osage women could "become respected and useful, and happy."[32] Of course the actual problem was that Americans generally, and missionaries specifically, could not comprehend a society built on gender equality.

A central aspect of "civilizing" the Osage required men to stop hunting and start farming. Hunting, primarily a leisure pursuit for Euro-Americans, did not constitute "legitimate" work, leading the missionaries to mistakenly believe Osage men were lazy, despised manual labor, and equated it with slavery; "perhaps there are no slave-holders who are more particular to have all their hard service done by their negroes, than these men are to have their drudgery performed by their women." Hunting, contrary to the missionaries' assertions, certainly qualified as manual labor. On hunting or war expeditions, Osage men often walked sixty miles in a day, went days without food or sleep, and overexerted themselves to the point of coughing up blood.[33] The real problem was not laziness; it was cosmology. Osage women grew plants because they were creators, spiritually and physically. Without this spiritual conditioning, Osage men could not excel at farming.

Nor did they need to because Osage women planted their crops in virtually every year well into the 1830s, although sometimes Native enemies destroyed fields and stole dried stores.[34] In 1820, Factor George Sibley reported that each Osage family "can save from ten to twenty bags of corn and beans, of a bushel and a half each; besides a quantity of dried pumpkins. On this they feast, with the dried meat saved in the summer, till September, when what remains is cashed, and they set out on the fall hunt."[35] Osage subagent John Richardson also noted the success Osage agriculture enjoyed in the late 1830s: "These Indians not only raised corn, beans, potatoes, etc., to an extent equal to the home consumption and demand, but generally produced a surplus."[36]

While Osage women successfully cultivated corn and other crops, the missionaries struggled with subsistence—a poor advertisement for the superiority of Euro-American life. Sometimes missionaries complained to Osage visitors "that we had given so much meat and bread to the Osage people of late, that we had scarcely any left," prompting hunters to bring in deer, and their wives to bring bison meat and venison. Facing starvation in 1823, missionaries had to buy nineteen bags of corn from an Arkansas Osage town, which arrived "packed in on four horses, under the charge of Tally's wife, who arrived much fatigued, having travelled most of the way on foot, with a child upon her back." Apparently women's food production continued to feed their own people and the missionaries.[37]

As the Arkansas Osage leader Tally (Tah-hah-ka-he or Ta-ha-ka-ha or Ta-Eh-Ga-Xe) and his wife indicated, food sharing was part of the hospitality Osage men and women used to maintain peaceful relations with Americans and other visitors throughout this period. And it worked; as one missionary reported, "They are remarkable for hospitality." Whenever Union missionaries visited an Arkansas Osage town, they were invited to visit and dine at dozens of Osage homes while the women took care of their horses. Women still did most of the cooking, including for visitors staying in their lodges, yet various outsiders noted the emergence of what appeared to be a new trend: male cooks. "They have a number of cooks, whose business it is to wait on visiters [sic], and conduct them from one lodge to another. . . . The cook if he chooses [eats the remaining food], and then leads you to another lodge."[38] Various scholars have argued that men took over this task when women "no longer had the time" due to the laborious hide trade. Descriptions of these men, though, often indicate their multifaceted role: "a great dignitary—combining grand chamberlain, minister of state, master of ceremonies and town crier." Typically "old and infirm," these men no longer participated in warfare. "Attached particularly to the family of some great man" or serving the community-at-large, these men were "supported by the public or their particular patron." Serving as a diplomatic host to outsiders, within Osage communities these men acted as a "newspaper" and gave "the order of the day," conveying important information and organizing events, especially feasts and ceremonies. One source described such a man as "a cook for the braves" and another said, "he tastes broth"; however, the majority of references to these men discussed serving, rather than actually preparing, the food. No doubt though, men could cook, as they had long done when away from home or during the grand buffalo hunts, while women were in fact too busy processing meat and hides. Thus this "herald" and "cook" seemed to be a position related to men's

Tál-lee, a Warrior of Distinction, painted by George Catlin (used with permission of the Smithsonian American Art Museum, gift of Mrs. Joseph Harrison Jr.). Tál-lee, known also as Tally, was an Arkansas Osage leader who had frequent contact with Americans, including missionaries and military personnel. George Catlin painted numerous portraits of Osage people while visiting Fort Gibson in 1834. He seemed particularly impressed by Tally's military feats. Catlin wrote that this portrait was a "fair specimen" of Osage dress and ornamentation, and he called Tally a "handsome and high-minded *gentleman*." Like many Osage men, Tally was known for his height, which can be seen relative to his seven-foot lance in this painting. (Emphasis original; George Catlin, *Letters and Notes on the Manners, Customs, and Condition of the North American Indians*, vol. 2, 3rd ed. [New York: Wiley and Putnam, 1844], 40–44; Louis F. Burns, *A History of the Osage People* [Tuscaloosa: University of Alabama Press, 2004], 61, 64, 205–206; J. Frederick Fausz, *Founding St. Louis: First City of the New West* [Charleston, SC: History Press, 2011], 112–113; and Willard H. Rollings, *The Osage: An Ethnohistorical Study of Hegemony on the Prairie-Plains* [Columbia: University of Missouri Press, 1992], 244–245.)

diplomatic and political leadership, which certainly remained important in navigating relationships with Americans. Yet, most of the actual food—cultivated, gathered, or dried—was still prepared by women.[39]

Warfare with refugee Native nations and the high demand for female labor, particularly in hide processing, meant polygynous marriage constructions and matrilocality remained the norm. Travelers and missionaries frequently noted men with a "plurality of wives." Prior to any marriage, a man still had to distinguish himself in hunting and warfare and he had to maintain or exceed this high level of achievement in order to subsequently marry his wife's sisters or cousins. Missionaries were particularly puzzled by the "peculiar attachment" of parents, especially fathers, toward the eldest daughter; "It is the custom of the Indians to treat the oldest daughter with the greatest care and attention. When a young man marries into a family, he usually takes the oldest sister," and then if qualified, he would marry the younger sisters. "This fact may account in some measure for the peculiar respect paid by the parents to their oldest daughter. They generally keep her near them, and if a young man speaks to her without their permission, they always consider it as an insult." In fact, the characteristics a man considered when selecting a wife were her family's reputation, her "interest in her work, and her physical strength," necessary for her economic role in the family. Focusing on their eldest daughter allowed parents to arrange her respectable, mi'-zhin marriage that influenced subsequent marriages, including of sisters or cousins to the same man, and leadership and priesthood participation by anyone in the extended family. One missionary noted in 1821, "As polygamy is common among them, it is not uncommon to see with one man in his lodge, three or four women, who are his wives, with fifteen or twenty children." Of course, in reality it was not "his lodge"; the husband joined his wife's family's household, and women owned the homes they built.[40] Divorce remained available to men and women. In one example, after convincing a man to come live with them, missionaries noticed he lacked the authority to compel his wife to follow suit; she did not join him, and their marriage ended once they no longer lived together. Another traveler observed that divorce could be conducted by "mutual consent" and a man simply reclaimed the gifts he had presented to his ex-wife's family at the time of the marriage. Marriage, polygyny, and divorce still rested on an Osage social organization that did not subordinate women to men.[41]

Numerous observers noted that female sexual freedom continued in the early nineteenth century for both married and unmarried women. Protestant missionaries repeatedly criticized "lewd and immodest conduct" or a lack of "chastity and modesty" among Osage women. The missionaries eventually asked some Osage women living near a mission school to move because of the "pernicious influence" they exerted over the older male students. The most "prevalent sins" they found among the Osage were "adultery, fornication and all manner of uncleanness." Much to the missionaries' dismay, Osage women continued to control their sexuality.[42]

To further the civilization program, missionaries established agricultural settlements, Hopefield in the south and Neosho in the north, at each mission where Osage families could, in theory, learn about Christianity and Euro-American-style agriculture.[43] For the Osage who settled here, this was more likely part of the ongoing decentralization of Osage society that eased subsistence burdens; potentially provided protection from attacks; and allowed individuals, in this case through alliances with missionaries, to achieve leadership status that would be unavailable in more established towns. Missionaries labeled the residents in these communities "half-breeds," believing white "blood" entailed more "civilized" behaviors. The Osage did not construct identity in this way, but regardless of Euro-American conceptions of race, historic gender roles remained evident.[44]

In the early years of these settlements, missionaries justified allowing women and children to continue removing trees and clearing fields because otherwise "there will not be sufficient domestic business to employ them." The women continued building their homes in the traditional fashion and they continued agricultural production of corn, beans, melons, and pumpkins while adding cotton and potatoes from seeds the missionaries provided. To supplement their subsistence base, women in these settlements also gathered wild foods, which proved the only food source in years when floods or other natural disasters destroyed the crops. And Osage men still went on communal summer hunts, sometimes delaying their return to the settlement well into December. Occasionally, missionaries claimed the men in these settlements were doing the cultivation, but women continued to direct most of the production, adhering to Osage cosmology, which allowed men to do agricultural labor under female direction, as she was considered the owner of the field. When the missionaries instructed some men on farming tasks, the missionaries simply filled the female-field-owner role and likely did not impact the Osage men's conception of gender. At the same time, missionaries provided livestock and implements for plowing, and it was plausible the

Osage viewed the animals, rather than their male drivers, as the true laborers. Worst of all for the missionaries, the corn raised in these settlements fed "the crowd of wild Indians, that have thronged about them, to live on the fruit of their industry." Families may have joined the missionary settlement as a way to gain food for their home Osage community and their extended families. Equally disappointing for the missionaries was the "settlers'" complete lack of interest in any Christian teachings. Regardless of the missionaries' intentions, these efforts at "civilizing" the Osage accomplished very little. These settlements remained connected to Osage social constructions through continued gender roles and communal sharing of food. It turned out the Osage "settlers" needed sustenance more than the Savior.[45]

The Protestant missions were surrounded by Osage towns, but they were significantly isolated from other American communities. The missionaries' frequent shortages of food and supplies allowed Osage labor to become part of Osage-American exchange. Though traditional gender construction continued to define subsistence practices, pressure from surrounding Native and Euro-American populations and declining hide trade prompted some Osage individuals to seek out other income. Some Osage men and women worked at the missions for wages, paid in cash or goods. An Osage individual could contribute to their family's subsistence with wage work, and they typically redistributed the payments within the family or community like other trade goods. In other words, much like hides, meat, or surplus crops, Osage labor constituted another "item" traded with Euro-Americans. Nevertheless, the missionaries hoped wage labor would teach Osage individuals the habits of "civilization."[46]

Missionary employers assigned tasks to these laborers based on the Euro-American gender construction. Agricultural wage work was supposed to encourage Osage men to take up farming for themselves. But this labor was not necessarily outside the male gender role because men were always able to help in the fields as long as they were under the direction of a woman. Men could have again viewed their agricultural labor in this same light because the missionaries directed their work. In the summer of 1822, during some of the most intense competition and violence with the Cherokee, Osage men started coming to the missions seeking work. Harmony missionaries sent the men to hoe corn, fed them an evening meal, and paid them somewhere around fifty cents in wages exchanged for a variety of goods, including bread, cornmeal, tobacco, and clothing. The number of employees ranged from three to fifteen at any one time at each mission. In 1823, one Osage man, Moineh-Perhsa, performed wage labor in exchange for the Union missionaries providing room, board, and clothing for his wife and child. In this context, male agricultural labor constituted a trade item, especially during times when violence inhibited acquiring other trade goods.[47]

Missionaries also used wages when they could not find any other way to convince Osage men in the agricultural settlements to farm. Reverend Epaphras Chapman, one of the missionaries to the Arkansas Osage, wrote that, "it was thought expedient to try their constancy by inviting them to labour with us previously for wages. By this means we became convinced, that it would be necessary to lead them on, in the accomplishment of their important undertaking."[48] While praising what looked like Osage male farming, the missionaries also remarked that the commitment to agricultural labor directly related to how punctually Osage men received payment. It seemed for these men the goal was immediate income.[49]

When the Harmony missionaries plowed a field in Pawhuska's (White Hair's) town in the spring of 1822, they marveled that "White-hair, the principal Chief, set an example of industry to his people. He was the first in the field, and assisted with a rake to clear the ground."[50] Pawhuska was certainly aware that missionaries wanted men to adopt farming, so by visibly doing this work, he could serve a dual purpose: gain missionaries' approval necessary for US diplomatic relationships, while aiding his female relatives as he—and many other Osage men—had always done. Again in 1824, Harmony missionaries Nathaniel Dodge, William Montgomery, and Otis Sprague visited Pawhuska's town, noticing "many of the men this season have assisted the women in cultivating corn."[51] But again, men were likely working under the direction of field-owning women, which fit inside their cosmology and established practices.[52] Missionaries thought they had encouraged Osage men to cultivate, but instead, they witnessed typical Osage gendered work.

Osage women also performed wage labor for the missionaries. They were assigned tasks Euro-Americans considered "women's" work, such as food preparation and sewing; however, this was also part of the established female role in Osage society. As Reverend William Vaill wrote in 1823, "A number of males as well as females have commenced manual labour. The women have taken hold of domestic business with admirable skillfulness, and have laboured for the Mission till they have purchased, in some instances, cloth for garments and made them with their own hands."[53] In trading their labor for wages or goods, Osage men and women continued to cooperate in ensuring their economic stability.

The Protestants did not limit their missionizing efforts to adults, and focused much of their attention on trying to instill Christian values and cultural change in children. However, only a small fraction of Osage youth attended the Protestant missionary schools and of these, only a few stayed for extended periods of time. Osage leaders, including Sans-Nerf of the Great Osage, began asking federal officials for secular, not religious, schools as early as 1819. He and others hoped schools would provide education on the skills needed to survive in the changing world around them. Instead, the Protestant's religious emphasis attempted to usurp Osage cosmology and the relationship with Wa-kon'-da. This was not what Sans-Nerf intended.[54] Limiting student attendance proved a primary method of resistance. At the same time, Cherokee attacks discouraged parents from parting with their children. Thus, federal disinterest in intervening in the Osage-Cherokee conflict, precipitated by removal policies, further undermined the civilization program.[55]

Osage leaders maintained friendly relations with the missionaries without sending their children to the schools. In May 1822, in the midst of warfare between the Osage and Cherokee, the Union missionaries held a council with various Arkansas Osage leaders, including Claremore and Tally, where they inquired about what prevented the Osages from sending their children to the schools. The Union Mission journal quoted the Osage council, "You must not blame us; but you must blame the people below, (meaning the Cherokees). It is owing to them that our children are not in your school."[56] By July, the missionaries held growing suspicions that Claremore did not intend to send his children to them regardless of peace with the Cherokee.[57] Once the Fort Osage trading factory closed, Little Osage chief Walkimain, who appeared supportive of education programs in the past, became increasingly indifferent to missionary requests for children.[58] The Osage frequently visited the missions when traveling or while out on hunts, but rarely left their children. Three hundred children passed through the missions in 1822, and none joined the schools. Bypassing chiefs or leaders, the missionaries started appealing to individual parents to gain students, but these parents also made excuses about relinquishing their children. Reverend Vaill wrote, "When they are asked, Do you not mean to leave this child? they reply, after we have got through with this hunt, or after we have seen such and such relations."[59] In October 1823, Reverend Vaill reported,

Wáh-chee-te, Wife of Cler-mónt, and Child, painted by George Catlin (used with permission of the Smithsonian American Art Museum, gift of Mrs. Joseph Harrison Jr.). While visiting Fort Gibson in 1834, George Catlin painted numerous portraits of Osage people, including one of Arkansas Osage chief Claremore (Clermont) and this portrait of his wife and child. Catlin described Wáh-chee-te as "richly dressed in costly cloths of civilized manufacture, which is almost a solitary instance amongst the Osages." However, Osage women had spent decades trading for European cloth and using it, along with skins, to fashion clothing out of a variety of materials. In Catlin's color original, the parting of Wáh-chee-te's hair is clearly painted red, denoting her observance of the daily prayer vigil. (George Catlin, *Letters and Notes on the Manners, Customs, and Condition of the North American Indians*, vol. 2, 3rd ed. [New York: Wiley and Putnam, 1844], 40–44.)

The Chiefs are friends to us, as citizens, and as the representatives of a great nation which they respect; but they cannot as yet be considered as Fathers of the School. They have not realized the benefit of civilization; have many fears lest they shall lose their influence by changing their habits; and have done very little, if anything, to make the School popular among their people.[60]

In 1825, Claremore confirmed the Union missionaries' former fears when he openly stated his opposition to the missionary efforts, both at agricultural settlements and at the schools, as noted in the Union Mission journal, "He now frankly acknowledges that his fathers walked in a good path, and he wishes to tread in their steps."[61]

Each mission school never had more than fifty students at any one time.[62] When missionization began, Superintendent of Indian Trade Thomas McKenney estimated the number of Osage children from all three divisions numbered approximately 4,500.[63] Two schools with less than 100 total students constituted a small fraction of Osage children. And by 1830, to fill their empty classrooms, missionaries admitted Cherokee and Creek children, who quickly made up a majority of the student body.[64] Nevertheless, in the midst of war with the Cherokees and continuing intrusion of both Native and Euro-American hunters and settlers, mission schools provided food and shelter, possibly supplementing lean months in Osage towns. The missionaries surmised that a mother who committed her two sons and one daughter to the Harmony Mission school in 1823 did so because of her poverty and lack of husband or relatives to provide assistance.[65] Boys and girls also earned wages at the Union Mission school, likely supplementing family income during difficult times.[66] In addition, parents may have sent their children to school to learn how to speak, read, and write English, increasingly important skills as the Osage navigated US colonization.[67]

The number of resident children may have been small, but Osage adults often visited the missions for extended periods. So many Osage individuals visited the Union Mission that the missionaries constructed a lodge in 1823 specifically for Osage guests and wage laborers. Osage women made up the majority of those who stayed long periods. Missionaries assumed they did so to learn Euro-American domestic arts, the fruits of which the missionaries were happy to consume; again, women's labor was producing traded goods. In April 1823, Osage women and girls crafted nine patchwork quilts and "performed nearly as much labour on shirts and other articles."[68] Osage women from the Hopefield settlement also joined in sewing and knitting for the mission community.[69] Osage women and girls assisted in other aspects of domestic life, including food production for themselves and the missionaries.[70] In exchange for their labor, these women received shelter, shared in food stores, and maintained diplomatic ties with Americans. These women may have also used the mission as a refuge during difficult times at home. Of course, food preparation and clothing manufacturing already comprised the gendered work of Osage women. Likewise, women had long used domestic production and hospitality to further diplomacy, which now included missionaries.

Most importantly, these women, and all the visitors, stayed close to the children in the school. It was well documented that Osage parents, grandparents, aunts, uncles, older siblings, and cousins loved their children, showered them with affection, took great care in child-rearing, and were averse to being separated from them. One visitor claimed, "Osage fathers and mothers show an extraordinary kindness and even weakness in regard to their children. If there are spoiled children in this world, they are those of the Osage."[71] It was not surprising then that Osage visitors had a variety of reasons to linger at the missions.

Some historians dismiss the mission schools as indicative of Osage social norms because the small number of students came from "mixed-blood" families. However, as Osage scholar Jean Dennison elucidated, "mixed-blood" people usually acquired this label based on their behaviors rather than their ancestry. As indicated above, so-called full-blood leaders had requested secular schools during treaty negotiations. Thus, interest in education was a response to living in the imperial United States, rather than a result of one's "blood."[72]

To that point, Osage gender construction remained evident among all the students in the schools. In addition to learning English, schoolgirls learned Euro-American-style sewing and clothing construction, very similar to the clothing manufacturing already defined as Osage female work. Missionaries frequently praised the girls' rapid "progress" in learning to sew and in creating articles of clothing for the mission families.[73] Harmony missionaries in 1823 started reporting each girl's specific completed sewing and hemming yardage and number of days she spent working in the kitchen.[74] By the end of the year, the Union Mission journal stated, "The female scholars had made, in five months, 16 garments for adults, and 61 for children, besides performing their full share of labour in the kitchen."[75] The missionaries never ceased applauding Osage girls' ability to quickly learn to "read, write and sew."[76]

Although both male and female students received praise for English proficiency, the missionaries struggled to make progress in teaching the boys to take up agriculture. As other scholars have argued, in some ways missionization demanded more profound changes of Indigenous men than of women.[77] In 1822, Harmony missionaries, while complimenting the sewing capacity of the girls, simply mentioned that "the boys were also taught to labour in the field," with no mention of the success or amount of work the boys completed.[78] In another report, Union missionary Reverend Vaill described the "rapid progress" of four teenage boys in reading and writing English, but at the same time he lamented their inability to learn agriculture because the "prejudices of this people, like those of most Indians, are much against the idea of laboring. They identify labour with slavery."[79] In reality, they identified cultivation with female physical and spiritual creativity. According to the missionaries, the only "successful" male graduates learned a trade. For example, a student whom the missionaries renamed Stephen Van Rensselaer learned blacksmithing, making nails, hinges, and small knives, and worked as a mission interpreter.[80] Abraham Swiss apprenticed with missionary Abraham Redfield in carpentry at the Union Mission.[81] Learning trades, particularly ones that centered on making weaponry or tools, fit into Osage gender roles much easier than agriculture. Plus, this training provided immediate benefit to the boys' families and the Osage economy of the time.[82]

Irregular attendance obviously hindered the missionary education agenda. Children frequently abandoned the schools of their own accord, and parents frequently took their children, sometimes repeatedly, from the schools.[83] Tally, as an Arkansas Osage leader, particularly struggled with balancing his role of appeasing the missionaries while leaving his son to their care. When Woh-sis-ter, whom the missionaries renamed Philip Milledoler, initially joined the school in May 1822 at approximately fifteen years old, Tally hesitated about leaving his son, but his wife insisted the boy join the school.[84] After reports that the missionaries used the children as slaves, Tally visited the Union Mission in July to investigate any mistreatment.[85] Though the missionaries thought they allayed his fears, Tally returned fifteen days later and took Woh-sis-ter with him to Fort Smith where Osage leaders negotiated a peace with Cherokee leaders. The Union Mission journal characterized

Woh-sis-ter's departure stating, "We have consented to have Philip go, both to please the father, and to benefit the child by enlarging his acquaintance with the white people."[86] Missionaries attempted to justify Woh-sis-ter's absence, but in reality Tally wanted to take his son, and so he did. More than a week later, Woh-sis-ter had not returned to the school, prompting the missionaries to travel to his hometown to reclaim him. Tally continued to make excuses about family members criticizing him for giving his son to the missionaries. Reverend Chapman and his wife Hannah described Woh-sis-ter,

> We found Philip divested of his clothes, with his hair shaved, and his face painted like an Osage. After some faint excuses, he said he would return with us. But when we were ready to leave the Village this morning, he pleaded for another day, that he might see his grand mother who had been absent.[87]

The next day, Woh-sis-ter returned to Union. After a few months at the school, in late October 1822, Tally returned to the mission to take his son on a hunt, complaining "that while others had three or four young men to help them, he was alone, was poor, and found it difficult to maintain his large family." In order to guarantee Woh-sis-ter's return, the missionaries had Tally sign a written contract agreeing to bring his son back to the mission in thirty days.[88] But in January 1823, Reverend Chapman confirmed Tally had permanently withdrawn his son from the mission school.[89] When Woh-sis-ter passed through the mission on the way to a bear hunt a few months later, the missionaries implored him to rejoin the school. He responded that "it was good for him to be a hunter and a warriour . . . [because] in these employments he must spend his days."[90] Woh-sis-ter retained his English reading skills; however, sedentary Euro-American farming held little value for his present or his future.[91]

Harmony Mission faced similar issues with keeping its students. In early 1822, Sans-Nerf (Great Osage leader) convinced his daughter to allow her two sons, ages thirteen and seven, to attend the mission school.[92] But within weeks, the children's mother came to the mission and

> requested permission to take the youngest home, alleging that he was yet too young to learn, and promising to return him when his age would admit. She was heedless of the opinion and advice of the Family; and the

boy was accordingly stript of his comfortable suit, wrapped in a tattered blanket, and taken from the school.[93]

A few days later, the older boy, whom the missionaries renamed George, left the mission on his own to return to his mother. Once home, "George's" mother cut up the majority of his mission clothing, repurposing it as she saw fit. When Sans-Nerf brought back the salvageable clothing, he told the missionaries that his eldest grandson was unwilling to return to school and "he thought it best not to compel him at present."[94] When the missionaries threatened to withhold the value of the clothing from federal annuity payments, Sans-Nerf responded that the Osage gave the missionaries "a great piece of land, and had not asked any thing for it" and if the missionaries wanted more land, then he would return another piece of "George's" clothing.[95] It appeared neither "George" nor his brother ever returned to the mission school.

Osage residents in the agricultural settlements avoided leaving their children at the mission schools for extended periods too.[96] In December 1824, Reverend Vaill complained about the Union Mission school losing students, including the son and daughter of Pau-hunk-sha, one of the original Hopefield settlers. Vaill commented on Pau-hunk-sha's actions, "We had some confidence in him, but he has again disappointed us, for this is not the first time he has taken his children from the school."[97] Another Osage Hopefield farmer, Waushingah-lagena (known as "Beautiful Bird"), had a son who came and went at the Union Mission school several times, once leaving with his grandmother to return to an Osage town.[98] Of the forty-one children at the Hopefield settlement in May 1825, only seven attended the Union Mission school.[99] Certainly some of them may have been too young for school, but inconsistent attendance indicated the Hopefield settlers also lacked a commitment to missionary education. In 1830, on the eve of the Protestant mission's closure, the Union Mission annual report blamed the school's failure to "civilize" the children on the "instability of the parents, in taking them away." Mothers, fathers, and grandparents remained the dominant influence over their children.[100]

Those who joined the agricultural settlements or sent their children to the schools faced widespread criticism from other Osage people. Hopefield residents in particular suffered extensive ridicule.[101] When disease spread through Hopefield in the summer of 1824, debilitating many and killing a few, a mission farmer noted in his journal that the Hopefield residents "were so credulous as to believe what their *sahka shingah*, or old men [*Non'-hon-zhin-ga*], told them, that their living among white people was the cause of the sickness and deaths among them."[102]

Parents of school children experienced similar reproach. "The mother of Jane R. Montgomery and Robert Finley took these children from the school, alleging 'that the Osages laugh at her, and call her a fool for keeping them where they are made slaves.'"[103] Tally too feared his son's enslavement and said that his "people laughed at him, and called him a man of no sense, for giving his son to the Missionaries to become a white man."[104] Charges of enslaving children were not without merit. By American standards, Osage parents spoiled their children, especially boys, who grew up to be "lazy" men, and the missionaries focused on teaching the Protestant work ethic by including laboring as part of the curriculum. For Osage parents, "civilized" life seemed to produce suffering, exploitation, and death. No wonder few parents sent their children to mission schools.

One of the missionaries' largest obstacles to changing Native lifeways lay in the Osage language. Even though several missionaries devoted sizable time and effort studying the language, they never achieved fluency and found it challenging to learn.[105] Reverend Pixley summed up the difficulty, "I am now more fully convinced than ever, that there is no alternative for me, but to abandon the thought of ever learning the Indian language to any useful purpose. . . . The difficulties of learning a language, not written, full of *dialects* and *contracts*, and altogether irregular, is not easy to be conceived."[106] The language "being almost entirely destitute of words by which to convey moral sentiments," meant the Osage worldview had no conception of sin, guilt, or forgiveness, frustrating the "lessons" missionaries tried to teach.[107]

The missionaries primarily relied on interpreters, presenting another set of problems. Intermarried Frenchmen constituted the majority of the "civilized" men with a suitable knowledge of the Osage language. They had a limited knowledge of English, though, while the missionaries had a limited knowledge of French.[108] Missionaries complained the Frenchmen's knowledge of the Osage language primarily related to trade or "domestic business" rather than spiritual or religious beliefs. The missionaries most vehemently opposed using French interpreters because "the language which the interpreters have acquired is generally such as is used by women and the most degraded of the community with whom they have associated, and theirs is a different dialect from that which is used by the majority, and the most respectable part of the nation."[109] It was unclear if Chapman believed the degraded status of all Osage women presented the language problem, or if the problem resulted from Frenchmen who, by Osage standards, illegitimately cohabited with Osage women in a *gashon'the migthonge* marriage. Either way, the language barrier presented a sizable obstacle in "civilizing" the Osage.

The Protestant missionaries eventually recognized their failure. As early as January 1823, Reverend Vaill reported to the United Foreign Missionary Society, "Already have we had cause for humiliation in not being able to accomplish the views of the Society, and our own views also."[110] In September 1824, the Union missionaries provided lengthy responses to questions about why missions to groups such as the Cherokees and Choctaws supposedly garnered immediate success while the Osage missions struggled. They pointed to the lack of "laboring white men" and the comparatively few "half-breed children" among the Osage in preventing their "witnessing the blessings of civilization and of the Gospel."[111] In other words, Osage men lacked a proper example to emulate, and intermarriage had not produced the deterioration of Osage culture.

Mobility was another factor. "Probably few portions of the heathen world are in circumstances more unfavorable to being affected by missionary labors, than the Osages. Their wandering and predatory habits render it exceedingly difficult for missionaries to have much intercourse with them; and what little instruction is communicated at any time is very soon forgotten, while on their periodical hunting or war expeditions."[112] Continued subsistence from agriculture, hunting, and trade—the product of complementary gendered work—prevented a "sense of their wretchedness," limiting Osage interest in changing their lifeways.[113] The missionaries also blamed federal Indian agents, who not coincidentally were Chouteau family members, for the failure, saying the Osages "for many years, have had no *resident* agent, and they were never favoured with one who did not make it his principal business to derive his wealth from their trade." Of course this led the missionaries to believe that "the influence of the trader is at war with missionary operations."[114] This was one of the contradictions of US Indian policy: trade, at least temporarily, supported established lifeways and undermined missionization. The Osage used this contradiction to protect themselves and their society.[115] In the summer of 1830, missionaries complained the Osage were "as regardless of the advantages of education, religion, and civilization, as ever, and that the chiefs taught their children to believe their old ways."[116]

Missionaries struggled to gain converts primarily because of the Osage interconnected view of the world, manifested directly in spiritually sanctioned gender roles. Reverend Montgomery of the Harmony Mission wrote in 1831 that the mission's failure resulted in part because the Osage believed "the arts, government, and religion of white people are viewed as a whole, inseparable from one another."[117] This presented problems because the missionaries "always found that much pains are requisite in order to prevent [the Osage] from confounding farming with religion."[118] Cornelia Pelham also noted that it was "extremely difficult for any of the missionaries to make an Osage man discriminate with any thing like clearness between religion and farming, if he ploughs and plants, and wears clothes like white men he seems to think himself a christian as a matter of course."[119] For the Osage, women cultivated because Wa-kon'-da favored them with the creative power necessary to bring crops to harvest. Thus, if an Osage man adopted farming, it constituted a spiritual act they correlated with Christianity. Protestant missionaries never convinced Osage men this was a worthwhile conversion.

Though the missionaries may have been disappointed with their results, or lack thereof, as historian Willard Rollings argued, the Osage "feigned interest in order to use the missionaries to their advantage."[120] The missionaries were another source of goods that could supplement the Osage economy and perhaps aid in relations with federal officials. Specifically, the Osage traded for, stole, or requested livestock as gifts from missionaries.[121] In 1831 Reverend Montgomery wrote about the difficulty in missionizing the Osage, and related Arkansas Osage leader Claremore's remarks on this issue, "You do nothing . . . but talk about books; you have never given me a plough, an axe, or a bake-oven; these are the things which I value. . . . Do you think the Cherokees who send their children to your school took books first? No. I suppose they first received cattle, etc, and afterwards schools."[122] This is why the traders had better relations with the Osage than the missionaries: traders provided things the Osage found useful. The Osage did not need religion and agriculture—they already had both.

Osage women happily used missionary-built mills though for their corn. As the Harmony Mission journal noted in December 1822, "The first corn for an Osage was ground at our mill to-day. Soon may this important engine of civilized man be the means of relieving the Osage females from the fatigueing task of making their corn soft by means of manual labour."[123] Within the week, Osage women brought ten to twelve bushels of corn at a time to grind in the mission's mill.[124] The missionaries believed the mills would decrease the overall amount of labor required for agriculture and encourage supposedly lazy men to take it up. Instead, a mill simply eased the female workload, like iron awls or cloth, without restructuring gender.

Osage leaders also wanted to use missionaries as intermediaries between themselves and federal officials, particularly concerning the ongoing conflict with the Cherokees. Not only did mission students acquire a working knowledge of English, benefiting government and trade negotiations, but the Osage also relied on missionaries to communicate on their behalf. In August 1821, three months after Harmony Mission's founding, Sans-Nerf came to the mission requesting the Protestants "aid him in preparing a communication for the Government, requesting that all white men, who have not been suitably authorized, might be kept from trading with his people."[125] In 1823, when federal officials demanded Claremore relinquish members of his community suspected of killing Cherokees, he responded by soliciting Reverend Chapman to come to his town to write a letter to Colonel Arbuckle at Fort Smith. Reverend Chapman's letter maintained the Osage only responded in self-defense to Cherokee attacks, thus declaring Osage innocence.[126] Similarly, trespassing white settlers increasingly stole Osage horses and property, prompting Claremore and his fellow townspeople to start leaving property with the missionaries when they traveled on hunts.[127] In these ways, the Osage made use of the missionary presence to mediate their interactions with US officials and settlers.

In the nineteenth century, Osage life involved continuity, change, and colonization. Initially the Osage remained in self-selected town sites in their historic territory. Subsistence practices continued and they remained commercial hunters. But the US settler empire intended to eliminate Indigenous people; hence, federal Indian policy forced eastern Native peoples into the Missouri and Arkansas River valleys, undermining Osage hegemony. These "proxy invaders" disrupted Osage life, and through coercion, federal officials acquired Osage land that quickly became home to the intended beneficiaries: American settlers.

In the meantime, federal officials supported missionization as another way to eliminate Native people. Protestant missionaries, despite their best efforts, could not alter Osage cosmology or gender construction. Missionaries tried to teach men to farm, but Osage women already excelled at this, and sometimes had to feed the starving Protestants. Instead, the Osage used missionaries to provide support to communities facing extensive disruption. Missionaries participated in Osage exchange and served diplomatic roles in Osage-US relations. The schools offered children and adults instruction in the English language, as well as temporary food and shelter.

Missionization may have failed, but US colonization succeeded in reducing Osage power and eventually eliminating their presence in Missouri and Arkansas. It seems Reverend Montgomery's observations were correct: the source of Osage troubles—including invasion, loss of game, warfare, and economic decline—could all be traced back to their interactions with Americans. This diminished the power of all Osage people, and though some social structures started to change, gender complementarity was not one of them. In 1825, the Great and Little Osage were forced to leave homes dating back to at least French contact. In 1839, the Arkansas Osage had to abandon towns they had created nearly eighty years earlier based on the Three Forks region's agricultural, hunting, and trade productivity. Women and men then had to build an Osage future in Kansas.

CHAPTER 4 "THE VEXATIONS THAT THE AMERICAN GOVERNMENT INFLICTED": OSAGE WOMEN AND MEN RESISTING ELIMINATION

In January of 1839, Captain Philip St. George Cooke, stationed at Fort Gibson, wrote a letter to his commander concerning the "condition and prospects of the Osage tribe." After recently visiting Osage communities, he noted they had been "driven from the land of their fathers and their own, and confined to a small district where there is no game"; a problem only aggravated by a drought that had destroyed their "little patches of corn" that season. He reviewed Osage land cession treaties from the beginning of the century, remarking on the US government's vast underpayment for Osage land, meaning that "the Osage tribe has an honest, matter of fact claim upon the equity of the Nation of millions of dollars." He predicted that "their *speedy* prospect is famine, and death to many; to the *remnant* great sufferings, and a gradual extinction." And finally, he concluded, "This, if permitted, must be pronounced, when the whole case is considered, the strongest proof offered in a century of the imputations on the American people, of oppression, and ill-faith to the indian, and an eternal reproach upon the Nation."[1] Victor Tixier, a French traveler who joined an Osage hunt in the summer of 1840, related similar sentiments based on a conversation he had with an Osage man, Big Soldier (Nika-ouassa-tanga), who also "complained of the vexations that the American Government inflicted upon his people by driving them farther away all the time, and by paying poorly for the lands which were bought from them."[2]

As Cooke and Big Soldier pointed out, the Osage were experiencing settler colonialism. Federal Indian policy had already impoverished the Osage by facilitating Native and American settler invasion, leveraged to acquire Osage land in Missouri and Arkansas without adequate compensation. In Kansas, these policies combined with a second attempt at missionization, an extremely disruptive settler invasion, a difficult climate for agriculture, and epidemics. It was seemingly the perfect recipe for elimination. The Kansas

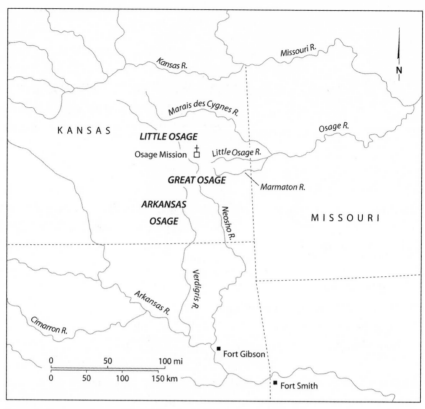

Osage in Kansas, 1830s–1860s. (Map by Bill Nelson.)

reservation presented challenges not only for survival, but also for continuing ritual practices and gender roles. Famine and suffering increased, but contrary to Cooke's prediction, extinction was not the result. The Osage used mobility to preserve people and culture. And, for a time, they maintained the agriculture-hunting-trading economy based on gender complementarity that facilitated spiritual and physical survival. Eventually though, colonization produced extraordinary population and economic decline, culminating in their expulsion from Kansas and confinement in Indian Territory.

By the 1820s, the Osage were facing the full force of US imperialism. Early in the century, the Osage lost land primarily because of federal removal policy that functioned as ethnic cleansing, expelling eastern Natives into Osage territory, where these refugees served as "proxy invaders," compromising Osage power and eventually survival. Then the federal government coerced Osage "consent" to treaties that ceded land, the terms of which were not clearly conveyed nor fully upheld. All of this was done to enable settlement by Americans. Settlers colonized because of economic inequalities within their own society. They were typically landless migrants from the United States or Europe who viewed land ownership as the only way to improve their status and achieve independence. Consequently, settlers invaded Native land. According to historian Alan Taylor, "One people's freedom came at another's expense." These settlers also quickly and aggressively established territorial, state, and county or municipal governments that shifted power away from Natives and federal officials to themselves. These new governments simultaneously gave settlers political and legal legitimacy at the local and national level, which aided in their efforts to colonize Natives and their land. As Patrick Wolfe has argued, "Settler colonialism is an inclusive, land-centered project that coordinates a comprehensive range of agencies, from the metropolitan centre to the frontier encampment, with a view of eliminating indigenous societies."[3]

In other words, the policies Thomas Jefferson, Meriwether Lewis, and William Clark had initiated two decades earlier were reaching their conclusion. The Osage were invaded and surrounded. Missouri statehood in 1821 underscored the population and power shift. Already warring with rival Natives, the Osage knew they could not afford to have Americans as an enemy. Therefore, they had little choice but to comply when Clark, still serving as superintendent of Indian affairs, demanded more land cessions in 1825. This treaty exemplified a common characteristic of US-Indian policy: land sales "took place within circumstances constructed by whites to yield a state of affairs in which selling was the lesser of evils." In another typical act of coercion, Clark required treaty negotiations in May, delaying the Osage summer hunt, which was central to their subsistence and economy. The most prominent leaders of the northern and southern Osage bands, including Pawhuska (White Hair), and Claremore, respectively, had to cede all their lands in Missouri and Arkansas Territory and most of their land in what became Kansas and Oklahoma. For their reservation, they retained a fifty-mile strip of land in what is now southern Kansas, extending to the western edge of their previous territory.[4]

Arkansas Osage leader Claremore and his followers, however, defiantly remained in their lower Verdigris River homes. But passage of the Indian Removal Act in 1830 subsequently forced thousands more eastern Native refugees into the region, resulting in even more violent competition over food sources that further undermined subsistence for this group. At the same time, invading American settlers wanted to own this land. Based on experience, many settlers knew "that initiating conflict with the Indians was the surest way to prod the federal government to buy the Indians' land." Acting on this decades-old tradition, Missouri settlers spread rumors in 1837 of Osage attacks on settlers, resulting in Governor Wilburn W. Boggs calling out a 500-man militia that intimidated and assaulted the few Osage individuals they could find, in an effort to expel them from the state. As anticipated, in 1839, federal officials provided an additional twenty years of annuities and thousands of head of livestock to motivate Claremore and his followers to finally move.[5]

In their old homes, the Osage had served as "caretakers" for the many "gifts" *Wa-kon'-da* (Mysterious Power) provided. Animals in particular were viewed as "brothers," and hunters sought ritual permission to acquire and utilize animal bodies. As discussed in chapter 2, it was not clear how the increased scale of commercial hunting impacted these relationships and responsibilities. Caretaking, though, seemed to involve preventing any other people from hunting their "brothers" on Osage land. Osage scholar John Joseph Mathews repeatedly characterized the period of Native and Euro-American invasion as one where the Osage were unable to properly protect their "brothers" from other "killers." This dereliction of duty was experienced as a continual spiritual failure only magnified by the loss of most of their land, which made caretaking impossible. As Osage historian Louis Burns characterized it, "We know the burden of guilt carried by the Osages was great. They had betrayed *Wa kon ta's* trust and given over the little brothers to a strange people. To what extent the retribution for this act affected the Osages we cannot know. . . . The foundation of Osage civilization was crumbling." Mathews agreed.

> And since [the Osage] had allowed *Mo'n-sho'n*, Mother Earth, the
> Sacred One, to grow smaller like an old woman. . . . *Wah'Kon-Tah* threw
> his crooked lance of fire more frequently at them and sent the earth-
> shaking thunder more often. . . . *Wah'Kon-Tah's* anger may have seemed
> more terrible and more frequent in their minds now because of their
> remissness, but still they belonged to him, and to him alone.[6]

In other words, US colonization prevented the Osage from upholding their spiritual responsibilities to their "brothers" and to *Wa-kon'-da*; and for this, there were spiritual and physical consequences.[7]

Predictably, the years surrounding Osage removal proved deadly. Since contact with French traders, beginning in the 1680s, the Osage had almost entirely avoided disease outbreaks. The arrival of Europeans did not produce immediate, inevitable, and extensive mortality because the Osage, like other Indigenous groups, were not an immunologically defenseless, "virgin" population. Throughout eighteenth-century European colonization, the Osage remained powerful, populous, and fully in control of their physical and spiritual lives. Not until the actions of Euro-American colonizers disrupted every aspect of Osage life did a context for epidemic death and sustained population loss emerge. The Osage did not die from accidentally introduced "virgin" soil epidemics. They died because US colonization, removal policies, reservation confinement, and assimilation programs severely and continuously undermined physical and spiritual health. Disease was the secondary killer.[8]

During the 1820s and 1830s, federal Indian policy severely threatened Osage survival through intensified encroachment by Natives and Americans, competition over game, and violence. All of this produced stress, inconsistent access to food, and malnutrition that left the Osage susceptible to disease. Epidemics in turn produced more stress, more malnutrition—which often inhibited hunting and farming—and a weakened immune system that left people vulnerable to more outbreaks. Mathews noted that in 1821, women worked hard to gather food because Cherokee violence had destroyed cached crops and limited hunting; prior to this, "starvation was practically unknown among them, at least having its source in enemy actions." Over the next several years, Protestant missionaries noted various "fevers" and illnesses, killing numerous Osage people, especially women.[9]

At the same time, missionaries made inflammatory claims: they noted repeated incidences of child abandonment and infanticide, including "in one instance, a child of two weeks old was buried alive with its mother." Missionary families allegedly adopted several children they found abandoned and "cast into the open prairie to perish." Josephine McDonagh has expertly argued that such claims were often falsified and used as a way to demonstrate "savagery," justifying the missionary work and hopefully spurring donations to support it. It was possible that infanticide took place in Osage society, conceivably in times of disease or other challenges. In Osage cosmology, "until the ceremonial naming the child has no place in the [nation's] organization, and it is not even regarded as a person." Typically, ceremonial naming took place when a child was between three and six months old. In theory, if a parent abandoned a child prior to naming, it might not be viewed as murder. But the Osage treasured children, the future of the nation. And these are the only examples of Osage infanticide, rendering the missionaries' assertions suspect.[10]

When the Great and Little Osage moved to their Kansas reservation, it took them five years to find adequate village sites, which undermined subsistence and trade; "and this compelled them to suffer a great deal for want of needed provisions."[11] Malnutrition only worsened during concurrent droughts and floods, resulting in influenza, dysentery, and smallpox outbreaks through 1830. And in 1839, when the Arkansas Osage were preparing to move to Kansas, smallpox broke out among them too, delaying their removal. Americans traveling on trails across the plains spread cholera to the Osage in the 1840s. The Osage died at higher rates from cholera than some Native groups because of their large towns, ranging from several hundred to sometimes over 1,000 residents, where individuals in a small geographical area were repeatedly exposed to the illness-causing bacteria. On the Kansas reservation, the unprecedented (in Osage history) close proximity of Osage settlements to one another limited their longstanding method of placing waste on the "outskirts" of town. Starting in the 1830s, the outskirts of multiple towns overlapped, contributing to poor sanitation and disease virulence.[12]

Epidemics and declining Osage health reduced fertility. A healthy diet and body fat are required for successful pregnancy and lactation, meaning malnutrition limited fertility. Mental and physical stress did too. Influenza, measles, and smallpox all lowered birth rates for months after an infection or disproportionately killed pregnant mothers and caused miscarriage. Children were especially vulnerable to diseases and often the most numerous causalities of a particular contagion. In sum, ongoing US colonization and its concomitant disruptions made the Osage vulnerable to disease, and inhibited population recovery in this period.[13]

Reduced population and fertility held spiritual significance because children were the greatest demonstration of Wa-kon'-da's desire for continued Osage existence. Could this have been, as Burns suggested, perceived as Wa-kon'-da's retribution for unfulfilled spiritual responsibilities brought on by US colonization and land loss? Certainly other Native groups perceived death during removal in this context, and the Osage likely did as well.[14] No doubt loss of fertility, children, and population also held significant implications for women, whose cultural and spiritual power manifested through their motherhood. This was comparable to the loss of military prowess in the last chapter that undermined masculinity. By midcentury, the entire society— men and women—struggled to fulfill their responsibilities and the power of the entire nation reflected it.

Forced relocation to Kansas meant for the first time the Osage were not choosing town locations based on their own motivations and needs. Instead they had to do so within prescribed reservation boundaries. This was a difficult task because Kansas's climate and geography was less hospitable to agriculture. "The valley of the Neosho and that of the Verdigris, being considered to have the best farming soil of the whole reservation, were chosen in progress of time for the principal Osage villages." They eventually settled into seventeen towns; the Great and Little Osage lived along the Upper Neosho, while the Arkansas Osage resided roughly sixty miles to the southwest along the Verdigris River.[15]

To many outsiders, the Osage were also divided into "mixed-bloods" and "full-bloods." The removal treaty demonstrated this by allowing some so-called half-breed families to retain sections of the ceded land. As many Osage scholars have argued, the construction of "half-breed" reflected American assumptions rather than Osage realities. Osage history going back to their origin story never privileged a single lineage and instead repeatedly noted various groups coming together and moving apart for a variety of reasons. As Osage anthropologist Jean Dennison has argued, "Osage citizenship [resulted from] one's location within a clan-based governance structure . . . and one's residence within Osage-controlled territory." Captives and European traders had been adopted into this structure for decades, as had been the case with outsiders long before colonization. Americans liked to believe that intermarriage diluted Native "blood" and resulted in more "civilized" offspring that inherited superior "racial" traits. This construction conveniently furthered the settler empire's goal of elimination by continually claiming fewer and fewer people qualified as "Indian" and thus fewer people could claim tribal land rights. Americans also associated "mixed-blood" people with various behaviors—notably, owning private property—that supposedly resulted from their inherited "white blood." Hence, missionaries liked to focus their efforts on "mixed-blood" children, who were ostensibly already closer to the intended "civilized" goal. By treating people differently based on this imposed hierarchy, Americans created new divisions in Native nations geographically, materially, and politically, all of which weakened their overall ability to resist colonization.[16]

On the Kansas reservation, the Osage continued their agriculture-hunting-trading economy, which was far better suited to the environment than sedentary agriculture American settlers eventually attempted in the region. The Osage spent the winters in forested areas along small streams, providing pasture for their horses, fuel, and protection from winter weather. Once spring commenced, they moved to higher ground to escape periodic floods along these water courses. On fertile creek banks, one Indian agent noted, the "women make some corn, beans, and pumpions [sic], which they raise entirely with hoes . . . this is done before they leave home on their summer hunt, which is about the first of June."[17] To encourage grass growth for their horses, and to attract deer, elk, and bison herds, the Osage burned the prairies in the early spring and late fall.[18] In dry weather, they set fire on the plains to drive game, particularly deer, toward streams; as one missionary observed, "Deer seem to be very much afraid of fire, and as soon as they notice smoke arising on the plains they start for the timber land along the river courses, where they fall an easy prey to the Indian hunter."[19] After the summer hunt, they returned home to harvest corn "while it is in its green state." In September they commenced the fall hunt, which supplied the thicker and more valuable buffalo hides. This lasted until the winter months when they returned to the sheltered, watered areas, awaiting spring.[20]

The records of federal agents, travelers, missionaries, and settlers document Osage women cultivating corn, pumpkins, squash, beans, and melons through the entire reservation period.[21] In a handful of years, an agricultural surplus allowed for continued cache storage for winter consumption.[22] Typically though, the harvests only produced enough "to feast on when they return from their hunting excursions on the plains."[23] The different environment, more prone to drought, and periodic flooding along creeks and tributaries, often ruined these fields and diminished or destroyed harvests. For example, in 1848, an Indian agent reported, "For two successive years having their crops entirely washed away by high waters, had the effect almost entirely to discourage [them]." In 1850 another agent wrote, "Owing to the drought the past summer, the corn was all ruined." For the next twenty years, agriculture failed about as often as it succeeded. In 1868, their agent recorded, "These Indians are reduced to a starving condition . . . their corn, pumpkins, and squashes, were almost an entire failure this year. The hot sun and dry weather, in July, were too severe for these articles, as they are cultivated by these Indians." No wonder they were discouraged.[24]

In this way, confinement to the Kansas reservation posed specific challenges to gendered work. Agriculture directly related to women's economic and spiritual position in the community. So when farming was undermined, this impacted women's roles. With farming in Kansas often failing and rarely producing significant harvests, it appears women continued cultivating, at least in part, because of its spiritual significance in reiterating women's creative role in terms of fertility and food production. Their "patches," as observers often called them, were still planted in the ceremonial hills, and the Osage, when possible, continued to celebrate the harvest corn feast (primarily of green corn), which honored women's role as life-givers and was one of the most joyous celebrations of the year.[25] Because bison and corn were viewed as equally important food sources, continued cultivation and relevant ritual also reiterated the importance of gendered duality in Osage subsistence and survival, even as the scale of agriculture declined and that of hunting increased.[26] Likewise, men continued their role of "protecting the fields where women worked," by preventing horses or cattle from grazing where Osage women planted their crops; this was no small feat, based on the sometimes large size of their herds and close proximity between towns.[27] In addition, all of the ritual knowledge Francis La Flesche collected from both men and women discussed at length the spiritual importance of corn and the prominent role of women as creators in Osage society. All of La Flesche's informants would have obtained their ceremonial knowledge in the Kansas reservation period, meaning the complementary gender construction remained central to their cosmology in that period.

Nevertheless, the Osage responded to the tenuous nature of reservation agriculture by depending more and more on hunting for subsistence and trade. This preserved significant aspects of the Osage economy—the male role of acquiring the game and the female role of processing the meat and hides. Missionaries and Indian agents frequently described how the Osage subsisted "entirely from the chase."[28] The whole community continued to travel together on the two large buffalo hunts, though men frequently made "short hunting excursions on the plains to get a constant supply of fresh meat."[29] Women continued to tan the hides and cure the meat.[30] Skins only became valuable trade items if thoroughly processed by Osage women. Trader James

Edwin Finney noted, "In addition to curing the meat and caring for their camp duties, the Osage women spent much time and effort in the work of tanning and dressing the skins of buffalo and making them into robes for domestic use and for barter with the traders." Traders evaluated skins "according to size, condition of the hair, thickness and texture of the skin, [and] care used in tanning."[31]

Throughout most of the reservation period, Osage hunters continued to bring in tens of thousands of skins for trade. In late 1847, Osage hunters had a "bad hunt," which limited trade; yet they still brought in over 16,000 robes and skins amounting to $28,000.[32] When necessary, hunting also allowed the Osage to barter valuable skins for Missouri farmers' crops, with a typical exchange rate of one buffalo robe for twenty to twenty-five bushels of corn.[33] In the 1850s, the

> buffalo were as yet numerous and [the Osage] used to kill every year an average of at least 20,000 of them for whose robes they sometime receive more than 5 dollars apiece. So their revenue arising from the sale of the same was a great one, to say nothing of the extra amount of money they were getting for small furs of which they always had a great variety.[34]

As late as 1874, on the Indian Territory reservation, Osage hunters killed over 10,000 bison, though by this point diminishing herds made this a rarity.[35]

To diversify their economic opportunities in Kansas, the Osage began trading with another imperial power in the region: the Comanche. Since the eighteenth century, the Comanche and their Kiowa allies had long excluded Osage hunters from accessing the sizable bison herds west of the Arkansas River along the Salt Plains, and warfare between these rivals was common. In the 1830s, Comanche and Kiowa warfare with the Cheyenne, Arapaho, and Texas settlers had limited their access to American trade goods. Thus, the Comanche, Kiowa, and Osage all had motivations to establish peace and open trade. The Osage then served as middlemen between the lucrative Comanche trade system and US traders. The Osage would take their annuity goods or purchase merchandise from US traders and, as one observer described it, "every year the day of the full moon in July is the meeting time for the two nations. The Osage bring red paint, kitchen utensils, blankets, cloth, iron, and the [Comanche] give in return horses which they breed, mules stolen from the Texans, all kinds of pelts, etc." According to historian Pekka Hämäläinen,

"The amount of goods exchanged at these meetings could be astounding." In 1847 alone, the Osage exchanged $24,000 worth of goods for 1,500 head of Comanche livestock, worth $60,000.[36]

During this period, the Osage still "measured their worldly wealth in horses."[37] Beyond the Comanche trade, horses gained even greater value as the Osage adjusted to plains life and traveled greater distances to access game. At the same time, horses proved a valuable trade good they could use in exchange for food, especially in years of poor weather or disease.[38] Federal agents estimated the Osage had between 10,000 and 12,000 head of horses during the 1830s and 1840s.[39] Neosho agent P. P. Elder reported in 1863, "The property of these Indians consists mostly in horses, ponies, and mules, of which they have large numbers, and of a superior quality."[40] Both Osage men and women rode horses and learned to do so at a young age. On the plains, young boys cared for the horses and trained them.[41] Visitors observed that Osage herds were well-kept, well-groomed, and watched with extreme care. There was still no evidence though that the Osage bred horses, and instead continued to acquire them in the male occupations of hunting, raiding, and trading.[42]

Peace with the Comanche not only provided trade income and livestock, but also it facilitated undisturbed access to large bison herds, providing another avenue to subsistence and profitable trade.[43] Unfortunately, this trade ended in 1853 when a treaty between the US government and the Comanche, Kiowa, and Apache provided the first annuities and direct provision of American goods to these nations. The Comanche no longer needed the Osage as trading partners, eliminating this critical income and renewing competition over the western bison herds. In 1858, the Comanche resumed attacking Osage hunting parties on the plains, limiting access to game and undercutting Osage economic stability.[44]

Needless to say, war, both physically and ritually, remained part of Osage life. Though conflict with eastern emigrant Natives had predominantly ended, competition over bison herds and plains territory continued with their longtime enemy, the Pawnee, and with other plains nations.[45] In 1840, Tixier witnessed a large, communal, multiday war ceremony in preparation for an attack on the Pawnee. In an effort to gain *Wa-kon'-da*'s assistance in this endeavor, there were days of fasting, dancing, ceremonial pipe smoking, preparation of sacred charcoal for blackening their faces like relentless fire, and women using prayer and painting to send good wishes for men's success. A member of the Non'-hon-zhin-ga (priesthood) ceremonially opened the sacred bird-hawk wa-xo'-be (sacred bundle), still "constantly carried by the brave's first wife," where the duality of the universe was reiterated, the role of warrior mothers acknowledged, and women and men's courage combined for the impending battle.[46] In the scalp dance, conducted when men returned from battle, women still dressed and danced like men while listening to their husbands and male relatives recite war achievements, all to demonstrate women and men's courageous success in warfare.[47]

Tattooing had always been tied closely with warfare, and this took on new importance both during the rise and fall of the Osage empire. By the nineteenth century, steel needles often replaced the previous bone-quills, but ceremonial marking still required a sizable payment of horses, robes, or blankets to the ritually initiated artist. A man who had achieved war honors could have war symbols ceremonially tattooed on his body, representing his achievements. This same man, if he could afford it, could have his wives and daughters similarly tattooed with symbols of life and female creative power, which the Osage continued to view as indicative of the female role in creating warriors, perpetuating the community, and spiritually guarding and protecting her home. The tattoos continued to request Wa-kon'-da's aid in maintaining the Osage nation into the future.[48] Various visitors noticed men's tattoos in the 1830s, and in 1840, Tixier noted that nearly all Osage females he encountered had tattoos: "Their necks, chests, backs, arms, the backs of their hands, their stomachs down to the hips, the lower part of their thighs, and their legs are marked with indelible blue lines."[49]

During the years of Osage imperial domination, many men had the requisite experience and wealth that facilitated tattooing on a man and his female relatives. As warfare and wealth declined, only elite warriors and their families could maintain the practice. In 1854, a missionary witnessed an Osage wedding ceremony, and he noted the bridegroom's appearance, including how "his body is all tattooed with such symbolic figures as chiefs alone are allowed to be marked with."[50] Late in the Kansas reservation period, as the opportunity to gain war honors diminished, tattooing became a way of sustaining younger individuals' observance of ritual traditions. As one man tattooed at age seventeen noted, the tattooing ceremony was done "to make him faithful in keeping the rites."[51] Thus, the cultural and spiritual significance associated with tattoo designs continued in some form, even if the achievements needed to obtain them began to change. Certainly, tattooing was not able to maintain

Chief Bacon Rind, Chief of the Osage Indians (used with permission of the Kansas State Historical Society). Born in 1860, Bacon Rind (Wa-tse-mon-in) became a prominent Osage leader
in the early twentieth century and was also one of Francis La Flesche's informants for his
research on Osage rituals and history. Bacon Rind was initiated as a priest of the Bear clan
before converting to Peyotism. This photograph, taken between 1870 and 1890, shows Bacon Rind's tattoos. Stretching from the middle of his chin to his abdomen was the sacred
ceremonial knife. The sacred pipe stretched from the middle of the knife over each shoulder. Thirteen rays of sun, indicative of the thirteen military honors (o'don), also stretched
from knife to shoulder. (Garrick A. Bailey, *The Osage and the Invisible World: From the Works of
Francis La Flesche* [Norman: University of Oklahoma Press, 1995], 23–24; Francis La Flesche,
"Researches among the Osage," *Smithsonian Miscellaneous Collections* 70, 2 [1919], 112–113;
and La Flesche, "The Osage Tribe: Rite of the Chiefs; Sayings of the Ancient Men," *Thirty-
Sixth Annual Report of the Bureau of American Ethnology* [1914–1915] [1921], 54.)

the breadth of values manifested in war rituals, but it was an effective adaptation that preserved at least some of these values in a changing world.

The greatest challenge the Osage faced in Kansas came from settler colonialism. As early as March 1853—more than a year before the Kansas-Nebraska Act passed, which officially created Kansas Territory—a congressional Indian appropriations bill included an authorization for the president of the United States to enter into negotiations with "Indian tribes west of the States of Missouri and Iowa for the purpose of securing the assent of said tribes to the settlement of the citizens of the United States upon the lands claimed by said Indians, and for the purpose of extinguishing the title of said Indian tribes in whole or in part to said lands."[52] The goal of Native elimination could not be clearer. The federal government had just signaled to eager speculators and squatters that Native land rights in Kansas were temporary, and if settlers wanted access to this newly available land, they should move now! And they did.

By the time Congress debated the Kansas-Nebraska Act a year later, Natives faced significant settler invasion.[53] One missionary noted that "squatters were not very particular about keeping in the lines . . . [never] caring about the limits of the Osage reservation."[54] From this point on, missionaries and government agents documented settlers coming into the region daily, disregarding reservation boundaries, building homes, tilling fields, destroying food sources, stealing horses, and using violence—including murder—to gain Osage land and resources.[55] Timber resources were often seized, as one federal official commented, "In the first place the Indian and his property is suffering materialy [sic] by the trespasses of the whites . . . but the stealing of thousands of dollars worth of timber and carrying to adjoining lands as merchandise is radicaly [sic] wrong. The Indian is not allowed any privileges

OPPOSITE: Eastman's Map of Kansas and Nebraska Territories (used with permission of the Kansas State Historical Society). In 1854, Commissioner of Indian Affairs George Manypenny certified this map, made by US Army captain Seth Eastman, as an accurate representation of reservation boundaries in the territories. Settlers were supposed to refer to this map to ensure they did not settle on reservations. However, the map was notoriously inaccurate. For example, the map portrayed a fictional gap between the southern border of the Shawnee lands and the northern border of the Kanza lands. Even though settlers liked to blame the inaccurate map for their illegal squatting on Native land, their settlements were on Native land even based on the inaccurate lines drawn here. The Osage reservation was properly identified, and still settlers illegally moved onto it in droves. (Ronald Parks, *The Darkest Period: The Kanza Indians and Their Last Homeland, 1846–1873* [Norman: University of Oklahoma Press, 2014], 68–69.)

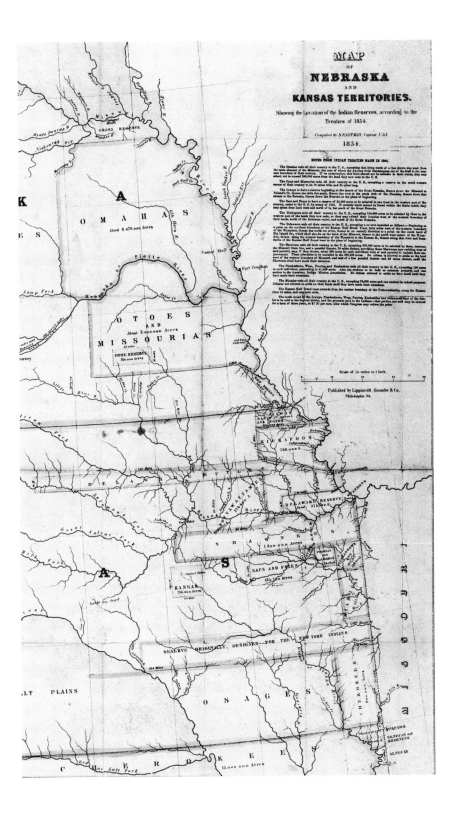

MAP
OF
NEBRASKA
AND
KANSAS TERRITORIES.

Showing the Location of the Indian Reserves, according to the
Treaties of 1854.

Compiled by S. EASTMAN, Captain U.S.A.

1854.

NOTES FROM INDIAN TREATIES MADE IN 1854.

Scale of 20 miles to 1 inch.

Published by Lippincott, Grambo & Co.
Philadelphia Pa.

on the wild lands of the whites if found gathering 'pop paws' they are driven off like wolves."[56]

Beginning in 1853, settlers accelerated the colonization of Indigenous people in Kansas. And they were well aware of their role in the settler empire.

> When they came there they knew they were trespassers, and had no right whatever to settle where they did; but they were men who wished to "fight for their rights." They became very much displeased that the government did not give them each at least a quarter section of this best land for the *great hardships* they had endured among those savages, and as a reward for their services in driving the Indians from their homes and the graves of their fathers, and occupying their best lands which they (the settlers) had no shadow of title to.[57]

"Speeches delivered by so-called leading men and newspaper articles" further convinced settlers that "Indians have no rights which should be respected by white men." Settlers "generally associated in clubs, pledged to defend each other in occupation of claims," created their own militias, organized at least three counties entirely inside the Osage reservation, and then applied to the governor for protection. All the while, Indian agents repeatedly requested the use of military force to guarantee reservation boundaries and remove squatters. But the "neglect of the [federal] Government to assert the supremacy of law over a few border men, professional squatters, was regarded as a tacit approval of criminal acts by men professing to be just and honest; hence, [more settlers] perpetrated the same crime, claiming the right to do what was allowed by others."[58] Why would the federal government bother enforcing temporary land rights? Congress had already made it clear that Natives in Kansas would be eliminated, and if settlers were willing to do the work, why not let them? All of this exhibited the systemic nature of US imperialism. In other words, "invasion is a structure not an event . . . [and therefore] elimination is an organizing principal of settler-colonial society rather than a one-off occurrence."[59]

Beyond being an attack on survival, settlers' actions also directly assaulted Osage gendered work. As agent Isaac Gibson reported,

> While absent on their winter hunt, cribs of corn, and other provisions, so hardly earned by their women's toil, were robbed. Their principal

village was pillaged of a large amount of puncheons, and wagon-loads of matting hauled away and used by the settlers in building and finishing houses for themselves. Even new-made graves were plundered, with the view of finding reassures, which the Indians often bury with their dead.[60]

Everything that Gibson listed was the product of female labor. Settlers not only stole cached corn, but also in other examples they let livestock graze, or they stole corn straight from the fields.[61] Women and men had gone to great lengths to continue agriculture in Kansas, not only for food but also for the spiritual significance corn and women's creative power played in Osage cosmology. Loss of crops produced starvation and made it impossible for the Osage to celebrate the corn harvest feast, which annually reiterated the central female creative role in society. Settlers also moved into Osage lodges or dismantled and rebuilt them elsewhere for their own families. Hence, women lost the woven mats and other building materials that had composed their homes, destroying significant female-owned property.

At least during their time in Kansas it appears women performed some, if not all, of the burials. The deceased were buried with goods deemed necessary to travel to the afterlife, including food and perhaps a sacrificed horse. Just as women were responsible for building homes for the living, women also used rocks or earth to build a mound over the deceased. When Americans robbed graves, Osage family and friends believed their departed loved one was suffering and possibly starving. Settlers had such disregard for the Osage that they harassed the living and the dead, and in this case also the labor of women charged with providing for the transition to the afterlife.[62]

The scope of settler pillaging also meant that men were not able to uphold their gendered responsibility of protecting women, children, homes, and fields. Beginning in the 1850s, "thievish white people" also stole "a large number of horses and mules," often numbering in the hundreds.[63] Sometimes Osage men would reclaim their livestock, after which the squatters complained to territorial, state, or federal officials that they were "victims" of Osage violence. Neosho agent George Snow reported in 1867,

Since the war, horse stealing has been carried on to an alarming extent. There is not a horse lost by these new settlers but what the "Osages have got it." The people of Neosho, Labette, Wilson, Greenwood, Woodson, and Allen counties claim that they have lost about 80 head of horses this spring and summer. A large portion of these "horses" were Osage ponies, bought of irresponsible traders, renegade Indians, and thieving white men for a mere trifle. Many of these "horses" stray away from their pretended owners and go back to the Indians. Most that are stolen are taken by white men who go to the Indian camps, so the theft may be charged to the Indians.[64]

From the late 1860s on, white settlers stole five to twenty horses from the Osage virtually every day, which never resulted in any prosecutions or a return of the livestock.[65] Horses had long been a source of Osage wealth, a valuable trade good, and a necessity in hunting. In Kansas, the primary method of subsistence was bison hunting, meaning men without horses could not effectively provide for their families, a central aspect of the male gender role. Their primary enemy had become Americans, but the Osage were well aware of their inferior power relative to Americans generally and settlers locally.[66] Violence in this context seemed useless. But men's inability to counter this immediate threat and to protect women's property and fields—considered the most prestigious o'don (war honor)—likely took a psychological toll on their masculinity. Because of settler colonialism, neither men nor women could effectively conduct many of their physical and spiritual responsibilities.

In Kansas, the Osage also had to contend with missionization, this time by Catholics. Beginning in the seventeenth century, Catholic missionaries periodically visited Osage communities. After the Osage started intermarrying with French traders, they had increasing contact with Catholics, and Osage marriages and baptisms appear in church records all across Missouri.[67] When the Osage moved to Kansas, Jesuits operated missions among the nearby Kickapoo and Potawatomi.[68] The first sustained Catholic missionary effort to the Osage began in April 1847 when Father John Schoenmakers arrived and "took formal possession of the two log houses put up by the Indian Department for the use of the mission."[69] The mission was located near the federal agency and an American Fur Company trading post, a few miles away from Flat Rock Creek's junction with the Neosho River (now St. Paul, Kansas).[70] On May 10, 1847, he opened the Osage Manual Labor School for boys. And on October 10, 1847, the Sisters of Loretto opened the female branch of the school.[71] Like the Protestants discussed in the last chapter, these seemingly well-intentioned Jesuit missionaries were also part of a systemic effort to eliminate Indigenous people. They were officially part of US Indian

Catholic Church at Osage Mission (used with permission of the Kansas State Historical Society). This photograph, taken between 1865 and 1875, shows the church at the Osage Mission (now St. Paul, Kansas). The center portion is the original mission building, erected in 1847. (Kansas State Historical Society, Kansas Memory: Catholic Church at Osage Mission, St. Paul, Kansas, accessed July 21, 2017, http://www.kansasmemory.org/item/215652.)

policy and thus instruments of the colonial state. Though focused on culture change, this did not diminish their role in genocide because attacking Native spirituality, identity, and relationships had "a direct impact on that people's capacity to stay alive."[72]

That being said, Catholic missionaries established more hospitable relationships with the Osage than the former Protestant missionaries. For one, the priests and nuns came without families or any other responsibilities. Father John Bax, one of the original Jesuit missionaries, wrote in 1850, "The Indians are attached to us, principally, say they, because we have no wives and children, 'if you had,' they say, 'you would do like the missionaries (the presbyterians) who preceded you, you would think too much of your families, and you would neglect the red-man and his children.'"[73] This demonstrates how, in the Osage estimation, missionaries could provide material aid while also serving as intermediaries for the Osage in dealings with invading Americans.[74] Though they were enduring acute suffering, abandoning established religion, gender roles, or their economy was not, however, on the Osage agenda.

Throughout their time in Kansas, the Jesuit fathers, among others, noted the maintenance of Osage gender constructions, and predictably, though mistakenly, associated the female role with slavery and the male role with laziness. Father Schoenmakers informed federal officials in 1854 that Osage parents "bring up their daughters under heavy burdens and in entire ignorance, to become, I might well say, slaves to their future husbands."[75] Father Paul Ponziglione, who joined the Osage Mission in 1851, reported that "among our pagan Indians, woman is as yet the wretched slave she used to be in ancient times."[76] In describing the daily routine in an Osage town, Ponziglione wrote, "To the poor squaws is left all the drudgery of the camp . . . they are, miserable contemptible slaves."[77] His assessment of Osage men was equally unflattering: "Hunting has so far been and is yet their only occupation. When not engaged in it, they spend their time playing cards or idling around with their friends."[78] In reality of course, the primary loci of female labor was in their towns, where missionaries could easily observe women working. Men performed the majority of their labor, which required a significant amount of skill and stamina, outside of town on hunting or war expeditions, and thus out of view to most local missionaries and other observers. Women's work was not evidence of their enslavement but, rather, evidence of their economic and spiritual prominence in Osage society derived from their creative (reproductive) power.

Women, as the missionaries witnessed, continued their sizable domestic production. Moccasins were often fashioned from hides, but leggings, breech cloths, and tunics were frequently made out of wool, calico, flannel, and muslin obtained through trade. Women also constructed both permanent and hunting lodges in the traditional style. On a hunt, Victor Tixier described women gathering twelve-foot branches they "planted" in the ground, bent into arches, and covered with buffalo skins to build lodges that were nearly five feet tall, fifteen feet long, and seven feet deep. Back in the permanent towns, bark, mats, and buffalo skins covered wood pole framed, rounded roof lodges with fire pits dug into the ground, roughly fifty feet long, twenty feet high, and twenty feet wide. Father Ponziglione watched women weaving the mats used for these structures through the 1860s: "The squaws occupied in weaving the flags they have just been gathering from the ponds . . . making their new stock of mats for the next winter." Watson Stewart, a settler in Kansas in 1856, marveled at how Osage women fashioned boards, wood poles, and skin mats to create their large lodges. Stewart and his neighbors

Osage Couple (used with permission of the Kansas State Historical Society). Osage women built and owned their homes, like the one featured in this photograph taken between 1880 and 1890. Women "planted" the wood poles in the ground and then covered them with a variety of materials, which were also a product of women's labor, including buffalo hides and woven reed mats. The couple's clothing was also typical of late nineteenth-century Osage dress, where women fashioned most of their apparel from trade cloth. (Victor Tixier, John Francis McDermott, and Albert Jacques Salvan, *Tixier's Travels on the Osage Prairies* [Norman: University of Oklahoma Press, 1940], 117, 134, 159–160, 170–171; Paul Mary Ponziglione, "The Osages and Father John Schoenmakers," unpublished manuscript, eds. Lowrie J. Daly and Garrick Alan Bailey [St. Louis, MO: Midwest Jesuit Archives], 164; and Eliza J. Wyckoff, "Reminiscences of Early Days in Kansas," *Manuscript Collections, Miscellaneous Collections: Jane Baude* [Topeka: Kansas State Historical Society, March 1, 1918], 7–8, 10.)

so admired the boards, they hauled off "wagon loads" from an "abandoned" Osage settlement to use in their own houses.[79]

Polygyny and matrilocality remained prominent through the Kansas reservation period too. While visiting the Osage, Tixier stayed in a guest lodge, under Ouichinghêh's care. He marveled at her husband Chabé-chinka's commitment to alternating each night sleeping in this lodge and that of his second wife.[80] Missionaries and federal agents often noted that plural marriages were "common," including among the people they labeled "mixed-blood," well into the late nineteenth century.[81] Polygyny continued to support population growth and cooperative labor among women, which proved more and more important as survival became increasingly difficult in Kansas. Continued sexual freedom and availability of divorce prevented polygyny from subordinating Osage women.[82] In addition, couples could easily divorce, the frequency and ease of which also inhibited missionary efforts to teach monogamous, patriarchal Christian marriage.[83]

In the Treaty of 1839 the federal government had pledged to build houses for twenty-two Osage leaders as part of an effort to encourage nuclear family households and sedentary farming.[84] In 1848 federal officials finally finished constructing the houses, built on high ground, far enough away from one another to allow for American-style cultivation, and supplied with furniture and agricultural implements. Father Schoenmakers tried to encourage the leaders and their families to live in these homes, but very few even tried because they did not want to live at such a distance from their family and friends. In addition, these homes presented specific challenges for women: "The poor squaws could neither supply wood for the wide fireplaces built in them, nor could they stand the labor of running up and down from the houses to the river for water; moreover, it was almost impossible for them to keep such dwellings warm and clean."[85] Osage families abandoned these houses for their hometowns and sold the furniture to western Missouri settlers.[86]

The Catholic missionaries devoted the majority of their attention to educating Osage children. The opportunity to learn English drew students to the mission school, where everyone—male and female—received instruction in reading, writing, and arithmetic. Father Schoenmakers repeatedly complimented the "rapid progress" students made in these subjects.[87] "They read fluently, understand the rules and operation of arithmetic, and love to study it." Unfortunately for the missionaries, parents often permanently withdrew their children after they could speak English, using them as family interpreters.[88]

Joseph Pawnee-no-pah-she (Pa-I'n-No-Pa-She, "Governor Joe," or "Big Hill Joe"), who became principal Osage chief in 1869, also learned English at the Osage Mission. Yet he rarely spoke English with whites and preferred using an interpreter—a useful strategy in discerning the motives of federal officials and other Americans.[89]

Catholic schooling made very little impact on altering Osage gender construction. In the school's first two years, both missionaries and Indian agents commented on the boys spending three hours outside of regular class time learning "the use of agricultural implements."[90] Apparently the boys needed extra incentives to do this work, leading Father Schoenmakers to start "paying them liberally" for agricultural labor.[91] Only with wages would the boys "act manly throughout the season."[92] Eventually, though, agricultural instruction became increasingly difficult and de-emphasized in the curriculum because "the soil on which our establishments have been located is, perhaps, the worst soil in the Osage country, which tends to discourage the energy of our young beginners."[93] Osage women already knew that. They had selected the most fertile land on the reservation for their towns, and even their farming regularly failed. Just as with the Protestant schools, the early Catholic mission graduates primarily gained employment in the trading posts, not in establishing individual farms.[94] As it turned out, the male students saw little use for learning agriculture when it did not fit into their gender role or local climate, and other aspects of their education proved far more useful in already male gendered contexts, such as diplomacy and trade.

The female department struggled to gain students and had lower enrollment than the male department for all but one year.[95] Beyond English and arithmetic, the girls spent their additional time learning skills already associated with Osage femininity, namely, gardening, sewing, knitting, and embroidery.[96] Father Schoenmakers remarked that the girls "are more industrious than the boys, always manifesting a willingness to do any kind of work required by their teachers."[97] The girls were not more industrious; they were instead being asked to do work that they already viewed as a legitimate female occupation.

Enrollment in the male department never exceeded 130 students, while the female department never reached 100 students.[98] The number of children in the Osage population for the corresponding period ranged between an estimated 800 and 1,600 children, meaning the missionary education only reached a small fraction of the population.[99] The Jesuits complained less than their Protestant counterparts about family interference and students leaving the school, but they experienced the same problems.[100] In reporting enrollment data to federal authorities, Father Schoenmakers started in 1853 differentiating the students in "constant attendance."[101] In 1854 he wrote, "We opened the school seven years ago, but on account of the inconstancy of their relations, and increasing pride and independence of these children, few have the perseverance of giving their youthful years to education. Of those now at school [fifty boys and thirty-one girls] only ten have attended regularly these four years."[102] Eventually, Father Schoenmakers appealed to federal officials, hoping they would withhold annuity payments for students in school until they completed their education, but this plan never came to fruition.[103] As discussed in the previous chapter, the Osage families had always had close, loving relationships with their children. Offspring were evidence of *Wa-kon'-da*'s favor and the embodiment of their people's future. As their agent noted in 1871, "the Osages . . . have strong affections for their children, and . . . are averse to sending them away." In a world of disease and population decline, relations were even less inclined to part with their children.[104]

The mission journal documented one couple, both graduates of the school, trying to individually farm, but living in poverty. "If both of them would [throw] away their French clothes (as the Osage call our way of dressing) and would return to the indian blanket, their friends and connections would give them plenty. But they prefer to labour hard and suffer rather than to act against the promises they made in baptism."[105] These two made a rare choice. Living on a small family farm in southern Kansas led to poverty and starvation (for many Americans too); whereas, living in an Osage town provided communal support and food production better suited to the environment, which was part of the reason most did not adopt the Euro-American lifestyle.

Mobility also proved one of the greatest obstacles the priests encountered in "civilizing" the Osage. Father Bax noted, "The mode of life that the Indians are obliged to lead . . . [t]hey commonly pass six months of the year in the chase, which forces them to remove from us, and exposes the morality of those who would wish to live as exemplary Christians, to great temptations and dangers."[106] Avoiding missionaries was part of the appeal of mobility, but it was also necessary for survival.[107] Because the climate did not consistently support agriculture, hunting provided a more reliable income. After more than a year of drought, one missionary described the Osage during the harsh winter of 1855–1856 as "being well housed in their winter towns with an abundance of fuel to keep themselves comfortable, having plenty of dry meat for daily use, and being most all well supplied with a large amount of buffalo robes for trade, they had nothing to envy of their white neighbors, and winter found them all prepared for it."[108] Periodic droughts, devastating to invading Euro-American settlers, sometimes proved advantageous for the Osage. For example, during the 1860 drought, the majority of Euro-American settlers "had to live on a half ration, for they had raised no crops of any kind . . . many of them had to travel over 2 miles to procure a barrel of water."[109] Meanwhile, the majority of Osage hunting bands abandoned the plains and instead sought game along the Arkansas River and its tributaries.

> In so doing, to use a western expression, they struck a real bonanza, for the dry season having compelled most all kind of game to come down to quench their thirst in the waters of the big rivers, the Osages had an excellent hunting season, they procured an abundance of meat and had an unexpected harvest of rare furs. Hence this drought which proves so ruinous to the new settlers as well as to the emigrants then on their way to Pike's Peak, was rather I might say beneficial to the Indians.[110]

The reservation also occasionally suffered from grasshopper plagues; through mobility, the Osage withstood these infestations far better than their Euro-American neighbors. In the summer of 1854, grasshoppers descended on southern Kansas—the first time in Osage memory this occurred—devouring dried meat and cached produce, and devastating the white settler's crops. So the Osage packed up and left immediately for their fall hunt, with some bands headed to the Platte River and the others toward Turkey Creek's junction with the Cimarron River. The latter hunting ground in particular had plentiful wood, water, pasture land for horses, and large bison herds yielding a successful hunt.[111] Back near their towns, Euro-American settlers who already lost their 1853 harvest due to drought suffered similarly dry weather in 1854, when the grasshoppers finished off what was left.[112] In the spring of 1855, grasshoppers started hatching, forcing Osage women to abandon planting their crops so everyone could commence hunting and escape the infestation. In this year again, the Osage had a successful hunt, obtaining a large amount of game and rare peltries that brought high trade prices.[113] When another grasshopper swarm arrived in August of 1866, the Osage immediately departed on another hunt to avoid the plague. Mobility and hunting provided enough protection to keep grasshoppers from totally undermining subsistence.[114]

Even though the Osage knew how to survive in Kansas better than their American counterparts, the missionaries repeatedly tried to teach Euro-American-style farming at agricultural settlements. It is likely Osage people joined these settlements for the same reasons some had joined the earlier Protestant settlements: decentralization of Osage-community structure; diversifying subsistence, which was especially challenging in Kansas; and maintaining positive relations with Americans. In 1849, three miles south of the mission, Osage men and women were paid to fell trees and split rails to fence in forty acres that Brother Thomas O'Donnell subdivided into individual family farm plots.[115] The Osage women in this settlement rearranged all of his plots, forcing O'Donnell to accept their conception of proper field organization.[116] He successfully persuaded Osage men to conduct the planting, which the men likely again viewed as inside the male gender role because O'Donnell seemingly owned the field and directed this labor, as Osage women had long done. But he could not persuade them to till or weed the fields. The Osage typically left on summer hunts while their crops matured; thus, these settlers did not see much need to tend the fields. After weeds took over and a drought dried out the soil, Father Ponziglione acknowledged the "total failure of their farming enterprise discouraged the [men] and they came to the conclusion that such a kind of work was not for them, and that the Great-Spirit had made them to be hunters, not farmers. Hence, as long as there was plenty of buffalo on the plains, they would be big fools if they would go to work."[117] All the Osage "farmers" abandoned this settlement.[118]

Six years later, after loss of the Comanche trade, diminishing access to the bison herds, and the end of previous treaty annuities, twenty-five families agreed to another missionary-sponsored farming experiment.[119] Again, subsistence challenges seem to have been a prime motivator for accommodating, in some way, missionary demands. But successive droughts led to four consecutive years of crop failure.[120] To preserve this settlement, Father Schoenmakers supplied the residents with seeds. "Let them have whatever they needed, free of all charges . . . and he would purchase from them whatever they could spare, paying them regular market prices." The settlement grew to fifty families by 1859, but even with these subsidies, the Osage settlers had to continue hunting just to survive.[121]

The 1860s provided the final blow to the second agricultural experiment. A drought in 1860 made the ground too hard for plowing, and the settlers dispersed to join their kin out hunting.[122] In 1861, after the Civil War began, the settlers saw "their houses and their improvements destroyed by roving incendiaries; their oats and corn fields [were] turned into pastures for cavalry horses, their hogs and cattle [were] butchered by unruly troopers."[123] Once again they joined their kin, depending on hunting for subsistence.[124] Throughout the rest of the war, soldiers and "desperadoes" burned the Osage settlers' fields and homes.[125] In desperation, Father Schoenmakers turned to exchanging food and cash with Osage men and women who cut firewood for the mission, paying $5.00 for every 1,000 rails.[126] After land cessions in 1865, all the Osage moved more than forty miles from the mission, and these settlers abandoned Euro-American-style agriculture altogether. If Osage women struggled to produce successful harvests, it was no surprise Osage men, as well as American missionaries and settlers, could not either.[127]

Overall, Catholic missionization failed. The mission journal in 1870 admitted the goal of the mission was "the instruction of the Osage Indian in all that concerns religion and civilization, so from the very first day we came here [and] tried all the means in our power to succeed in this work [and] we must acknowledge that we did not do much."[128] In 1872, Father Ponziglione visited the Osage, now settled on their Indian Territory reservation, commenting, "They listened to my instruction, but I doubt very much they will follow my advises: their will I think is good, but their nature is weak, and the power of old habits is very strong."[129] More accurately, the Osage utilized missionaries in ways that addressed Osage needs, which did not involve Christian conversion or adoption of Euro-American gender roles. Joseph Pawnee-no-pah-she summed it up well, "It took Father Schoenmakers fifteen years to make a white man out of me, and it will take just fifteen minutes to make an Osage out of myself."[130]

Daily prayer vigils, one of the most ubiquitous aspects of Osage spirituality, remained a prominent part of their lives in Kansas. Tixier documented men, women, and children's lamentations, and while traveling with a hunting party, he too was awakened by the sound of wailing: "This religious song was addressed to the Great Spirit (*Oua-Kondah*) to ask of him a good hunt and to avert the wrath of the Evil Spirit. This supplication was accompanied by abundant tears."[131] In describing this period, John Joseph Mathews proudly declared,

After more than 150 years in contact with European manners and mores and greed and fears . . . each morning when the morning star came up, men went to the high places to chant their prayers while the women stayed in their lodges or came out to stand in front of them facing east. Grandfather rose each morning bringing the light of day, in which they desired to live into old age.[132]

Missionaries similarly recorded how at daybreak, noon, and sunset, Osage men and women daubed their faces with mud or covered their heads with dust and ashes and made their "daily supplications to the Great Spirit" through pitiful cries and lamentations for their lost family members.[133] In 1868, a nearby white settler, Eliza Wyckoff, wrote, "At day-break, every morning, they made a hideous singsong noise lasting a half-hour, mourning for their dead."[134] Hence, the Non'-hon-zhin-ga's understanding of the sunrise embodying the merging of masculine (day) and feminine (night) forces and denoting the circular nature of life and death, remained a time when all Osage people appealed to Wa-kon'-da for their individual and nation's long life.

But other ritual practices were changing. By the 1860s and 1870s, warfare and raiding were markedly decreasing for the Osage as they struggled more with the American invasion than with rival Native nations; thus, opportunities to perform war-related ceremonies similarly declined.[135] What did this mean for the persistence of the values these rituals conveyed and reiterated? All of the late nineteenth-century and early twentieth-century ethnographers gathered their material from Osage informants who had personally practiced the rituals they relayed. Reverend James Owen Dorsey, for example, interviewed Red Corn (Ha pa Shu tsy) somewhere around 1884 where he provided a detailed description of the war ceremonies, including the scalp dance, indicating these were practiced during his lifetime.[136] Several women still possessed the ritual knowledge associated with weaving and caring for with the wa-xo'-be they had utilized while living in Kansas when La Flesche conducted his interviews in the early twentieth century. And even the material La Flesche gathered from male members of the Non'-hon-zhin-ga provided signficant discussion of women's roles in warfare as warrior mothers.[137] So the construction of gender complementarity embodied in war rituals remained part of Osage cosmology in Kansas, at least for those who were alive and probably adults during the early reservation period. But over time, the decline of warfare and the corresponding ritual practices meant that this manifestation of the gender construction deteriorated.[138]

Throughout the Kansas reservation period, federal policies and settler invasion produced stress and malnutrition that heightened Osage susceptibility to disease. Repeatedly delayed annuities prevented the Osage from obtaining goods necessary for all manner of women's and men's work and for trade, which simultaneously undermined subsistence. Combine this with poor weather, and in 1852, the result was measles, typhoid fever, whooping cough, and scurvy killing at least 1,000 people.[139] Drought, floods, grasshoppers, and the settler invasion contributed to malnutrition throughout the 1850s, enabling multiple waves of smallpox and other contagious diseases to kill hundreds at a time.[140] And unfortunately, disease sometimes proved a weapon between rival Native nations. While out on the winter hunt in November 1854, Osage warriors came upon a small, Comanche camp; because the two nations were again enemies by this point, the Osage attacked.

> At that time [the Comanches] happened to have in their camps a poor man afflicted with a most loathsome and contagious distemper resembling leprosy, and they agree to sacrifice this unfortunate to avenge themselves of the Osages. The poor Indian being in the very last stage of his sickness, not able to survive but few days, was then painted all over with vermilion and dressed up in rich style as chiefs are accustomed to be buried. They place by him his arms, his pipe, and a good supply of tobacco, their object being to entice their enemies to rob the sick man of all he had, knowing that by so doing they would most certainly contract the same sickness, and this by gradually developing in the coming spring would most likely cause the death of many of them! This really most barbarious [sic] and wicked stratagem proved in due time terribly successful, and produced the intended result.[141]

Smallpox, not leprosy, killed an estimated 400 people in the spring of 1855.[142] The challenges facing the Osage only worsened in the 1860s, leaving them starving and desperate. More droughts, floods, grasshoppers, and settlers kept devastating agriculture, perpetuating malnutrition and disease. Even in years with successful hunts, dietary reliance almost exclusively on meat led to scurvy—also a deadly killer. Sometimes horses were the only trade good the

Osage could use to procure food. And with frequent settler theft, this safety-net exchange item was also in rapid decline. [143]

Needless to say, Osage population dramatically declined in Kansas. Estimates indicate in 1820, prior to moving to Kansas, the Osage numbered 10,000–12,000. By 1850, the total was an estimated 8,000. In 1860, the population was near 3,500; and in 1870, somewhere around 3,000. When the Osage were expelled from Kansas, it is believed one in four died within the first year in Indian Territory. Throughout this period, there were years of population growth and increasing birth rates, but colonial disruptions never abated; thus, the population could not recover. Overall, the population continued to decline through the 1880s. [144] As was common for Natives across the continent, land loss yielded demographic collapse. Native elimination was not just in terms of land title, it was also literal—a genocide of "sustained duration." [145]

How did the Osage understand this misery? Simply put, as a result of the "vexations" produced by US Indian policy and invading Americans, "almost all their troubles are ascribed to their connection with the white people." [146] Once forced to move, they could not uphold their sacred responsibilities in their old homeland, and thus they had betrayed Wa-kon'-da's blessings. As a result, John Joseph Mathews said the people wondered if Wa-kon'-da was angry. All of their struggles seemed to "indicate that he was at least displeased." Likewise, Mathews said the Osage saw "overwhelming evidence that they were being defeated by the great mysteries of the Heavy Eyebrows (Americans) . . . the strong medicine of [their] God . . . was tragically disturbing." Even though Mathews said the Osage were "resistant as ever" to abandoning their "prayers . . . and ceremonial dances," Louis Burns contended that in Kansas "their religion was shaken." These unparalleled compounding tragedies impacted them, like everything else, in both a physical and spiritual sense. Neither men nor women could effectively conduct their work, and this was jeopardizing their existence in the present and potentially the future. [147]

In addition to settler invasion, the Civil War also significantly disrupted Osage lives and federal Indian policy. Osage leaders remained well informed about the US political situation, and at the outbreak of the war retreated across the plains to the mountains, before settling in temporary camps in Indian Territory (Oklahoma) along the Cimarron and Washita Rivers. [148] After completing a successful hunt in late 1862, the Osage returned to their Kansas reservation communities. [149] Situated in a borderland between the Confederacy

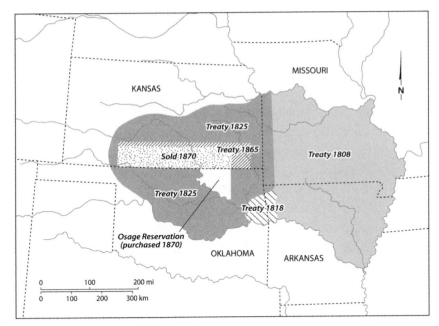

Osage Land Loss. (Map by Bill Nelson.)

and the Union, the Osage reservation attracted roaming regiments and rob-
bers who plundered or burned agricultural fields, homes, and horse herds
throughout the war.[150] Thus, hunting expeditions became exceedingly dangerous, and many Osage families dispersed to live in smaller family units
during the war.[151] Over the course of the war, various Osage bands and individuals served both for the Union and Confederate armies.[152] However, it
seems the Osage remained relatively neutral during the Civil War, concerned
primarily with subsistence and survival rather than taking sides. The war
also interrupted funding for Indian policy, federal agents, and missionaries,
hampering the civilization program. Therefore, federal inconsistency again
facilitated continued resistance to efforts to change lives and culture as Osage
families continued to rely on kin networks and agriculture, hunting, and trading to survive.

   In this chaos, federal and state officials saw an opportunity to try to force
the Osage to relinquish their Kansas reservation and move to Indian Territory.
Again, settler invasions had devastated the Osage, and every level of government had cooperated to dispossess them; hence, they had little choice but to
"consent" in 1863 to ceding the eastern portion of the Kansas reservation and

moving their towns farther west onto a "diminished reservation." However, the treaty languished in Congress, and in 1865 the Osage had to "consent" to another version, finally ratified in 1866, with funding for removal approved in 1867.[153]

After the initial negotiations in 1863, settlers started to flood into the newly "ceded" land. In 1866 Pawhuska (White Hair) complained to federal officials that when the Osage returned from their winter hunt they found "whites settled on some of our towns, they cut down our timber and eat our bottom grass, which we need for our ponies."[154] As Neosho agent George Snow witnessed, "It has not been two years yet since these Indians relinquished near 2,000,000 acres of their lands to the white settler. Still they are not satisfied. Immigration rolls on, like the tornado which meets nothing to check it. They have overrun all the trust lands, and are now settling on the diminished reservation."[155] In 1867 Agent Snow visited these nearly seventy families and ordered them to leave, but they said they would not remove until he had sufficient arms to force them. "They say that laws always have been made to protect the squatter, and they think they will not be left out in the cold when the governor of the State is 'determined to protect them at all hazards.'" Hostilities reached such proportions that "four companies of 'militia' [were] organized on the border by the State authority . . . threatening the Indians with 'extermination.'"[156] By 1869, five hundred families made illegal claims on the diminished reservation. These squatters built houses, began farming, stole Osage crops, allowed their livestock to graze in Osage fields, and prevented Osage women from gathering timber on their "claims."[157]

To make matters worse, in the fall of 1867, the Osage were attacked by the Arapaho while out buffalo hunting—preventing the acquisition of meat and hides. They were so destitute that federal officials provided rations in February 1868 to combat starvation. Then, in May 1868, the commissioner of Indian affairs personally met with the Osage, demanding they leave Kansas, which Osage leaders refused. Hence, he threatened to end rations; to allow angry settlers in attendance at the negotiations to exact violent revenge; and finally with outright extermination. As a result, the Osage "agreed" to transfer their Kansas reservation land directly to a railroad company, which was illegal. Heated debates eventually erupted in Congress over the treaty's questionable legality, preventing ratification. Finally, in July 1870, Congress added provisions to an Indian appropriation bill to buy the Osage land and provide for their confinement in Indian Territory. The new reservation, situated inside Cherokee lands, required an additional three years of negotiations to secure Osage title. In the spring of 1872, the majority of the Osage left Kansas for their final reservation in Indian Territory.[158] These "repeat removals, excisions from reservations, grants of the same land to different tribes, all conducted against a background of endless pressure for new or revised treaties," were the hallmarks of an Indian policy relentlessly working toward "extinguishment of native title." In terms of the Osage in Kansas, mission accomplished.[159]

For the Osage, confinement to a Kansas reservation meant they could no longer utilize or protect the "gifts" Wa-kon'-da had provided in their old homeland. Yet they kept praying daily for Wa-kon'-da's assistance in all their endeavors and for community perpetuation. They continued to conduct their physical work in a spiritual context: women planted crops, men hunted, and women processed hides and meat. However, men's and women's work became increasingly difficult over time. Weather, insects, and settlers destroyed agriculture. Hunting and trade opportunities declined. And the result included epidemics, starvation, and population decline. All of this undermined men and women's gender roles and the associated ritual practices. Mobility and increasing reliance on hunting was the best way to preserve people and culture.

Summing up the settler empire's exploitive land acquisition policies, Captain Cooke at Fort Gibson in 1839 predicted famine, death to many, significant suffering, and eventual extinction for the Osage.[160] He accurately anticipated that life on the Kansas reservation would be extremely difficult and deadly, and he correctly pointed the blame at American colonization. Kansas was the last place the agriculture-hunting-trading economy and their established cosmological structure defined Osage life. Most importantly, Captain Cooke was wrong about extinction. Continuing the spiritual and physical gendered work that had—at least since colonization—defined their lives, ensured the Osage persisted as a nation through this brutal time. The surviving women and men withstood this together, indicating Wa-kon'-da's enduring desire for "a never-ending line of descendants," which they maintain to this day.[161]

CONCLUSION RECOVERING THE FEMININE IN THE OSAGE EMPIRE AND BEYOND

Long before Europeans arrived in the Americas, the ancient Osage *Non'-hon-zhin-ga* (priesthood) concluded that *Wa-kon'-da*'s (Mysterious Power) creative power manifested in a duality-based universe, where procreative forces united to perpetuate celestial and seasonal cycles. In order to secure *Wa-kon'-da*'s blessings and assistance in their lives, the *Non'-hon-zhin-ga* organized Osage society as a mirror image of the universe *Wa-kon'-da* created, embodied in gender complementarity. Through rituals, all Osage people continually sought *Wa-kon'-da*'s aid in the dual aspects essential for community existence: women's fecundity and men's courageous protection of women and everything women produced. Both women and men had interdependent, important, varied, and highly valued roles that ensured their nation's continued existence.[1]

By the seventeenth century, they had settled in a region of significant geographic advantages, in modern-day western Missouri, bordering forests, prairies, and plains. Their homeland was filled with diverse gatherable plants, large and small game, and fertile soil for agriculture. At the same time, this was highly defensible territory, bordered on three sides by large rivers, with the Ozarks near their towns as a place to retreat from invasion. From this base, the very cosmopolitan Osage people had a long history of both cultural and material exchange. In this productive and protected landscape, the Osage population grew (estimates indicate over 10,000). By adhering to the *Non'-hon-zhin-ga*'s understanding of the universe, including gender complementarity, clearly they had acquired *Wa-kon'-da*'s greatest blessing: "a never-ending line of descendants," manifested in women's creative power and fertility.[2]

When French traders arrived, the Osage seized the opportunity to reserve access to European trade goods for themselves by preventing French exchange with other Native groups. This involved expanded raiding and warfare, which in Osage society involved women and men. Women, as warrior mothers, were "regarded as no less important [than] men who face death upon the fields of conflict." Most rituals, especially those related to warfare, involved ceremonially opening of the sacred bird-hawk *wa-xo'-be* (sacred bundle), which also embodied this duality. In peacetime, women cared for the *wa-xo'-be* because it signified life for the Osage, just like women via their fertility. In war, men carried it into battle because it served as a supplication to *Wa-kon'-da* for hawk-like courage while also representing death to Osage enemies. But men needed more than the hawk's courage, they needed women's courage too. All "the Little Ones"—men and women—"placed bravery above all other virtues." Women used ceremonial singing, praying, and dancing, that was conducted before, during, and after war expeditions to spiritually combine their courage with men's, and ensure military victories. The scalp dance most obviously conveyed this throughout their time in Missouri, Arkansas, and Kansas, when women, dressed as male warriors, danced with enemy scalps as a demonstration of women's spiritual vanquishing of the enemy that corresponded with men's ritual and physical triumph on the battlefield. As it turned out, brave Osage warrior mothers, in addition to their courageous husbands and sons, proved a formidable foe. Together, they built an empire.[3]

In Osage cosmology, hunting was viewed as "a war for survival [just like] warfare against humans." Hence, much of the ritual involved with hunting mirrored the ritual involved with warfare, which required women's participation for success. Of course, the most obvious aspect of women's role in hunting came from the voluminous hide and meat processing that created something useful out of the slain animals. In the eighteenth century, the Osage became the "true bankers of this region" because women manufactured tens of thousands of hides that fetched "the best prices in the coffeehouse auctions of Montreal and London." But in the nineteenth century, the US settler empire wanted Native elimination in order to acquire their land. As a result, the Osage were confined to a virtually untillable Kansas reservation, while American settlers invaded and confiscated Osage property. To survive this colonization, the Osage relied increasingly on hunting and trade for subsistence, which continued to reiterate *Wa-kon'-da*'s duality-based universe, via an economy of complementary labor.[4]

By "recovering the feminine," as Paula Gunn Allen termed it, we see that women *and* men were the main actors in both the rise and fall of the Osage empire. The scholarly misconception has been that men's actions produced this empire, and as a result, women's status presumably declined. In reality, the Osage conception of the world and their place in it involved gender complementarity. The only way they could survive and succeed was to manifest this duality through their spiritual and physical actions. And they did, even as American settler colonialism nearly obliterated everything. In less than a century, the Osage lost upward of seventy percent of their population and retained only a small piece of their once immense territory. For Americans, this destruction was intentional and habitual. Even under this extreme duress, the surviving Osage people maintained much of their established religious and economic practices through most of the nineteenth century; and gender complementarity—being directly connected to both—also endured.[5]

However, by the late 1870s, the subsistence and trade activities that had sustained Osage life since at least the early eighteenth century were disappearing.[6] Prior to this, Osage towns had functioned as ceremonially independent communities, containing Non'-hon-zhin-ga from all twenty-four clans, all of which cooperated to perform rituals. Population decline devastated this system. As many Non'-hon-zhin-ga passed away, so did the clan wi'-gi-e (ritual chant) and the cosmological knowledge contained therein. As towns and clans lost members, multiple communities combined to provide the full clan representation necessary for rituals.[7] At the same time, these rituals that secured Wa-kon'-da's aid in warfare, hunting, and agriculture held little relevance on a reservation where none of these things could sustain them.[8] In this context, the Osage made another "move to a new country," with many adopting Big Moon Peyotism, or joining Catholic, Quaker, or Baptist congregations.[9] When reflecting on this period, Osage scholar Jean Dennison of course acknowledged the massive trauma and devastation caused by colonization, but she also described these changes as encompassing "more than loss." It was a time when the Osage decided to "put the bundles away" because they no longer held meaning in their lives. Pragmatically, the Osage people conscientiously decided "what they would bring forward and what they would leave behind."[10]

In spite of Indian policy's efforts to the contrary, the Osage entered the twentieth century with relatively sizable financial wealth. Osage leaders intentionally sold, rather than ceded, their Kansas reservation lands. As the proceeds grew to over one million dollars in the US treasury, the Osage people were starving, aggravated by the fact that Indian agents used meager food rations to coerce cooperation with assimilation programs. Osage governance was also undermined when an Indian agent created a new tribal council, full of his appointees. Fed up with all of this, Osage leaders traveled to Washington, DC, in 1879 and convinced the commissioner of Indian Affairs to allow quarterly cash payments to each person from their Kansas land sales. In return, though, the Osage had to adopt a "civilized" American-style constitutional government, culminating in what Dennison and Osage scholar Robert Warrior described as another "move to a new country." The newly established government then started granting grazing leases to Texas cattlemen and neighboring Kansas farmers, which also produced annual per-capita payments. This economic self-sufficiency, entirely due to Osage initiatives and ingenuity, finally put an end to half a century of population decline, ultimately preventing their elimination.[11]

This relative wealth certainly made the Osage experience unique in comparison to that of other Indigenous communities confined to reservations at the same time. Nevertheless, this prosperity came at a price, as virtual carnivals sprang up around Osage payment days when all manner of swindlers and thieves descended on the reservation. The discovery of oil only amplified these problems, as murders, crime, and fraud became commonplace in what was known as the "Osage reign of terror."[12] At the same time, federal policy continued its effort to eliminate communal land rights and thus the Indigenous nations that held them. Passage of the Dawes Act (1887) and the infamous Oklahoma settler invasions eventually led to Osage allotment in 1906. But Osage allotment followed an unusual trajectory, in part because the Osage nation maintained collective mineral rights, creating an "underground reservation." And instead of dividing the reservation between tribe-member allotments and surplus land for white settlers, the Osage retained all of their land, with all members, including women, receiving equal allotments of the entire reservation.[13]

Parents had avoided long-term American schooling for their children through the 1870s, but on the Indian Territory reservation, Indian agents compelled boarding school attendance by withholding children's income payments. Even so, Osage parents overwhelming opposed separation from their children. Runaways were frequent, and Osage parents were so notoriously lax in ensuring student attendance, the Bureau of Indian Affairs again authorized withholding payments to minors in 1913 to coerce school attendance. Parents resisted because Euro-American education assaulted virtually every aspect of Osage culture, including language, spirituality, and familial and communal relationships.[14] By the early twentieth century, assimilation efforts seemed successful as most Osage individuals spoke English, wore western-style clothing, and cut their hair based on fashionable trends.

Wood-frame bungalows or two-story brick homes replaced lodges. And food primarily came from local stores. However, these changes did not indicate the elimination of Osage identity or nationhood.[15]

Though many Osage beliefs and practices "had to be left behind," others like gender complementarity continued to play an important role in community life. In the late nineteenth century, the Osage adapted a ceremony from the Ponca and Kansa, called the I'n-Lon-Schka, which even in the twenty-first century serves as the most significant ritual and social activity for the Osage nation. As most of the Osage adopted Peyotism and Christianity, various Non'-hon-zhin-ga adapted the I'n-Lon-Schka as a way to preserve and perpetuate Osage spiritual beliefs and ideals in familiar prayers, songs, and rituals relevant to their changing lives. This annual ceremony embodied oral history and maintained Osage identity and solidarity. Osage scholar Alice Anne Callahan translated I'n-Lon-Schka as "playground of the eldest son." The selection of a young boy or man as the Drumkeeper recognized "outstanding youth" in the nation, demonstrating the continued prominence of Osage children in their society. The I'n-Lon-Schka began as a warrior society dance, but after World War II, Osage women joined the dance. As Callahan and Osage scholar Jami Powell have argued, the prominent role of men in leading the dance has obscured the roles played by women in the I'n-Lon-Schka, which replicated the historic gender construction. Mothers taught and trained the dancers; thus, women's attitudes, ideas, and understandings of the dance directed its form and meaning. This multiday ceremony also involved feasting, and the female head cook instructed and organized the "committee cooks"; hence, the "preparation of the food as well as the cooking is all a part of the ceremony."[16]

Most importantly, women created the regalia worn by their family members in I'n-Lon-Schka, including the ribbon work adornments. Osage women initially obtained ribbons through trade with the French, and ever since, women have reformed these ribbons into "uniquely Osage" designs. Mrs. Fred Lookout (Julia)—who also served as one of Francis La Flesche's informants—was credited with helping to ensure this art form remained a prominent demonstration of Osage identity by passing on patterns and techniques to other Osage mothers who made I'n-Lon-Schka regalia for their children.[17] One manifestation of this continuity involved the "traditional Osage wedding dress," which dates back to the first Osage meeting with Thomas Jefferson in 1804. As was common in such meetings, Jefferson distributed gifts to the Osage delegation, including several US military officer's coats and stovepipe

Osage Wedding (Western History Collections, University of Oklahoma Libraries, Cunningham-Dillon Collection, number 517). This photograph of an Osage wedding was taken in the early twentieth century. The women in the carriage wear decorated stovepipe hats and military-style coats that by this point had been part of the "traditional Osage wedding dress" for over a century. Today, Osage women still make and wear this regalia as part of *I'n-Lon-Schka*. University of Oklahoma records label this a photograph of Bill Fletcher's Osage wedding on July 14, 1918. However, Daniel Swan and Jim Cooley's research labels this image "Annie Collum Others's wedding in Fairfax, Oklahoma, ca. 1916." (Alice Anne Callahan, *The Osage Ceremonial Dance* I'n-Lon-Schka [Norman: University of Oklahoma Press, 1990], 64–65; Daniel C. Swan and Jim Cooley, "Chiefs, Brides, and Drum Keepers: Material Culture, Ceremonial Exchange, and Osage Community Life," in *Material Vernaculars: Objects, Images, and Their Social Worlds*, ed. Jason Baird Jackson [Bloomington: Indiana University Press, 2016], 161, 175–176, 180–181.)

hats. The famously tall Osage men could not fit in the coats though, so the men gave the clothing to their daughters, who started wearing the coats and hats in wedding ceremonies. Over time, this became part of traditional wedding ceremony attire, as Osage women continued to make coats, complete with gold epaulettes, brass buttons, and a significant amount of ribbon work, finger weaving, and beadwork paired with, among other things, top hats adorned with feathers and ribbons. Today Osage women still make and wear the "wedding dress" in *I'n-Lon-Schka* and for other special occasions and ceremonies.[18] In these ways, Osage women's distinctive creations served "as a visual marker of belonging, strengthening community ties." Of course that was exactly what settler colonialism endeavored to eliminate, and as such, this artistry "must be understood as an essential part of. . .decolonization."[19]

Both Powell and Dennison credit *I'n-Lon-Schka*, ribbon work, and women with maintaining and strengthening Osage identity and nationhood in the face of ongoing US imperialism. Dennison, Powell, and Callahan, among others, are doing the same with their scholarship. The *I'n-Lon-Schka*, as Powell argued, "resists the logic of elimination through its emphasis on the future," namely, by emphasizing the role of families and young people in the dance. Powell concluded *I'n-Lon-Schka* "provides a space in which Osage families imagine an Osage future through their children." All of the time, expense, and artistry involved with preparing for *I'n-Lon-Schka* demonstrated "the pride that Osage parents feel when they watch their children dance." Clearly, the preeminence of Osage mothers and children—and their association with future nationhood—remains central to Osage life. Therefore, gender construction was a pivotal site of experiencing, adapting to, and resisting colonization.[20]

NOTES

ACKNOWLEDGMENTS

1. George E. Tinker, *Missionary Conquest: The Gospel and Native American Cultural Genocide* (Minneapolis: Fortress Press, 1993), 115–116; Walter L. Hixson, *American Settler Colonialism: A History* (New York: Palgrave Macmillan, 2013), 197–200; and Andrea Smith, "Queer Theory and Native Studies: The Heteronormativity of Settler Colonialism," in *Queer Indigenous Studies: Critical Interventions in Theory, Politics, and Literature*, ed. Qwo-Li Driskill, et al. (Tucson: University of Arizona Press, 2011), 45–46.

INTRODUCTION

1. Alice B. Kehoe, "The Shackles of Tradition," in *The Hidden Half: Studies of Plains Indian Women*, ed. Patricia Albers and Beatrice Medicine (Lanham, MD: University Press of America, 1983), 56; and Gunlög Fur, "'Some Women Are Wiser Than Some Men': Gender and Native American History," in *Clearing a Path: Theorizing the Past in Native American Studies*, ed. Nancy Shoemaker (New York: Routledge, 2002), 83.

2. Sarah Tuttle, *Letters on the Chickasaw and Osage Missions*, 2nd ed. (Boston: Massachusetts Sabbath School Society, 1833), 120–121.

3. Emphasis original; "Osage Indians: Account of Their Conditions, Manners, Etc.," *Missionary Herald* 23, no. 5 (May 1827): 146–147.

4. Kehoe, "The Shackles of Tradition," 56–57; Chris Finley, "Decolonizing the Queer Native Body (and Recovering the Native Bull-Dyke): Bringing 'Sexy Back' and out of Native Studies' Closet," in *Queer Indigenous Studies: Critical Interventions in Theory, Politics, and Literature*, ed. Qwo-Li Driskill et al. (Tucson: University of Arizona Press, 2011), 34–36; Linda Tuhiwai Smith, *Decolonizing Methodologies: Research and Indigenous Peoples* (New York: Zed Books, 1999), 8–9; Carol Devens, *Countering Colonization: Native American Women and Great Lakes Missions, 1630–1900* (Berkeley: University of California Press, 1992), 2–3; and Nancy Shoemaker, ed. *Negotiators of Change: Historical Perspectives on Native American Women* (New York: Routledge, 1995), 3–4, 7.

5. Michelle Zimbalist Rosaldo and Louise Lamphere, eds., *Woman, Culture, and Society* (Stanford, CA: Stanford University Press, 1974); Joan W. Scott, "Gender: A Useful Category of Historical Analysis," *American Historical Review* 91, no. 5 (December 1986): 1054; Theda Perdue, *Cherokee Women: Gender and Culture Change, 1700–1835* (Lincoln: University of Nebraska Press, 1998), 3–5; Gunlög Fur, *A Nation of Women: Gender and*

Colonial Encounters among the Delaware Indians, Early American Studies (Philadelphia: University of Pennsylvania Press, 2009), 3–5, 8; James Axtell, "Ethnohistory: An Historian's Viewpoint," Ethnohistory 26, no. 1 (Winter 1979); and Fur, "'Some Women Are Wiser Than Some Men': Gender and Native American History," 82.

6. Scott, "Gender: A Useful Category of Historical Analysis," 1056–1057; Perdue, Cherokee Women, 7; and Albert L. Hurtado, "Sex, Gender, Culture, and a Great Event: The California Gold Rush," Pacific Historical Review 68, no. 1 (1999): 2.

7. Will Roscoe, Changing Ones: Third and Fourth Genders in Native North America, 1st ed. (New York: St. Martin's Press, 1998), 7, 21; Laura F. Klein and Lillian A. Ackerman, "Introduction," in Women and Power in Native North America, ed. Laura F. Klein and Lillian A. Ackerman (Norman: University of Oklahoma Press, 1995), 12–14; Scott, "Gender: A Useful Category of Historical Analysis," 1054; Juliana Barr, Peace Came in the Form of a Woman: Indians and Spaniards in the Texas Borderlands (Chapel Hill: University of North Carolina Press, 2007), 2, 8–9, 11, 13; Lillian A. Ackerman, A Necessary Balance: Gender and Power among Indians of the Columbia Plateau (Norman: University of Oklahoma Press, 2003), 3–5, 22–24, 117, 250; Perdue, Cherokee Women, 7; Loretta Fowler, Wives and Husbands: Gender and Age in Southern Arapaho History (Norman: University of Oklahoma Press, 2010), 5, 302; Nancy Shoemaker, "Introduction," in Negotiators of Change: Historical Perspectives on Native American Women, ed. Nancy Shoemaker (New York: Routledge, 1995), 5–9; Daniel Maltz and JoAllyn Archambault, "Gender and Power in Native North America: Concluding Remarks," in Women and Power in Native North America, ed. Laura F. Klein and Lillian A. Ackerman (Norman: University of Oklahoma Press, 1995), 230–232; and Lillian A. Ackerman, "Complementary but Equal: Gender Status in the Plateau," in Women and Power in Native North America, ed. Laura F. Klein and Lillian A. Ackerman (Norman: University of Oklahoma Press, 1995), 77–78.

8. Sylvia Van Kirk, Many Tender Ties: Women in Fur-Trade Society, 1670–1870, 1st American ed. (Norman: University of Oklahoma Press, 1983), 4–8; Barr, Peace Came in the Form of a Woman, 2, 5, 7, 13, 15, 287–289; Michelene E. Pesantubbee, Choctaw Women in a Chaotic World: The Clash of Cultures in the Colonial Southeast (Albuquerque: University of New Mexico Press, 2005), 4–6, 114, 141–143, 173–175; Ackerman, A Necessary Balance, 35, 229–230, 238; Perdue, Cherokee Women, 9–10; Fowler, Wives and Husbands, 6, 288–299; and Shoemaker, "Introduction," 13–20.

9. Several scholars refer to women as having an important role in Osage society, but Garrick Bailey is the only one to explicitly say they had "complementary" gender roles. Garrick Alan Bailey and Daniel C. Swan, Art of the Osage (Seattle: St. Louis Art Museum in association with University of Washington Press, 2004), 63; Willard H. Rollings, The Osage: An Ethnohistorical Study of Hegemony on the Prairie-Plains (Columbia: University of Missouri Press, 1992), 16–21, 69–74; and J. Frederick Fausz, "Becoming

'a Nation of Quakers': The Removal of the Osage Indians from Missouri," *Gateway Heritage: Quarterly Journal of the Missouri Historical Society* 21 (Summer 2000): 31.

10. Rollings, *The Osage*, 89–91, 106, 111, 116; Louis F. Burns, *A History of the Osage People* (Tuscaloosa: The University of Alabama Press, 2004), 242–243; Kathleen Du-Val, "'A Good Relationship, & Commerce': The Native Political Economy of the Arkansas River Valley," *Early American Studies* 1, no. 1 (Spring 2003): 80–82; and Kathleen DuVal, *The Native Ground: Indians and Colonists in the Heart of the Continent* (Philadelphia: University of Pennsylvania Press, 2006), 103, 106–107, 109.

11. Historian Willard Rollings, in numerous texts specifically examining the Osage, avoided using the term "empire," instead describing their power as "hegemony." Terence N. D'Altroy, "Empires in a Wider World," in *Empires: Perspectives from Archaeology and History*, ed. Susan E. Alcock, et al. (New York: Cambridge University Press, 2001), 125; DuVal, *The Native Ground*, 4–5, 8, 103–104; Gilbert C. Din and Abraham Phineas Nasatir, *The Imperial Osages: Spanish-Indian Diplomacy in the Mississippi Valley* (Norman: University of Oklahoma Press, 1983), 385–390; Rollings, *The Osage: An Ethnohistorical Study of Hegemony on the Prairie-Plains*, 7–8; and Willard H. Rollings, *Unaffected by the Gospel: The Osage Resistance to the Christian Invasion (1673–1906): A Cultural Victory* (Albuquerque: University of New Mexico Press, 2004), chapter 2.

12. Burns, *A History of the Osage People*, 23–37, 85–86, 89–95, 447.

13. In discussing relations between Native nations, Hämäläinen did not refer to the Osage as an empire in the main text, instead using terms such as "formidable, dominant, expansionist, and conquering." However, he called the Powhatan, Iroquois confederacy, and Lakota "imperialistic or quasi-imperialistic" and then, in a corresponding footnote, said the "Osages, too should be mentioned here." Pekka Hämäläinen, *The Comanche Empire* (New Haven, CT: Yale University Press, 2008), 2–4, 32, 96, 98, 147, 349–353, 357, 366n3.

14. DuVal, *The Native Ground*, 114; DuVal, "'A Good Relationship, & Commerce,'" 80–88; Garrick Alan Bailey, *Changes in Osage Social Organization: 1673–1906*, University of Oregon Anthropological Papers No. 5 (Eugene: University of Oregon Press, 1973), 40–43; and Rollings, *The Osage*, chapters 4–5.

15. Some of the predominant texts on the Osage include Rollings, *The Osage*; DuVal, *The Native Ground*; Rollings, *Unaffected by the Gospel*; Din and Nasatir, *The Imperial Osages*; Bailey, *Changes in Osage Social Organization*; and Garrick Alan Bailey, ed. *The Osage and the Invisible World: From the Works of Francis La Flesche* (Norman: University of Oklahoma Press, 1995).

16. Hämäläinen, *The Comanche Empire*; Richard White, "The Winning of the West: The Expansion of the Western Sioux in the Eighteenth and Nineteenth Centuries," *Journal of American History* 65, no. 2 (September 1978); and James Axtell, *The Rise and*

Fall of the Powhatan Empire: Indians in Seventeenth-Century Virginia (Williamsburg, VA: Colonial Williamsburg Foundation, 1995).

17. DuVal, *The Native Ground*, 103–105, 127; DuVal, "'A Good Relationship, & Commerce,'" 81–83; and Rollings, *The Osage*, 7–8, 11–12.

18. Scott, "Gender: A Useful Category of Historical Analysis," 1054, 1056–1057, 1073.

19. Rollings, *The Osage*, 80–81, 159; DuVal, *The Native Ground*, 127; and Fausz, "Becoming 'a Nation of Quakers,'" 31.

20. DuVal, *The Native Ground*, 179, 196, 198, 200, 202–204, 208–209; Andrea Smith, "Queer Theory and Native Studies: The Heteronormativity of Settler Colonialism," in *Queer Indigenous Studies: Critical Interventions in Theory, Politics, and Literature*, ed. Qwo-Li Driskill et al. (Tucson: University of Arizona Press, 2011), 50–51; David La Vere, *Contrary Neighbors: Southern Plains and Removed Indians in Indian Territory* (Norman: University of Oklahoma Press, 2000), 7, 44–45, 48, 50–51; Rollings, *The Osage*, 220–221; Bernard W. Sheehan, *Seeds of Extinction: Jeffersonian Philanthropy and the American Indian* (Chapel Hill: University of North Carolina Press, 1973), 7, 125–129, 246–247; Anthony F. C. Wallace, *Jefferson and the Indians: The Tragic Fate of the First Americans* (Cambridge, MA: Belknap Press of Harvard University Press, 1999), 226, 274; and Patrick Wolfe, "Settler Colonialism and the Elimination of the Native," *Journal of Genocide Research* 8, no. 4 (2006): 387–389, 393, 399–400, 402–403.

21. DuVal, *The Native Ground*, 224–226; Rollings, *The Osage*, 253–256; and Rollings, *Unaffected by the Gospel*, 118.

22. Tai S. Edwards, "Disruption and Disease: The Osage Struggle to Survive in the Nineteenth-Century Trans-Missouri West," *Kansas History: A Journal of the Central Plains* 36, no. 4 (Winter 2013–2014).

23. ARCIA, 1869, "Annual Report of G. C. Snow, Agent for Osages and Other Tribes," 380–381; and Wolfe, "Settler Colonialism and the Elimination of the Native," 391–393.

24. Rollings, *Unaffected by the Gospel*, 166–168, 171.

25. DuVal, *The Native Ground*, 127.

26. Susan A. Miller, "Native Historians Write Back: The Indigenous Paradigm in American Indian Historiography," in *Native Historians Write Back: Decolonizing American Indian History*, ed. Susan A. Miller and James Riding (Lubbock: Texas Tech University Press, 2011), 37.

27. Robert Allen Warrior, *Tribal Secrets: Recovering American Indian Intellectual Traditions* (Minneapolis: University of Minnesota Press, 1995), 2, 87–88, 124–125.

28. Francis La Flesche, "Tribal Rites of Osage Indians," *Smithsonian Miscellaneous Collections* 68, no. 12 (1918): 86–90; Bailey, ed. *The Osage and the Invisible World*, 7, 11–12, 17–18, 26; Francis La Flesche, "A Dictionary of the Osage Language," *Smithsonian*

Institution: Bureau of American Ethnology, Bulletin 109 (Washington, DC: Government Printing Office, 1932): 2; Kehoe, "The Shackles of Tradition," 53–55; Francis La Flesche, "The Osage Tribe: Rite of the Wa-Xo'-Be," Forty-Fifth Annual Report of the Bureau of American Ethnology (1927–1928) (1930): 694–695; and Francis La Flesh, "Ethnology of the Osage Indians," Smithsonian Miscellaneous Collections 76, no. 10 (1924): 104–105.

29. William N. Fenton, "Indian and White Relations in Eastern North America: A Common Ground for History and Ethnology," in American Indian and White Relations to 1830: Needs and Opportunities for Study (Chapel Hill: University of North Carolina Press, 1957), 21–22; and Perdue, Cherokee Women, 8.

30. Maltz and Archambault, "Gender and Power in Native North America: Concluding Remarks," 231, 233–234, 245–249. For further discussion of gender complementarity, particularly in "myth," see Victoria D. Patterson, "Evolving Gender Roles in Pomo Society," in Women and Power in Native North America, ed. Laura F. Klein and Lillian A. Ackerman (Norman: University of Oklahoma Press, 1995), 129–132.

31. DuVal, The Native Ground, 5, 104–105.

32. Ibid., 4–5, 12, 103–107, 127; and Richard White, The Middle Ground: Indians, Empires, and Republics in the Great Lakes Region, 1650–1815 (Cambridge: Cambridge University Press, 1991).

33. Devens, Countering Colonization, 3; and Theda Perdue and Michael D. Green, North American Indians: A Very Short Introduction (New York: Oxford University Press, 2010), 18–19.

34. Rollings, Unaffected by the Gospel, 174–175, 182.

35. Wolfe, "Settler Colonialism and the Elimination of the Native," 388–389.

36. Paula Gunn Allen, The Sacred Hoop: Recovering the Feminine in American Indian Traditions (Boston: Beacon Press, 1986).

CHAPTER I. COSMOLOGY AND COMPLEMENTARY GENDER ROLES

1. Francis La Flesche, "The Osage Tribe: Rite of the Chiefs; Sayings of the Ancient Men," Thirty-Sixth Annual Report of the Bureau of American Ethnology (1914–1915) (1921): 43–45; Willard H. Rollings, The Osage: An Ethnohistorical Study of Hegemony on the Prairie-Plains (Columbia: University of Missouri Press, 1992), 5, 98–100; Garrick Alan Bailey, ed., The Osage and the Invisible World: From the Works of Francis La Flesche (Norman: University of Oklahoma Press, 1995), 27–28; David La Vere, Contrary Neighbors: Southern Plains and Removed Indians in Indian Territory (Norman: University of Oklahoma Press, 2000), 30–31; Marvin D. Jeter, "From Prehistory through Protohistory to Ethnohistory in and near the Northern Lower Mississippi Valley," in The Transformation of the Southeastern Indians, 1540–1760, ed. Robbie Franklyn Ethridge and Charles M. Hudson (Jackson: University Press of Mississippi, 2002), 216–218; Alice B. Kehoe, "Osage Texts and

Cahokia Data," in *Ancient Objects and Sacred Realms: Interpretations of Mississippian Iconography*, ed. F. Kent Reilly and James Garber (Austin: University of Texas Press, 2007), 249–250, 260; Louis F. Burns, *A History of the Osage People* (Tuscaloosa: The University of Alabama Press, 2004), 3, 22; and *The Osage Timeline*, Osage Tribal Museum (now the Osage Nation Museum), Pawhuska, OK, visited February 12, 2010.

2. Rollings, *The Osage*, 20–21, 68–79; Alice C. Fletcher and Francis La Flesche, *The Omaha Tribe*, vol. 1 (Lincoln: University of Nebraska Press, 1992), 270–271; Louis F. Burns, *Osage Indian Customs and Myths* (Tuscaloosa: University of Alabama Press, 1984), 97, 105–110; Andrea A. Hunter, "An Ethnoarchaeological Analysis of the Women's Role in Osage Society" (MA thesis, University of Missouri, 1985), 3–4; and Gilbert C. Din and Abraham Phineas Nasatir, *The Imperial Osages: Spanish-Indian Diplomacy in the Mississippi Valley* (Norman: University of Oklahoma Press, 1983), 8–9.

3. Francis La Flesche, "The Osage Tribe: Rite of the Chiefs; Sayings of the Ancient Men," *Thirty-Sixth Annual Report of the Bureau of American Ethnology* (1914–1915) (1921): 59–62, 157–185, 219–237, 254–269, 272–285; Thomas Edward Smith, "Who We Were, Is Not Who We Are: Wa.Zha.Zhe Representations, 1960–2010" (MA thesis, University of Kansas, 2013), 2; Francis La Flesche, "A Dictionary of the Osage Language," *Smithsonian Institution: Bureau of American Ethnology, Bulletin* 109 (Washington, DC: Government Printing Office, 1932): 209–210; Burns, *Osage Indian Customs and Myths*, 177–193; Burns, *A History of the Osage People*, 12–14, 21; and John Joseph Mathews, *The Osages: Children of the Middle Waters* (Norman: University of Oklahoma Press, 1961), 7–10.

4. La Flesche, "The Osage Tribe: Rite of the Chiefs; Sayings of the Ancient Men," 47–48, 60–62; Mathews, *The Osages*, 53–56, 75–79, 144–145; Garrick Alan Bailey, *Changes in Osage Social Organization: 1673–1906*, University of Oregon Anthropological Papers No. 5 (Eugene: University of Oregon Press, 1973), 18–19; and Rollings, *The Osage*, 21.

5. Rollings, *The Osage*, 7–8, 28; and Willard H. Rollings, *Unaffected by the Gospel: The Osage Resistance to the Christian Invasion (1673–1906): A Cultural Victory* (Albuquerque: University of New Mexico Press, 2004), 66–67, 70–71.

6. Francis La Flesche, "The Osage Tribe: Two Versions of the Child-Naming Rite," *Forty-Third Annual Report of the Bureau of American Ethnology* (1925–1926) (1928): 29–30; La Flesche, "The Symbolic Man of the Osage Tribe," *Art and Archaeology* 9 (February 1920): 69; and La Flesche, "The Osage Tribe: Rite of the Chiefs; Sayings of the Ancient Men," 48–51.

7. Francis La Flesche, "The Osage Tribe: The Rite of Vigil," *Thirty-Ninth Annual Report of the Bureau of American Ethnology* (1917–1918) (1925): 66–67, 365.

8. Rollings, *Unaffected by the Gospel*, 68–69.

9. La Flesche, "The Osage Tribe: Rite of the Chiefs; Sayings of the Ancient Men," 49–50; Francis La Flesche, "War Ceremony and Peace Ceremony of the Osage Indians," *Smithsonian Institution: Bureau of American Ethnology*, Bulletin 101 (Washington, DC: Government Printing Office, 1939), 75; Mathews, *The Osages*, 327; La Flesche, "The Osage Tribe: The Rite of Vigil," 364; Burns, *A History of the Osage People*, 208; Alice C. Fletcher and Francis La Flesche, *The Omaha Tribe*, vol. 2 (Lincoln: University of Nebraska Press, 1992), 493–494; and Francis La Flesche, "The Osage Tribe: Rite of the Wa-Xo'-Be," *Forty-Fifth Annual Report of the Bureau of American Ethnology (1927–1928)* (1930): 550.

10. The *Hon'-ga* (earth) moiety had two subdivisions representing the earth's dry land and water.

11. There is some discrepancy in the number of clans. Anthropologist Garrick Bailey identified twenty-four clans, while Francis La Flesche identified twenty-one. La Flesche qualified the three remaining clans as "separate when speaking of the gentile order [social organization] for the purpose of commemorating certain portions of the story of the tribe." However, historian Willard H. Rollings argued the *Non'-hon-zhin-ga* increased the number of clans over time, "perhaps to incorporate new people into the group or to expand the number to accommodate a growing population." Bailey, ed. *The Osage and the Invisible World*, 40–41; La Flesche, "The Osage Tribe: Rite of the Chiefs; Sayings of the Ancient Men," 52–54; and Rollings, *Unaffected by the Gospel*, 67.

12. Exogamy symbolically bound the two tribal divisions, but it also physically prevented tribal inbreeding. La Flesche, "The Symbolic Man of the Osage Tribe," 69–70; La Flesche, "The Osage Tribe: Rite of the Chiefs; Sayings of the Ancient Men," 47–48, 51, 59; La Flesche, "The Osage Tribe: The Rite of Vigil," 302, 360–361; Alice C. Fletcher and Francis La Flesche, *The Omaha Tribe*, vol. 1, 141; and Francis La Flesche, "Right and Left in Osage Ceremonies," in *Holmes Anniversary Volume: Anthropological Essays* (Washington, DC: J. W. Bryan Press, 1916), 278.

13. La Flesche, "The Osage Tribe: The Rite of Vigil," 238.

14. La Flesche, "The Osage Tribe: Rite of the Wa-Xo'-Be," 635; and La Flesche, "The Osage Tribe: The Rite of Vigil," 288.

15. La Flesche, "The Osage Tribe: The Rite of Vigil," 364.

16. The Osage Tribal Museum, now the Osage Nation Museum, had an exhibit relating to the structure of the cosmos and definitions of associated terms. *Osage Cosmos*, Osage Tribal Museum, Pawhuska, OK, visited February 12, 2010; and La Fleshe, "A Dictionary of the Osage Language," 193.

17. Josiah Gregg and Max L. Moorhead, ed., *Commerce of the Prairies* (Norman: University of Oklahoma Press, 1954), 419; Alice B. Kehoe, "Blackfoot Persons," in *Women and Power in Native North America*, ed. Laura F. Klein and Lillian A. Ackerman (Norman:

University of Oklahoma Press, 1995), 120–121; Zebulon Montgomery Pike, *The Expeditions of Zebulon Montgomery Pike, to Headwaters of the Mississippi River, through Louisiana Territory, and in New Spain, During the Years 1805–6–7*, ed. Elliott Coues, vol. 2 (New York: F. P. Harper, 1895), 532; La Flesche, "A Dictionary of the Osage Language," 38; Victor Tixier, John Francis McDermott, and Albert Jacques Salvan, *Tixier's Travels on the Osage Prairies* (Norman: University of Oklahoma Press, 1940), 251; and Thomas Nuttall, *A Journal of Travels into the Arkansa Territory During the Year 1819. With Occasional Observations on the Manners of the Aborigines*. (Philadelphia: Thos. H. Palmer, 1821), 193.

18. La Flesche, "War Ceremony and Peace Ceremony of the Osage Indians," 24–25; La Fleshe, "The Symbolic Man of the Osage Tribe," 70; and La Fleshe, "The Osage Tribe: The Rite of Vigil," 288.

19. La Flesche, "War Ceremony and Peace Ceremony of the Osage Indians," 228; and La Flesche, "The Osage Tribe: The Rite of Vigil," 288.

20. Burns, *Osage Indian Customs and Myths*, 97; and Mathews, *The Osages*, 80.

21. See also Janet D. Spector, "Male/Female Task Differentiation among the Hidatsa: Toward the Development of an Archeological Approach to the Study of Gender," in *The Hidden Half: Studies of Plains Indian Women*, ed. Patricia Albers and Beatrice Medicine (Lanham, MD: University Press of America, 1983), 95; Alice B. Kehoe, "The Shackles of Tradition," in *The Hidden Half: Studies of Plains Indian Women*, ed. Patricia Albers and Beatrice Medicine (Lanham, MD: University Press of America, 1983), 53–73; and Kehoe, "Blackfoot Persons."

22. La Flesche, "The Osage Tribe: The Rite of Vigil," 195, 238; La Flesche, "The Osage Tribe: Rite of the Wa-Xo'-Be," 624, 635; Fletcher and La Flesche, *The Omaha Tribe*, vol. 2, 338–339; and La Flesche, "War Ceremony and Peace Ceremony of the Osage Indians," 228.

23. Walter L. Williams, *The Spirit and the Flesh: Sexual Diversity in American Indian Culture* (Boston: Beacon Press, 1986), 81, 84, 242; Sue-Ellen Jacobs, Wesley Thomas, and Sabine Lang, "Introduction," in *Two-Spirit People: Native American Gender Identity, Sexuality, and Spirituality*, ed. Sue-Ellen Jacobs et al. (Urbana: University of Illinois Press, 1997), 1–2; and Will Roscoe, *Changing Ones: Third and Fourth Genders in Native North America*, 1st ed. (New York: St. Martin's Press, 1998), 7, 126–129.

24. John Bradbury, *Travels in the Interior of America, in the Years 1809, 1810, and 1811: Including a Description of Upper Louisiana, Together with the States of Ohio, Kentucky, Indiana, and Tennessee, with the Illinois and Western Territories, and Containing Remarks and Observations Useful to Persons Emigrating to Those Countries* (Liverpool: Printed for the author, by Smith and Galway, and published by Sherwood, Neely, and Jones, London, 1817), 40–41; Isaac McCoy, *History of Baptist Indian Missions: Embracing Aboriginal Tribes; Their Settlement within the Indian Territory, and Their Future Prospects* (Washington, DC: William

M. Morrison, 1840), 360–361; and Tixier, McDermott, and Salvan, *Tixier's Travels on the Osage Prairies*, 234.

25. Fletcher and La Flesche, *The Omaha Tribe*, vol. 1, 132–133; and Sabine Lang, *Men as Women, Women as Men: Changing Gender in Native American Cultures*, trans. John L. Vantine (Austin: University of Texas Press, 1998), 63–64.

26. "Introduction," in *Queer Indigenous Studies: Critical Interventions in Theory, Politics, and Literature*, ed. Qwo-Li Driskill et al. (Tucson: University of Arizona Press, 2011), 10–18; Jacobs, Thomas, and Lang, "Introduction," 2–3; and Gilbert Herdt, "The Dilemmas of Desire: From 'Berdache' To Two-Spirit," in *Two-Spirit People: Native American Gender Identity, Sexuality, and Spirituality*, ed. Sue-Ellen Jacobs et al. (Urbana: University of Illinois Press, 1997), 277–278.

27. Garrick Bailey, *Traditions of the Osage: Stories Collected and Translated by Francis La Flesche* (Albuquerque: University of New Mexico Press, 2010), 95–101.

28. W. B. Royall to R. Jones, June 21, 1848, in *Manuscript Collections, Miscellaneous Collections: W. B. Royall* (Topeka: Kansas State Historical Society).

29. Tixier, McDermott, and Salvan, *Tixier's Travels on the Osage Prairies*, 143, 219, 234; Burns, *A History of the Osage People*, 517n26; and Rollings, *The Osage*, 276–277.

30. Emphasis original; Tixier, McDermott, and Salvan, *Tixier's Travels on the Osage Prairies*, 234.

31. Ibid., 140–141, 234; and Rollings, *The Osage*, 276–277.

32. Evelyn Blackwood, "Sexuality and Gender in Certain Native American Tribes: The Case of Cross-Gender Females," *Signs* 10, no. 1 (Autumn, 1984): 36–39. Certainly many other examples document "female" alternative genders in Indigenous America. See Beatrice Medicine, "'Warrior Women'—Sex Role Alternatives for Plains Indian Women," in *The Hidden Half: Studies of Plains Indian Women*, ed. Patricia Albers and Beatrice Medicine (Lanham, MD: University Press of America, 1983).

33. Louis F. Burns, *Osage Indian Customs and Myths*, 177–193; Francis La Flesche, "The Osage Tribe: Rite of the Chiefs; Sayings of the Ancient Men," *Thirty-Sixth Annual Report of the Bureau of American Ethnology* (1914–1915) (1921), 47–48, 152–153; and La Flesche, "War Ceremony and Peace Ceremony of the Osage Indians," 202.

34. La Flesche, "The Osage Tribe: Rite of the Chiefs; Sayings of the Ancient Men," 152–153; La Flesche, "The Osage Tribe: Rite of the Wa-Xo'-Be," 532, 543–544; Burns, *Osage Indian Customs and Myths*, 3–6; La Flesche, "The Osage Tribe: The Rite of Vigil," 46–47; and Bailey, ed. *The Osage and the Invisible World*, 49–50.

35. Burns, *Osage Indian Customs and Myths*, 7; La Flesche, "The Osage Tribe: Rite of the Wa-Xo'-Be," 624; La Flesche, "The Osage Tribe: Rite of the Chiefs; Sayings of the Ancient Men," 140, 144, 270–272; La Flesche, "The Osage Tribe: The Rite of Vigil," 285; and La Flesche, "The Osage Tribe: Two Versions of the Child-Naming Rite," 54.

36. Burns, *Osage Indian Customs and Myths*, 7; La Flesche, "The Osage Tribe: Rite of the Wa-Xo'-Be," 535; and La Flesche, "The Osage Tribe: The Rite of Vigil," 238.

37. Francis La Flesche, "Tribal Rites of Osage Indians," *Smithsonian Miscellaneous Collections* 68, no. 12 (1918): 86–88; La Flesche, "A Dictionary of the Osage Language," 208; La Flesche, "The Osage Tribe: Rite of the Wa-Xo'-Be," 694; and La Flesche, "War Ceremony and Peace Ceremony of the Osage Indians," 59.

38. Willard Rollings argued, "Both women and men could acquire a [priesthood] degree if they could pay for it, although it seems that in the eighteenth and nineteenth centuries only men participated." His footnote provided no relevant information. But Rollings (in the same text) later contradicted this: "Although women were assuming positions within the Non-hon-zhin-ga by the late nineteenth century, this was apparently a later adaptation, for no women are mentioned in earlier accounts as being members of Non-hon-zhin-ga, and clearly the name—Little Old Men—suggests that males made up the membership of the early Osage religious council." Rollings left this uncited. La Flesche, "The Osage Tribe: The Rite of Vigil," 46–47, 238; James Owen Dorsey, "A Study of Siouan Cults," *Eleventh Annual Report of the Bureau of Ethnology to the Secretary of the Smithsonian Institution 1889–90* (1894): 391; Rollings, *The Osage*, 31, 51; La Flesche, "The Osage Tribe: Rite of the Chiefs; Sayings of the Ancient Men," 47–48, 281–282; and La Flesche, "War Ceremony and Peace Ceremony of the Osage Indians," 59.

39. Rollings, *The Osage*, 47–51; Bailey, ed., *The Osage and the Invisible World*, 42–45; Mathews, *The Osages*, 80; Bailey, *Changes in Osage Social Organization*, 18–22, 27; and La Flesche, "The Osage Tribe: Rite of the Chiefs; Sayings of the Ancient Men," 67–68.

40. Squash (*wa-ton'*) was also deemed a sacred food. La Flesche, "The Osage Tribe: The Rite of Vigil," 196, 207, 284, 288; Mathews, *The Osages*, 449; Francis La Flesche, "Ethnology of the Osage Indians," *Smithsonian Miscellaneous Collections* 76, no. 10 (1924): 107; La Flesche, "The Osage Tribe: Rite of the Wa-Xo'-Be," 624, 629, 632; and La Flesche, "The Osage Tribe: Rite of the Chiefs; Sayings of the Ancient Men," 279–281.

41. When an Osage community departed for the buffalo hunt, the Tsi'-zhu Ga-hi'-ge led the first day and Hon'-ga the second, continuing this alternating until they reached the hunting camp site. La Flesche, "The Osage Tribe: Rite of the Wa-Xo'-Be," 561–562, 632; Fletcher and La Flesche, *The Omaha Tribe*, vol. 1, 271; Rollings, *The Osage*, 47–50, 53; Mathews, *The Osages*, 80–81; and Burns, *Osage Indian Customs and Myths*, 97–98, 101.

42. Mathews, *The Osages*, 80–84; Burns, *Osage Indian Customs and Myths*, 101–104; La Flesche, "The Osage Tribe: Rite of the Chiefs; Sayings of the Ancient Men," 61, 257–269; and Dorsey, "A Study of Siouan Cults," 375–376.

43. La Flesche, "The Osage Tribe: The Rite of Vigil," 238, 288, 302; La Flesche, "The Osage Tribe: Rite of the Wa-Xo'-Be," 635, 681–682; and La Flesche, "War Ceremony and Peace Ceremony of the Osage Indians," 24–25.

44. La Flesche, "The Osage Tribe: Rite of the Chiefs; Sayings of the Ancient Men," 185–191.

45. "Home Proceedings: Great Osage Mission," *American Missionary Register* 5, no. 4 (April 1824): 112.

46. Carl Haley Chapman and Eleanor F. Chapman, *Indians and Archaeology of Missouri*, Missouri Handbook, no. 6 (Columbia: University of Missouri Press 1964), 101–103; Hunter, "An Ethnoarchaeological Analysis of the Women's Role in Osage Society," 24–28; Burns, *Osage Indian Customs and Myths*, 104–107; Mathews, *The Osages*, 84, 456–457; Gregg and Moorhead, *Commerce of the Prairies*, 422–423; and Tom McHugh, *The Time of the Buffalo* (New York: Alfred A. Knopf, 1972), 95–96.

47. Hunter, "An Ethnoarchaeological Analysis of the Women's Role in Osage Society," 3, 47–49.

48. La Flesche, "The Osage Tribe: Rite of the Wa-Xo'-Be," 624.

49. Ibid., 635; and La Flesche, "The Osage Tribe: The Rite of Vigil," 288.

50. La Flesche, "The Osage Tribe: Rite of the Wa-Xo'-Be," 624.

51. La Flesche, "The Osage Tribe: The Rite of Vigil," 194–196, 288; Mathews, *The Osages*, 449; La Flesche, "Ethnology of the Osage Indians," 104–105; Burns, *A History of the Osage People*, 12–13; La Flesche, "The Osage Tribe: Rite of the Chiefs; Sayings of the Ancient Men," 294–295; and La Flesche, "The Osage Tribe: Rite of the Wa-Xo'-Be," 624, 628–629, 631, 634.

52. John D. Hunter, *Manners and Customs of Several Indian Tribes Located West of the Mississippi: Including Some Account of the Soil, Climate, and Vegetable Productions, and the Indian Materia Medica: To Which Is Prefixed the History of the Author's Life During a Residence of Several Years among Them* (Philadelphia: J. Maxwell, 1823), 281–282.

53. Ibid., 281–283; and S. M. Barrett, *Shinkah: The Osage Indian* (Oklahoma City: Harlow Publishing, 1916), 41–42.

54. Hunter, *Manners and Customs of Several Indian Tribes Located West of the Mississippi*, 283; and La Flesche, "The Osage Tribe: Rite of the Wa-Xo'-Be," 624, 635–639.

55. Susan Post, "Species Spotlight: American Lotus," *Illinois Natural History Survey Report* (July–August 1997).

56. In addition to *Nelumbo lutea* (water chinquapin), La Flesche recorded the Puma clan's creation story, listing "*Glycine apios*" (probably ground nut, though this is not an actual scientific species name), "*Sagittaria latifolia*" (broadleaf arrowhead or "Indian potato"), and "*Falcata comosa*" (American hogpeanut, now known as *Amphicarpaea bracteata*) as early gathered foods (primarily consuming the roots). By the eighteenth

century, corn, squash, water chinquapin, and persimmons constituted the Osage's most valued plants because of their dependable food supply. La Flesche, "Ethnology of the Osage Indians," 104, 106–107; La Flesche, "The Osage Tribe: The Rite of Vigil," 195; La Flesche, "The Osage Tribe: Two Versions of the Child-Naming Rite," 55; and La Flesche, "The Osage Tribe: Rite of the Chiefs; Sayings of the Ancient Men," 109, 181–185, 261–262.

57. Jedidiah Morse, *A Report to the Secretary of War of the United States, on Indian Affairs, Comprising a Narrative of a Tour Performed in the Summer of 1820* (New Haven, CT: Converse, 1822), 206; Burns, *Osage Indian Customs and Myths,* 118–121; Mathews, *The Osages,* 29, 443; and Hunter, *Manners and Customs of Several Indian Tribes Located West of the Mississippi,* 265.

58. John Bradbury, *Travels in the Interior of America, in the Years 1809, 1810, and 1811,* 37; La Flesche, "The Osage Tribe: The Rite of Vigil," 238; Mathews, *The Osages,* 7, 9, 84, 457; La Flesche, "Ethnology of the Osage Indians," 106–107; Burns, *Osage Indian Customs and Myths,* 109–110, 118–122; Hunter, *Manners and Customs of Several Indian Tribes Located West of the Mississippi,* 84, 100, 106, 209, 264, 267–269; L. Bringier, "L. Bringier, Esq. On the Region of the Mississippi, Etc.," *American Journal of Science and Arts* 3 (1821): 31; Nuttall, *A Journal of Travels into the Arkansa Territory During the Year 1819,* 191, 194; "Home Proceedings: Union Mission," *American Missionary Register* 2, no. 2 (August 1821): 59; "Indian Mode of Life in Missouri and Kansas: George C. Sibley to Thomas L. Mckenney, October 1, 1820," *Missouri Historical Review* 9 (1914): 47; "Home Proceedings: Union Mission," *American Missionary Register* 3, no. 1 (July 1822): 13; "Home Proceedings: Great Osage Mission," *American Missionary Register* 5, no. 2 (February 1824): 48; "Home Proceedings: Great Osage Mission," *American Missionary Register* 5, no. 4 (April 1824): 112–113; and Jules Louis Renâe de Mun et al., *Journals of Jules De Mun* (St. Louis, 1928), 27.

59. "Osage Indians," *Missionary Herald* 22, no. 9 (September 1826): 268; Sarah Tuttle, *Letters on the Chickasaw and Osage Missions,* 2nd ed. (Boston: Massachusetts Sabbath School Society, 1833), 47–48; "Home Proceedings: Union Mission," *American Missionary Register* 3, no. 1 (July 1822): 13; and Tixier, McDermott, and Salvan, *Tixier's Travels on the Osage Prairies,* 136.

60. Mathews, *The Osages,* 165–167, 198–199.

61. La Flesche, "The Osage Tribe: Rite of the Wa-Xo'-Be," 681–682.

62. Mathews, *The Osages,* 65.

63. Ibid., 66.

64. La Flesche, "Tribal Rites of Osage Indians," 87–88; and La Flesche, "The Osage Tribe: Rite of the Wa-Xo'-Be," 694–695.

65. La Flesche, "The Osage Tribe: The Rite of Vigil," 302.

66. La Flesche, "The Osage Tribe: Rite of the Wa-Xo'-Be," 531, 681–682; La Flesche, "The Osage Tribe: The Rite of Vigil," 296, 301, 364–365; La Flesche, "War Ceremony and Peace Ceremony of the Osage Indians," 24–25; La Flesche, "Right and Left in Osage Ceremonies," 281–282; Mathews, *The Osages*, 64–66; and Rollings, *The Osage*, 30.

67. La Flesche, "The Osage Tribe: Rite of the Wa-Xo'-Be," 687, 693–695, 697–699.

68. La Flesche, "The Osage Tribe: The Rite of Vigil," 301–303; and La Flesche, "War Ceremony and Peace Ceremony of the Osage Indians," 59–60.

69. La Flesche, "The Osage Tribe: The Rite of Vigil," 192–194, 285.

70. Ibid., 284–285; La Flesche, "The Osage Tribe: Rite of the Chiefs; Sayings of the Ancient Men," 185.

71. J. Owen Dorsey, "An Account of the War Customs of the Osages," *The American Naturalist* 18, no. 2 (1884): 127–128.

72. Edwin James, *Part 2 of James's Account of S. H. Long's Expedition, 1819–1820*, ed. Reuben Gold Thwaites, vol. 15, Early Western Travels, 1748–1846 (Cleveland: A. H. Clark, 1905), 85.

73. Emphasis original; Mathews, *The Osages*, 324.

74. La Flesche, "War Ceremony and Peace Ceremony of the Osage Indians," 59–61; La Flesche, "The Osage Tribe: Rite of the Chiefs; Sayings of the Ancient Men," 152–153; La Flesche, "Right and Left in Osage Ceremonies," 282; La Flesche, "A Dictionary of the Osage Language," 101; and Fletcher and La Flesche, *The Omaha Tribe*, vol. 2, 339–340.

75. Mathews, *The Osages*, 325–326. For more images of male and female tattoos, see Francis La Flesche, "Researches among the Osage," *Smithsonian Miscellaneous Collections* 70, no. 2 (1918): 111–113.

76. Francis La Flesche, "Researches among the Osage," *Smithsonian Miscellaneous Collections* 70, no. 2 (1919): 112–113.

77. Ibid., 113.

78. La Flesche, "The Osage Tribe: Rite of the Wa-Xo'-Be," 531; Mathews, *The Osages*, 325–326; Francis La Flesche, "Ceremonies and Rituals of the Osage," *Smithsonian Miscellaneous Collections* 63, no. 8 (1914): 66–69; La Flesche, "A Dictionary of the Osage Language," 37; Fletcher and La Flesche, *The Omaha Tribe*, vol. 1, 221; and La Flesche, "Researches among the Osage," 112–113.

CHAPTER 2. "GENERAL HAPPINESS": GENDER AND THE OSAGE EMPIRE

1. George R. Brooks, "George C. Sibley's Journal of a Trip to the Salines in 1811," *Missouri Historical Society Bulletin* 21 (April 1965): 198–199.

2. Margaret Kohn, "Colonialism," in ed. Edward N. Zalta, Spring 2014, *The Stanford Encyclopedia of Philosophy*, accessed May 11, 2017, https://plato.stanford.edu/archives /spr2014/entries/colonialism/; Theda Perdue and Michael D. Green, *North American Indians: A Very Short Introduction* (New York: Oxford University Press, 2010), 18–19; and Robert J. Miller, *Native America, Discovered and Conquered: Thomas Jefferson, Lewis & Clark, and Manifest Destiny* (Westport, CT: Praeger, 2006), 1–5, 9.

3. Kathleen DuVal, *The Native Ground: Indians and Colonists in the Heart of the Continent* (Philadelphia: University of Pennsylvania Press, 2006), 4–6, 10, 108–109, 112; and W. J. Eccles, "The Fur Trade and Eighteenth-Century Imperialism," *William and Mary Quarterly* 40, no. 3 (July 1983): 344–345, 349, 355–356.

4. DuVal, *The Native Ground*, 103, 108–112, 117–127; and Willard H. Rollings, *The Osage: An Ethnohistorical Study of Hegemony on the Prairie-Plains* (Columbia: University of Missouri Press, 1992), 127–128, 130–138.

5. DuVal, *The Native Ground*, 118–122; J. Frederick Fausz, "Becoming 'a Nation of Quakers': The Removal of the Osage Indians from Missouri," *Gateway Heritage: Quarterly Journal of the Missouri Historical Society* 21 (2000): 30–31; and Rollings, *The Osage*, 108–109, 130.

6. Governor Alexandre O'Reilly outlawed the Native slave trade in Louisiana via proclamation on December 7, 1769; Lawrence Kinnaird, ed. *Spain in the Mississippi Valley, 1765–1794: Part 1, the Revolutionary Period, 1765–1781*, Annual Report of the American Historical Association for the Year 1945 (Washington, DC: US Government. Printing Office, 1949), 125–126.

7. Rollings, *The Osage*, 130–131.

8. Lawrence Kinnaird, ed., *Spain in the Mississippi Valley, 1765–1794: Part 3, Problems of Frontier Defense, 1792–1794*, Annual Report of the American Historical Association for the Year 1945 (Washington, DC: US Government Printing Office, 1946), 107.

9. Gilbert C. Din and Abraham Phineas Nasatir, *The Imperial Osages: Spanish-Indian Diplomacy in the Mississippi Valley* (Norman: University of Oklahoma Press, 1983), 72; and Rollings, *The Osage*, 131, 134–135.

10. Abraham Phineas Nasatir, ed., *Before Lewis and Clark: Documents Illustrating the History of the Missouri, 1785–1804*, vol. 2 (St. Louis: St. Louis Historical Documents Foundation, 1952), 539.

11. Emphasis original; Louis F. Burns, *A History of the Osage People* (Tuscaloosa: The University of Alabama Press, 2004), 89–95, 447.

12. Rollings, *The Osage*, 21, 58, 113, 135, 143, 195; and Carl Chapman, "The Indomitable Osage in Spanish Illinois (Upper Louisiana), 1763–1804," in *The Spanish in the Mississippi Valley, 1762–1804*, ed. John Francis McDermott (Urbana: University of Illinois Press, 1974), 289.

13. Louis Burns argued the oldest Osage word for horse was *Shon ka Cee Tun ka* (Big Yellow Dog), which was later replaced by *ka wa*. Rollings, *The Osage*, 82–83; Burns, *A History of the Osage People*, 498n33; Francis La Flesche, "A Dictionary of the Osage Language," *Smithsonian Institution: Bureau of American Ethnology*, Bulletin 109 (Washington, DC: Government Printing Office, 1932): 82; and John Joseph Mathews, *The Osages: Children of the Middle Waters* (Norman: University of Oklahoma Press, 1961), 126–128.

14. Rollings, *The Osage*, 82, 88.

15. Willard Hughes Rollings, "Prairie Hegemony: An Ethnohistorical Study of the Osage, from Early Times to 1840" (PhD diss., Texas Tech University, 1983), 255; and Rollings, *The Osage*, 6, 108, 122.

16. Louis Hennepin and Reuben Gold Thwaites, ed., *A New Discovery of a Vast Country in America, Volume 1* (Chicago: A. C. McClurg,1903), 177.

17. Jesuits and Reuben Gold Thwaites, *The Jesuit Relations and Allied Documents: Travels and Explorations of the Jesuit Missionaries in New France, 1610–1791*, vol. 64 (New York: Pageant Book, 1959), 170–171; Gilbert J. Garraghan, *Chapters in Frontier History: Research Studies in the Making of the West* (Milwaukee: Bruce Publishing, 1934), 57–58; Rollings, *The Osage*, 88–89; and Rollings, "Prairie Hegemony: An Ethnohistorical Study of the Osage, from Early Times to 1840," 258.

18. The "Illinois Country" (*le pays des Illinois*) generically referred to the Illinois peoples' homeland; east to the Alleghenies, west to the Rockies, north to modern Peoria, IL, and south to the Arkansas Post. Nancy Maria Miller Surrey, *The Commerce of Louisiana During the French Régime, 1699–1763* (New York: Columbia University Press, 1916), 269–270, 293, 297–298; Daniel H. Usner Jr., *Indians, Settlers & Slaves in a Frontier Exchange Economy: The Lower Mississippi Valley before 1783* (Chapel Hill: University of North Carolina Press, 1992), 196, 198; Rollings, *The Osage*, 94, 109, 116, 128; and Theodore Calvin Pease and Ernestine Jenison, *Illinois on the Eve of the Seven Years' War, 1747–1755*, Collections of the Illinois State Historical Library, vol. 29, Springfield, IL, Trustees of the State Historical Library, 1940, 377–379.

19. Zebulon Montgomery Pike, *The Expeditions of Zebulon Montgomery Pike, to Headwaters of the Mississippi River, through Louisiana Territory, and in New Spain, During the Years 1805–6–7*, ed. Elliott Coues, vol. 2 (New York: F. P. Harper, 1895), 532.

20. L. Bringier, "L. Bringier, Esq. On the Region of the Mississippi, Etc.," *American Journal of Science and Arts* 3 (1821): 34. For more on Bringier's travels, see W. D. Williams and Louis Bringier, "Louis Bringier and His Description of Arkansas in 1812," *The Arkansas Historical Quarterly* 48, no. 2 (1989).

21. John D. Hunter, *Manners and Customs of Several Indian Tribes Located West of the Mississippi: Including Some Account of the Soil, Climate, and Vegetable Productions, and the Indian*

Materia Medica: To Which Is Prefixed the History of the Author's Life During a Residence of Several Years among Them (Philadelphia: J. Maxwell, 1823), 265.

22. Louis F. Burns, *Osage Indian Customs and Myths* (Tuscaloosa: University of Alabama Press, 1984), 110–111.

23. Jules Louis Renâe de Mun et al., *Journals of Jules De Mun* (St. Louis, 1928), 26–27.

24. Hunter, *Manners and Customs of Several Indian Tribes Located West of the Mississippi*, 281–283; S. M. Barrett, *Shinkah: The Osage Indian* (Oklahoma City: Harlow Publishing, 1916), 41–42; and Thomas Nuttall, *A Journal of Travels into the Arkansa Territory During the Year 1819. With Occasional Observations on the Manners of the Aborigines* (Philadelphia: Thos. H. Palmer, 1821), 191.

25. Surrey, *The Commerce of Louisiana During the French Régime, 1699–1763*, 344–345. Some of these trading posts included Fort de Chartres, Fort Orleans, and Fort Cavagnolle. Rollings, *The Osage*, 89–91.

26. Carl Chapman, "The Little Osage and Missouri Indian Village Sites, Ca. 1727–1777 A.D.," *The Missouri Archaeologist* 21 (December 1959): 21.

27. Rollings, *The Osage*, 106, 111, 116; Kathleen DuVal, "'A Good Relationship, & Commerce': The Native Political Economy of the Arkansas River Valley," *Early American Studies* 1, no. 1 (Spring 2003): 80–82; DuVal, *The Native Ground*, 106–107, 109, 112; and Burns, *A History of the Osage People*, 103, 105–106, 242–243.

28. Fausz, "Becoming 'a Nation of Quakers,'" 30; and Rollings, *The Osage*, 94.

29. Surrey, *The Commerce of Louisiana During the French Régime*, 345, 347; and Rollings, *The Osage*, 93.

30. Rollings, *The Osage*, 93–94; and Linea Sundstrom, "Steel Awls for Stone Age Plainswomen: Rock Art, Religion, and the Hide Trade on the Northern Plains," *Plains Anthropologist* 47, no. 181 (May 2002): 114.

31. Chapman, "The Little Osage and Missouri Indian Village Sites," 14, 30; Carl Haley Chapman, "The Origin of the Osage Indian Tribe: An Ethnographical, Historical and Archaeological Study" (University of Michigan, 1959), 111, 114; Brewton Berry, Carl Chapman, and John Mack, "Archaeological Remains of the Osage," *American Antiquity* 10, no. 1 (1944): 5; and Carl Haley Chapman and Eleanor F. Chapman, *Indians and Archaeology of Missouri*, Missouri Handbook, no. 6 (Columbia: University of Missouri Press, 1964), 96–97.

32. Nuttall, *A Journal of Travels into the Arkansa Territory During the Year 1819*, 192–193; Hunter, *Manners and Customs of Several Indian Tribes Located West of the Mississippi*, 343–345; Mathews, *The Osages*, 234; La Flesche, "A Dictionary of the Osage Language," 58; and "Osages: Their Character, Manners, and Condition," *Missionary Herald* 24, no. 3 (March 1828): 79.

33. "The distribution of the tools and material items from the Scotten Site show a definite tendency toward the women being the dominant utilizer." The Scotten site is

the southeastern portion of an excavated Great Osage town known as the Brown site (23VE3), located approximately ten miles northeast of present-day Nevada, Missouri. Dr. Carl Chapman directed excavations of this site in 1941, 1947, 1964, and 1983. The Brown site is the "earliest known Osage village site," which Chapman argued "was evidenced by the greater amount of non-European materials found, especially the native made pottery." Andrea A. Hunter, "An Ethnoarchaeological Analysis of the Women's Role in Osage Society" (Thesis, University of Missouri, 1985), 2, 38–49; Nancy Shoemaker, "Introduction," in *Negotiators of Change: Historical Perspectives on Native American Women*, ed. Nancy Shoemaker (New York: Routledge, 1995), 7; and Chapman, "The Origin of the Osage Indian Tribe," 132–133.

34. Fausz, "Becoming 'a Nation of Quakers,'" 31.

35. Sundstrom, "Steel Awls for Stone Age Plainswomen," 114–115; Henry S. Sharp, "Asymmetric Equals: Women and Men among the Chipewyan," in *Women and Power in Native North America*, ed. Laura F. Klein and Lillian A. Ackerman (Norman: University of Oklahoma Press, 1995), 58; and David Wishart, "The Roles and Status of Men and Women in Nineteenth Century Omaha and Pawnee Societies: Postmodernist Uncertainties and Empirical Evidence," *American Indian Quarterly* 19, no. 4 (Autumn 1995): 514.

36. Burns, *A History of the Osage People*, 29, 487; and Mathews, *The Osages*, 64.

37. Treat to Davy, April 15, 1806, in "Letter Book of the Arkansas Trading House, 1805–1810," Records of the Office of Indian Trade, National Archives, Record Group 75, Microfilm, 61–66; Kathryn E. Holland Braund, *Deerskins and Duffels: The Creek Indian Trade with Anglo-America, 1685–1815* (Lincoln: University of Nebraska Press, 1993), 88–89; J. Frederick Fausz, *Founding St. Louis: First City of the New West* (Charleston, SC: The History Press, 2011), 151; Fausz, "Becoming 'a Nation of Quakers,'" 30–31; Rollings, *The Osage*, 93–94, 137–138, 219–220; Louis Houck, ed. *The Spanish Regime in Missouri*, vol. 1 (Chicago: R. R. Donnelley, 1909), 139; and Abraham Phineas Nasatir, ed. *Before Lewis and Clark: Documents Illustrating the History of the Missouri, 1785–1804*, vol. 1 (St. Louis: St. Louis Historical Documents Foundation, 1952), 209–211, 321, 539.

38. Mildred Mott Wedel, "Claude-Charles Dutisne: A Review of His 1719 Journeys (Parts 1 and 2)," *Great Plains Journal* 12, no. 1–2 (Fall 1972–Spring 1973): 151; Willard H. Rollings, *Unaffected by the Gospel: The Osage Resistance to the Christian Invasion (1673–1906): A Cultural Victory* (Albuquerque: University of New Mexico Press, 2004), 72; Anna Lewis, "Du Tisne's Expedition into Oklahoma," *Chronicles of Oklahoma* 3, no. 4 (December 1925): 320; Brooks, "George C. Sibley's Journal of a Trip to the Salines in 1811," 198; Thomas D. Isern, "Exploration and Diplomacy: George Champlin Sibley's Report to William Clark, 1811," *Missouri Historical Review* 73 (October 1978): 96–99; Major George C. Sibley, "Extracts from the Diary of Major Sibley," *Chronicles of Oklahoma* 5, no. 2 (June 1927): 210–211; "Home Proceedings: Union Mission," *American*

Missionary Register 2, no. 6 (December 1821): 223; Washington Irving, William Peter-field Trent, and George S. Hellman, *The Journals of Washington Irving (Hitherto Unpub-lished)*, vol. 3 (Boston: The Bibliophile Society, 1919), 124; and "Osage Indians," *Mis-sionary Herald* 22, no. 9 (September 1826): 268.

39. Irving, Trent, and Hellman, *The Journals of Washington Irving*, 124; Mathews, *The Osages*, 306–307; and Burns, *Osage Indian Customs and Myths*, 102–104.

40. Caddoan-speaking nations included Paninoir, Panimaha, Wichita, Tawakanis, Iscanis, Tonkawas, and Kichais. Nasatir, ed. *Before Lewis and Clark*, 18–19, 124–125; Burns, *A History of the Osage People*, 486; Nuttall, *A Journal of Travels into the Arkansa Ter-ritory During the Year 1819*, 183; Mathews, *The Osages*, 128, 138, 242, 252; Rollings, *The Osage*, 101–102, 106, 113; H. M. Brackenridge, *Views of Louisiana: Together with a Journal of a Voyage up the Missouri River, in 1811*, Nineteenth Century American Literature, Series A: The Ohio Valley; (Pittsburgh: Cramer, Spear, and Eichbaum, 1814), 71; and Edwin James, *Part 3 of James's Account of S. H. Long's Expedition, 1819–1820*, ed. Reuben Gold Thwaites, vol. 16, Early Western Travels, 1748–1846 (Cleveland: A. H. Clark, 1905), 272–273.

41. Hunter, *Manners and Customs of Several Indian Tribes Located West of the Mississippi*, 43–44.

42. La Flesche noted that some captives may have made up a servant class, who sometimes served as ceremonial messengers. William Vaill to David Greene, May 10, 1833 (frame 445–452) and William Vaill to David Greene, May 10, 1833 (frame 462–467), microfilm reel 779, in "Missions on the American Continents and to the Islands of the Pacific, 1811–1919 (ABC 18–19), 1830–1837," in *American Board of Com-missioners for Foreign Missions Archives, 1810–1961 (ABC 1–91)* Houghton Library, Har-vard University; "Osage Indians," *Missionary Herald* 22, no. 9 (September 1826): 268; Brett Rushforth, *Bonds of Alliance: Indigenous and Atlantic Slaveries in New France* (Chapel Hill: Unveristy of North Carolina Press, 2012), 9–10, 242; Rollings, *The Osage*, 109–111, 131; Brett Rushforth, "'A Little Flesh We Offer You': The Origins of Indian Slavery in New France," *William and Mary Quarterly* 60, no. 4 (2003): 785–789, 798, 801, 808; Robert P. Wiegers, "A Proposal for Indian Slave Trading in the Mississippi Valley and Its Impact on the Osage," *Plains Anthropologist* 33, no. 120 (May 1988): 194–195; Fran-cis La Flesche, "Right and Left in Osage Ceremonies," in *Holmes Anniversary Volume: Anthropological Essays* (Washington, DC: J. W. Bryan Press, 1916), 287; La Flesche, "A Dictionary of the Osage Language," 35, 132; and Hunter, *Manners and Customs of Several Indian Tribes Located West of the Mississippi*, 255–257.

43. Caddoan slaves also came from the Kichai, Taovaya, Iscani, Guichita, Tawa-koni peoples, and the later Wichita, Caddo, and Pawnee confederacies. Nasatir, ed. *Before Lewis and Clark*, 19; Rushforth, *Bonds of Alliance*, 169; Wiegers, "A Proposal for In-dian Slave Trading in the Mississippi Valley and Its Impact on the Osage," 196; DuVal,

The *Native Ground*, 27, 108–110; Garrick Alan Bailey, *Changes in Osage Social Organization: 1673–1906*, University of Oregon Anthropological Papers No. 5 (Eugene: University of Oregon Press, 1973), 35; Mathews, *The Osages*, 157; and Catherine M. Cameron, "The Effects of Warfare and Captive-Taking on Indigenous Mortality in Postcontact North America," in *Beyond Germs: Native Depopulation in North America*, ed. Catherine M. Cameron, Paul Kelton, and Alan C. Swedlund (Tucson: University of Arizona Press, 2015), 176–178.

44. Hunter, *Manners and Customs of Several Indian Tribes Located West of the Mississippi*, 365–366; Zebulon Montgomery Pike and Donald Dean Jackson, *The Journals of Zebulon Montgomery Pike, with Letters and Related Documents*, vol. 1, The American Exploration and Travel Series (Norman: University of Oklahoma Press, 1966), 295; Brackenridge, *Views of Louisiana*, 219; John Bradbury, *Travels in the Interior of America, in the Years 1809, 1810, and 1811: Including a Description of Upper Louisiana, Together with the States of Ohio, Kentucky, Indiana, and Tennessee, with the Illinois and Western Territories, and Containing Remarks and Observations Useful to Persons Emigrating to Those Countries* (Liverpool: Printed for the author, by Smith and Galway, and published by Sherwood, Neely, and Jones, London, 1817), 39–40; "Osage Indians: Account of Their Conditions, Manners, Etc," *Missionary Herald* 23, no. 5 (May 1827): 148; "Osages: Miscellaneous Communications Respecting the Mission," *Missionary Herald* 25, no. 4 (April 1829): 123–124.

45. Hunter, *Manners and Customs of Several Indian Tribes Located West of the Mississippi*, 77, 275, 316.

46. Rollings, *The Osage*, 7–8, 31, 64–66; Rollings, *Unaffected by the Gospel*, 67–75, 83–85; and Bailey, *Changes in Osage Social Organization*, 44–45.

47. Francis La Flesche, "The Osage Tribe: Rite of the Chiefs; Sayings of the Ancient Men," *Thirty-Sixth Annual Report of the Bureau of American Ethnology* (1914–1915) (1921): 59–67; and Rollings, *Unaffected by the Gospel*, 67–75.

48. Rollings, *The Osage*, 33–34; Rollings, *Unaffected by the Gospel*, 71–72; DuVal, *The Native Ground*, 114; Mathews, *The Osages*, 75–76, 160–163; La Flesche, "The Osage Tribe: Rite of the Chiefs; Sayings of the Ancient Men," 66; and La Flesche, "War Ceremony and Peace Ceremony of the Osage Indians," *Smithsonian Institution: Bureau of American Ethnology*, Bulletin 101 (Washington, DC: Government Printing Office, 1939): 3–6, 60, 77–78.

49. "Home Proceedings: Great Osage Mission," *American Missionary Register* 2, 6 (December 1821), 226; "Home Proceedings: Extracts of Private Letters from Members of the Union Mission," *American Missionary Register* 1, 11 (May 1821), 436; "Osage Indians," *Missionary Herald* 22, 9 (September 1826), 268; Cooke to Arbuckle, January 8, 1839, *Letters Received by the Office of Indian Affairs, 1824–1880: Osage Agency, 1824–1841*, National Archives Record Group 75, M234 (roll 631, frames 734–774); Brackenridge, *Views of Louisiana*, 72; and Bradbury, *Travels in the Interior of America*, 42.

50. George Catlin, *Letters and Notes on the Manners, Customs, and Condition of the North American Indians*, 3rd ed., vol. 2 (New York: Wiley and Putnam, 1844), 40.

51. Fausz, *Founding St. Louis*, 46.

52. Sarah Tuttle, *Letters on the Chickasaw and Osage Missions*, 2nd ed. (Boston: Massachusetts Sabbath School Society, 1833), 47.

53. Fausz, *Founding St. Louis*, 112–113; Washington Irving, *A Tour on the Prairies* (Paris: A. and W. Galignani 1835), 10–11; James, *Part 3 of James's Account of S. H. Long's Expedition, 1819–1820*, 271; Paul Mary Ponziglione, "The Osages and Father John Schoenmakers," unpublished manuscript, ed. Lowrie J. Daly and Garrick Alan Bailey (St. Louis: Midwest Jesuit Archives), 129; Fausz, "Becoming 'a Nation of Quakers,'" 29–30; and Burns, *Osage Indian Customs and Myths*, 132.

54. Thomas Jefferson to Albert Gallatin, July 12, 1804, in *Founders Online*, National Archives, accessed on June 22, 2017, https://founders.archives.gov/documents/Jefferson/99-01-02-0058.

55. Fausz, *Founding St. Louis*, 112–113.

56. Rollings, *The Osage*, 8; DuVal, *The Native Ground*, 105, 127; and Du Val, "'A Good Relationship, & Commerce,'" 81–83.

57. Emphasis original; Hunter, *Manners and Customs of Several Indian Tribes Located West of the Mississippi*, 272–273.

58. Ibid., 250, 258, 272–273, 281; and Burns, *Osage Indian Customs and Myths*, 93–94.

59. Hunter, *Manners and Customs of Several Indian Tribes Located West of the Mississippi*, 224–226; and Mathews, *The Osages*, 160–163.

60. Bradbury, *Travels in the Interior of America*, 36–37, 42–43; Edwin James, *Part 2 of James's Account of S. H. Long's Expedition, 1819–1820*, ed. Reuben Gold Thwaites, vol. 15, *Early Western Travels, 1748–1846* (Cleveland: A. H. Clark, 1905), 85; and Hunter, *Manners and Customs of Several Indian Tribes Located West of the Mississippi*, 59, 91.

61. Hunter, *Manners and Customs of Several Indian Tribes Located West of the Mississippi*, 340–341.

62. Rollings, *The Osage*, 42; and Bailey, *Changes in Osage Social Organization*, 16.

63. Rollings, *The Osage*, 42; Betty R. Nett, "Historical Changes in the Osage Kinship System," *Southwestern Journal of Anthropology* 8, no. 2 (1952): 168; and Bailey, *Changes in Osage Social Organization*, 13.

64. Alice C. Fletcher and Francis La Flesche, *The Omaha Tribe*, vol. 1 (Lincoln: University of Nebraska Press, 1992), 58; Rollings, *The Osage*, 42; and Bailey, *Changes in Osage Social Organization*, 43.

65. Bailey, *Changes in Osage Social Organization*, 43–44.

66. Ibid., 44.

67. Ibid.; and Wiegers, "A Proposal for Indian Slave Trading in the Mississippi Valley and Its Impact on the Osage," 196.

68. Rollings, *The Osage*, 66.

69. Hunter, *Manners and Customs of Several Indian Tribes Located West of the Mississippi*, 240.

70. Rollings, *The Osage*, 159.

71. Hunter stated that Cler-mont and Was-saw-be-ton-ga had four wives and twenty children each; O-kon-now had six or seven wives and seventeen to eighteen children. Hunter, *Manners and Customs of Several Indian Tribes Located West of the Mississippi*, 240, 250–252; Jedidiah Morse, *A Report to the Secretary of War of the United States, on Indian Affairs, Comprising a Narrative of a Tour Performed in the Summer of 1820* (New Haven, CT: Converse, 1822), 219; Nuttall, *A Journal of Travels into the Arkansa Territory During the Year 1819*, 185; and "Home Proceedings: Union Mission," *American Missionary Register* 2, no. 2 (August 1821): 59.

72. Lillian A. Ackerman, "Complementary but Equal: Gender Status in the Plateau," in *Women and Power in Native North America*, ed. Laura F. Klein and Lillian A. Ackerman (Norman: University of Oklahoma Press, 1995), 86.

73. Ibid.

74. Wishart, "The Roles and Status of Men and Women in Nineteenth Century Omaha and Pawnee Societies: Postmodernist Uncertainties and Empirical Evidence," 513.

75. Mun et al., *Journals of Jules De Mun*, 30.

76. Bradbury, *Travels in the Interior of America*, 36.

77. George William Featherstonhaugh, *Excursion through the Slave States, from Washington on the Potomac, to the Frontier of Mexico; with Sketches of Popular Manners and Geological Notices* (New York: Harper and Brothers, 1844), 71; Burns, *A History of the Osage People*, 360; Garrick Bailey, *Traditions of the Osage: Stories Collected and Translated by Francis La Flesche* (Albuquerque: University of New Mexico Press, 2010), 127; Victor Tixier, John Francis McDermott, and Albert Jacques Salvan, *Tixier's Travels on the Osage Prairies* (Norman: University of Oklahoma Press, 1940), 184, 258; and Hunter, *Manners and Customs of Several Indian Tribes Located West of the Mississippi*, 203, 241–242, 329–330.

78. Hunter, *Manners and Customs of Several Indian Tribes Located West of the Mississippi*, 252–255; Burns, *A History of the Osage People*, 210; and Bringier, "L. Bringier, Esq. On the Region of the Mississippi, Etc.," 34.

79. Mathews, *The Osages*, 308–311; Hunter, *Manners and Customs of Several Indian Tribes Located West of the Mississippi*, 243–244; and Francis La Flesche, "Osage Marriage Customs," *American Anthropologist* 14, no. 1 (1912): 127–128.

80. La Flesche, "Osage Marriage Customs," 128–130; La Flesche, "A Dictionary of the Osage Language," 94–95, 121; Ponziglione, "The Osages and Father John Schoenmakers," 145–146; Hunter, *Manners and Customs of Several Indian Tribes Located West of the Mississippi*, 247–248; and Mathews, *The Osages*, 312–323.

81. Rollings, *The Osage*, 126–129; and DuVal, *The Native Ground*, 117.

82. Tanis C. Thorne, *The Many Hands of My Relations: French and Indians on the Lower Missouri* (Columbia: University of Missouri Press, 1996), 88; Kathleen DuVal, "Indian Intermarriage and Metissage in Colonial Louisiana," *The William and Mary Quarterly* 65, no. 2 (April 2008): 267–271, 302–303; and Du Val, "'A Good Relationship, & Commerce,'" 82–83.

83. Emphasis original; Thorne, *The Many Hands of My Relations*, 66–71, 88; Fausz, *Founding St. Louis*, 20–21, 113, 116–117, 120–121, 150–151, 155–157; Tanis C. Thorne, "The Chouteau Family and the Osage Trade: A Generational Study," in *Rendezvous: Selected Papers of the Fourth North American Fur Trade Conference, 1981*, ed. Thomas C. Buckley (1984): 109–110; William E. Foley and C. David Rice, *The First Chouteaus: River Barons of Early St. Louis* (Urbana: University of Illinois Press, 1983), 7; and Fausz, "Becoming 'a Nation of Quakers,'" 30–32.

84. Michael Lansing, "Plains Indian Women and Interracial Marriage in the Upper Missouri Trade, 1804–1868," *Western Historical Quarterly* 31, no. 4 (Winter 2000): 423.

85. Mathews, *The Osages*, 164, 308.

86. Bradbury, *Travels in the Interior of America*, 36.

87. Thorne, "The Chouteau Family and the Osage Trade: A Generational Study," 111; Fausz, "Becoming 'a Nation of Quakers,'" 31; Sylvia Van Kirk, *Many Tender Ties: Women in Fur-Trade Society, 1670–1870*, 1st American ed. (Norman: University of Oklahoma Press, 1983), 4, 7–8; Lansing, "Plains Indian Women and Interracial Marriage in the Upper Missouri Trade," 418; and Thorne, *The Many Hands of My Relations*, 94–95.

88. Lansing, "Plains Indian Women and Interracial Marriage in the Upper Missouri Trade," 414–415; Van Kirk, *Many Tender Ties*, 30; and Clara Sue Kidwell, "Indian Women as Cultural Mediators," *Ethnohistory* 39, no. 2 (Spring 1992): 97.

89. Thorne, *The Many Hands of My Relations*, 92–96, 146–148, 172–173; Thorne, "The Chouteau Family and the Osage Trade," 110–112, 114; Mathews, *The Osages*, 285; Foley and Rice, *The First Chouteaus*, 45; and Stan Hoig, *The Chouteaus: First Family of the Fur Trade* (Albuquerque: University of New Mexico Press, 2008), 249–254.

90. Brooks, "George C. Sibley's Journal of a Trip to the Salines in 1811," 198–199.

CHAPTER 3. "A VERY UNFAVORABLE CHANGE IN THEIR CIRCUMSTANCES": THE OSAGE AND US IMPERIALISM

1. Kathleen DuVal, *The Native Ground: Indians and Colonists in the Heart of the Continent* (Philadelphia: University of Pennsylvania Press, 2006), 5–7, 10–11; J. Frederick Fausz, *Founding St. Louis: First City of the New West* (Charleston, SC: The History Press, 2011), 183; and Patrick Wolfe, "Settler Colonialism and the Elimination of the Native," *Journal of Genocide Research* 8, no. 4 (2006): 388.

2. "Osages," *Missionary Herald* 30, no. 1 (January 1834): 23.

3. Stuart Banner, *How the Indians Lost Their Land: Law and Power on the Frontier* (Cambridge, MA: Belknap Press of Harvard University Press, 2005), 121–122, 124–125, 127–129, 139, 144; and Theda Perdue and Michael D. Green, *The Cherokee Removal: A Brief History with Documents*, 2nd ed. (Boston/New York: Bedford/St. Martin's, 2005), 6–9.

4. DuVal, *The Native Ground*, 196–200; David La Vere, *Contrary Neighbors: Southern Plains and Removed Indians in Indian Territory* (Norman: University of Oklahoma Press, 2000), 7, 44–45, 48–51; and Willard H. Rollings, *The Osage: An Ethnohistorical Study of Hegemony on the Prairie-Plains* (Columbia: University of Missouri Press, 1992), 220–222.

5. Robert J. Miller, *Native America, Discovered and Conquered: Thomas Jefferson, Lewis & Clark, and Manifest Destiny* (Westport, CT: Praeger, 2006), 1–5, 59, 70–73, 77; Wolfe, "Settler Colonialism and the Elimination of the Native," 399; and Fausz, *Founding St. Louis*, 186.

6. Miller, *Native America, Discovered and Conquered*, 39, 78, 90–91; Wolfe, "Settler Colonialism and the Elimination of the Native," 399; John Mack Faragher, "'More Motley than Mackinaw': From Ethnic Mixing to Ethnic Cleansing on the Frontier of the Lower Missouri, 1783–1833," in *Contact Points: American Frontiers from the Mohawk Valley to the Mississippi, 1750–1830*, ed. Andrew R. L. Cayton and Fredrika J. Teute (Chapel Hill: University of North Carolina Press, 1998), 305; James H. Merrell, "Second Thoughts on Colonial Historians and American Indians," *William and Mary Quarterly* 69, no. 3 (July 2012): 509; and Gary Clayton Anderson, "The Native Peoples of the American West: Genocide or Ethnic Cleansing?" *Western Historical Quarterly* 47, no. 4 (Winter 2016): 409.

7. United Nations, "Convention on the Prevention and Punishment of the Crime of Genocide," 1, accessed July 17, 2017, www.un.org/en/genocideprevention/documents /atrocity-crimes/Doc.1_Convention on the Prevention and Punishment of the Crime of Genocide.pdf; Anthony F. C. Wallace, *Jefferson and the Indians: The Tragic Fate of the First Americans* (Cambridge, MA: Belknap Press of Harvard University Press, 1999), 226, 241–244, 248, 274; Miller, *Native America, Discovered and Conquered*, 91–92; Wolfe, "Settler Colonialism and the Elimination of the Native," 398–399; George E. Tinker, *Missionary Conquest: The Gospel and Native American Cultural Genocide* (Minneapolis: Fortress Press, 1993), 5–8; J. Frederick Fausz, "Becoming 'a Nation of Quakers': The Removal of the Osage Indians from Missouri," *Gateway Heritage: Quarterly Journal of the Missouri Historical Society* 21 (Summer 2000): 36; DuVal, *The Native Ground*, 179–180; Bernard W. Sheehan, *Seeds of Extinction: Jeffersonian Philanthropy and the American Indian* (Chapel Hill: University of North Carolina Press, 1973), 7, 125–129; and Willard H. Rollings, *Unaffected by the Gospel: The Osage Resistance to the Christian Invasion (1673–1906): A Cultural Victory* (Albuquerque: University of New Mexico Press, 2004), 49–50.

8. Rollings, *Unaffected by the Gospel*, 36; John Joseph Mathews, *The Osages: Children of the Middle Waters* (Norman: University of Oklahoma Press, 1961), 356–357; Miller,

Native America, Discovered and Conquered, 80–81, 99–107; and Fausz, *Founding St. Louis*, 188.

9. Jefferson wrote this infamous letter to William Henry Harrison one month after Jefferson had already privately appealed to Congress to fund the Lewis and Clark expedition but before word arrived of the official Louisiana Purchase in July. Thomas Jefferson to William Henry Harrison, February 27, 1803, in *Founders Online*, National Archives, accessed June 8, 2017, https://founders.archives.gov/documents/Jefferson /01–39–02–0500; Fausz, *Founding St. Louis*, 185, 188; and Miller, *Native America, Discovered and Conquered*, 45, 87–88, 101–102.

10. DuVal, *The Native Ground*, 196–201; Fausz, "Becoming 'a Nation of Quakers,'" 33–37; Miller, *Native America, Discovered and Conquered*, 92–93; and Rollings, *The Osage*, 220–222.

11. Wolfe, "Settler Colonialism and the Elimination of the Native," 391; Banner, *How the Indians Lost Their Land*, 148; and Theda Perdue and Michael D. Green, *North American Indians: A Very Short Introduction* (New York: Oxford University Press, 2010), 36, 40, 42–43.

12. Meriwether Lewis, "Upper Louisiana Territorial Governor, to President Thomas Jefferson, December 15, 1808," in *American State Papers: Indian Affairs*, vol. 1 (Washington, DC: Gales and Seaton, 1832), 766–767; Fausz, *Founding St. Louis*, 190; Louis F. Burns, *A History of the Osage People* (Tuscaloosa: The University of Alabama Press, 2004), 168; W. A. Croffut, ed., *Fifty Years in Camp and Field: Diary of Major-General Ethan Allen Hitchcock, U.S.A.* (New York: G. P. Putnam's Sons, 1909), 140; Fausz, "Becoming 'a Nation of Quakers,'" 34–37; DuVal, *The Native Ground*, 200–205; Banner, *How the Indians Lost Their Land*, 142, 197–198; Rollings, *The Osage*, 224–230; and Charles J. Kappler, ed. *Indian Affairs: Laws and Treaties, Vol. 2 (Treaties)* (Washington, DC: Government Printing Office, 1904), 95–99.

13. Calhoun to Clark, May 8, 1818, in Clarence Edwin Carter, ed., *The Territorial Papers of the United States*, v. 15 (Washington, DC: Government Printing Office, 1951), 391; DuVal, *The Native Ground*, 196–200, 208–216, 224–226, 231–237; Miller, *Native America, Discovered and Conquered*, 80; Wolfe, "Settler Colonialism and the Elimination of the Native," 388; Rollings, *The Osage*, 235–245, 252–256; and Banner, *How the Indians Lost Their Land*, 145–146.

14. H. M. Brackenridge, *Views of Louisiana: Together with a Journal of a Voyage up the Missouri River, in 1811*, Nineteenth Century American Literature, Series A: The Ohio Valley (Pittsburgh: Cramer, Spear, and Eichbaum, 1814), 70; L. Bringier, "L. Bringier, Esq. On the Region of the Mississippi, Etc.," *American Journal of Science and Arts* 3 (1821): 33; Rollings, *Unaffected by the Gospel*, 46; Rollings, *The Osage*, 216–217; Stan Hoig, *The Chouteaus: First Family of the Fur Trade* (Albuquerque: University of New Mexico Press, 2008), 28, 45.

15. Fausz, "Becoming 'a Nation of Quakers,'" 32, 37; Garrick Alan Bailey, *Changes in Osage Social Organization: 1673–1906*, University of Oregon Anthropological Papers No. 5 (Eugene: University of Oregon Press, 1973), 60–61; Burns, *A History of the Osage People*, 242–243; DuVal, *The Native Ground*, 170–171, 213; "Home Proceedings: Union Mission," *American Missionary Register* 6, no. 9 (September 1825): 272; "Home Proceedings: Journal of the Union Mission," *American Missionary Register* 6, no. 7 (July 1825): 216–217; "Osage Indians," *Missionary Herald* 22, no. 9 (September 1826): 271; Rollings, *The Osage*, 30, 173–177, 259; Rollings, *Unaffected by the Gospel*, 83–85, 116–117; Victor Tixier, John Francis McDermott, and Albert Jacques Salvan, *Tixier's Travels on the Osage Prairies* (Norman: University of Oklahoma Press, 1940), 217–218.

16. Josiah Gregg, *Part 2 of Gregg's Commerce of the Prairies, 1831–1839*, ed. Reuben Gold Thwaites, vol. 20, *Early Western Travels, 1748–1846* (Cleveland: A. H. Clark, 1904), 339–340; "Home Proceedings: Great Osage Mission," *American Missionary Register* 2, no. 10 (April 1822): 434–435; "Reports of Societies: Third Report of the United Foreign Missionary Society," *American Missionary Register* 1 (July 1820): 18; "Home Proceedings: Union Mission," *American Missionary Register* 2, no. 6 (December 1821): 223; "Home Proceedings: Union Mission," *American Missionary Register* 2, no. 3 (September 1821): 116; "Miscellanies: The Arkansas Territory," *American Missionary Register* 1, no. 7 (January 1821): 287; "Home Proceedings: Union Mission," *American Missionary Register* 5, no. 2 (February 1824): 38; "Home Proceedings: Great Osage Mission," *American Missionary Register* 5, no. 2 (February 1824): 45; Sarah Tuttle, *Letters on the Chickasaw and Osage Missions*, 2nd ed. (Boston: Massachusetts Sabbath School Society, 1833), 133–134; "Reports of Societies: Union Mission," *American Missionary Register* 2, no. 12 (June 1822): 466; "Osages: Miscellaneous Communications Respecting the Mission," *Missionary Herald* 25, no. 4 (April 1829): 123–124; "Home Proceedings: Union Mission," *American Missionary Register* 3, no. 1 (July 1822): 13; "Osage Indians: Account of Their Conditions, Manners, Etc," *Missionary Herald* 23, no. 5 (May 1827): 148; and Tixier, McDermott, and Salvan, *Tixier's Travels on the Osage Prairies*, 164–165.

17. William Vaill to David Greene, June 20, 1832 (frame 410–416), William Vaill to David Greene, May 6, 1833 (frame 437–444), William Vaill to David Greene, May 10, 1833 (frame 462–467), microfilm reel 779, in "Missions on the American Continents and to the Islands of the Pacific, 1811–1919 (ABC 18–19), 1830–1837," in *American Board of Commissioners for Foreign Missions Archives, 1810–1961* (ABC 1–91) Houghton Library, Harvard University; "Home Proceedings: Union Mission," *American Missionary Register* 5, no. 12 (December 1824): 363; "Home Proceedings: Union Mission," *American Missionary Register* 5, no. 2 (February 1824): 38; and Tixier, McDermott, and Salvan, *Tixier's Travels on the Osage Prairies*, 210–215.

18. William Vaill to David Greene, May 17, 1833 (frame 453–459), microfilm reel 779, in "Missions on the American Continents and to the Islands of the Pacific,

1811–1919 (ABC 18–19), 1830–1837," in *American Board of Commissioners for Foreign Missions Archives*, 1810–1961 (ABC 1–91) Houghton Library, Harvard University.

19. William Vaill to David Greene, June 20, 1832 (frame 410–416), William Vaill to David Greene, May 6, 1833 (frame 437–444), William Vaill to David Greene, May 17, 1833 (frame 453–459), microfilm reel 779, in "Missions on the American Continents and to the Islands of the Pacific, 1811–1919 (ABC 18–19), 1830–1837," in *American Board of Commissioners for Foreign Missions Archives*, 1810–1961 (ABC 1–91) Houghton Library, Harvard University; and "Osages: Journal of Mr. Vaill, During a Preaching Tour," *Missionary Herald* 29, no. 10 (October 1833): 370–371.

20. Mathews, *The Osages*, 594.

21. Ibid., 593–595; and Rollings, *The Osage*, 239–249.

22. Louis F. Burns, *Osage Indian Customs and Myths* (Tuscaloosa: University of Alabama Press, 1984), 119; Wolfe, "Settler Colonialism and the Elimination of the Native," 388; Fausz, "Becoming 'a Nation of Quakers,'" 35; Rollings, *The Osage*, 239, 246–248, 254; and DuVal, *The Native Ground*, 224.

23. Wallace, *Jefferson and the Indians*, 226, 247; Wolfe, "Settler Colonialism and the Elimination of the Native," 395–396; Miller, *Native America, Discovered and Conquered*, 91–92; DuVal, *The Native Ground*, 180; and Fausz, "Becoming 'a Nation of Quakers,'" 33, 36–37.

24. "Home Proceedings: Great Osage Mission," *American Missionary Register* 5, no. 2 (February 1824): 47; Tixier, McDermott, and Salvan, *Tixier's Travels on the Osage Prairies*, 172–174.

25. Rollings, *The Osage*, 219–220, 230–234; Tuttle, *Letters on the Chickasaw and Osage Missions*, 95–96; and Fausz, "Becoming 'a Nation of Quakers,'" 34.

26. Fausz, "Becoming 'a Nation of Quakers,'" 31, 36; Rollings, *The Osage*, 258; "Home Proceedings: Union Mission," *American Missionary Register* 2, no. 6 (December 1821): 223; Tuttle, *Letters on the Chickasaw and Osage Missions*, 92–93, 96–99; "Home Proceedings: Union Mission," *American Missionary Register* 4, no. 8 (August 1823): 235; Josiah Gregg and Max L. Moorhead, ed., *Commerce of the Prairies* (Norman: University of Oklahoma Press, 1954), 417, 422–423; "Home Proceedings: Great Osage Mission," *American Missionary Register* 5, no. 4 (April 1824): 112; "Home Proceedings: Union Mission," *American Missionary Register* 6, no. 9 (September 1825): 272; and "Osage Indians," 268.

27. Sheehan, *Seeds of Extinction*, 120–122; and Tinker, *Missionary Conquest*, viii, 4–10.

28. Prior to Protestant missionization, various Osage towns, families, and individuals had sporadic contact with Catholic missionaries in the eighteenth and early nineteenth centuries. Rollings, *Unaffected by the Gospel*, 7, 46, 49–53, 82, 85, 105–106, 112.

29. "Osages: Their Character, Manners, and Condition," *Missionary Herald* 24, no. 3 (March 1828): 80.

30. "Home Proceedings: Union Mission," *American Missionary Register* 2, no. 3 (September 1821): 115.

31. T. F. Morrison, "Mission Neosho: The First Kansas Mission," *Kansas Historical Quarterly* 4, no. 3 (August 1935): 229; and Tuttle, *Letters on the Chickasaw and Osage Missions*, 90–91, 128–129.

32. "Osage Indians: Account of Their Conditions, Manners, Etc.," 146–147.

33. Fausz, "Becoming 'a Nation of Quakers,'" 30; "Home Proceedings: Great Osage Mission," *American Missionary Register* 3, no. 4 (October 1822): 147; "Home Proceedings: Union Mission," *American Missionary Register* 4, no. 8 (August 1823): 237; "Home Proceedings: Union Mission," *American Missionary Register* 4, no. 9 (September 1823): 274; and Burns, *Osage Indian Customs and Myths*, 74.

34. For some examples, see "Home Proceedings: Union Mission," *American Missionary Register* 2, no. 3 (September 1821): 115; Carl H. Chapman, "Journey to the Land of the Osages, 1835–1836, by Louis Cortambert," *Missouri Historical Society Bulletin* 19 (April 1963): 217; "Home Proceedings: Union Mission," *American Missionary Register* 5, no. 12 (December 1824): 363; "Home Proceedings: Great Osage Mission," *American Missionary Register* 5, no. 9 (September 1824): 275; and "Osages: Journal of Mr. Vaill, During a Preaching Tour," 371.

35. "G. C. Sibley, Factor, Fort Osage, to Thomas McKenney, Superintendent of Indian Trade, October 1, 1820," in Jedidiah Morse, *A Report to the Secretary of War of the United States, on Indian Affairs, Comprising a Narrative of a Tour Performed in the Summer of 1820* (New Haven, CT: Converse, 1822), 205.

36. "Report of J. M. Richardson, Sub-Agent for the Osages, and Missionary and School Reports for that Sub-Agency," in ARCIA, 1848, 156.

37. Tally's Osage name is somewhat debated. Rollings uses Ta-hah-ka-he, which he translates as "Deer with Branching Horns." Mathews uses the English name "Tallai," with an Osage spelling of Ta-Eh-Ga-Xe, meaning "Buck-making Horns." According to Louis Burns, Tally was a close advisor to Black Dog and an acting chief at various points. "Home Proceedings: Union Mission," *American Missionary Register* 4, no. 9 (September 1823): 274; Burns, *A History of the Osage People*, 64; "Home Proceedings: Union Mission," *American Missionary Register* 3, no. 5 (November 1822): 185; Mathews, *The Osages*, 432; and Rollings, *Unaffected by the Gospel*, 9.

38. Emphasis added; "Home Proceedings: Union Mission," *American Missionary Register* 2, no. 3 (September 1821), 115.

39. French visitor Victor Tixier and French immigrant Louis Cortambert (married to a Chouteau daughter) called these male cooks "marmiton," which signified that this man was a herald, dignitary, and a cook. Fausz, "Becoming 'a Nation of Quakers,'" 31; Chapman, "Journey to the Land of the Osages, 1835–1836, by Louis Cortambert," 216–217; Washington Irving, William Peterfield Trent, and George S. Hellman,

The Journals of Washington Irving (Hitherto Unpublished), vol. 3 (Boston: The Bibliophile Society, 1919), 156; Zebulon Montgomery Pike, *The Expeditions of Zebulon Montgomery Pike, to Headwaters of the Mississippi River, through Louisiana Territory, and in New Spain, During the Years 1805–6–7*, ed. Elliott Coues, vol. 2 (New York: F. P. Harper, 1895), 527–528; Tixier, McDermott, and Salvan, *Tixier's Travels on the Osage Prairies*, 98–99, 120, 172, 199–200; Grant Foreman, "Our Indian Ambassadors to Europe," *Missouri Historical Society Collections* 5 (February 1928): 127n59; Paul Mary Ponziglione, "The Osages and Father John Schoenmakers," unpublished manuscript, ed. Lowrie J. Daly and Garrick Alan Bailey (St. Louis: Midwest Jesuit Archives), 113; and DuVal, *The Native Ground*, 109.

40. Gregg, Part 2 of *Gregg's Commerce of the Prairies, 1831–1839*, 338–339; Chapman, "Journey to the Land of the Osages, 1835–1836, by Louis Cortambert," 217; Tixier, McDermott, and Salvan, *Tixier's Travels on the Osage Prairies*, 124, 182–183; "Reports of Societies: Union Mission," *American Missionary Register* 2, no. 12 (June 1822): 466; "Home Proceedings: Union Mission," *American Missionary Register* 6, no. 8 (August 1825): 244; "Home Proceedings: Union Mission," *American Missionary Register* 2, no. 5 (November 1821): 183; "Osage Indians: Account of Their Conditions, Manners, Etc.," 146; Tuttle, *Letters on the Chickasaw and Osage Missions*, 129, 154; "Home Proceedings: Union Mission," *American Missionary Register* 2, no. 3 (September 1821): 108, 115–116; and "Home Proceedings: Union Mission," *American Missionary Register* 4, no. 7 (July 1823): 204.

41. Tixier, McDermott, and Salvan, *Tixier's Travels on the Osage Prairies*, 182–183; and "Home Proceedings: Great Osage Mission," *American Missionary Register* 3, no. 3 (September 1822): 93–94.

42. William Requa to David Greene, June 23, 1833 (frame 890–893), microfilm reel 779, in "Missions on the American Continents and to the Islands of the Pacific, 1811–1919 (ABC 18–19), 1830–1837," in *American Board of Commissioners for Foreign Missions Archives, 1810–1961* (ABC 1–91) Houghton Library, Harvard University; "Home Proceedings: Great Osage Mission," *American Missionary Register* 4, no. 7 (July 1823): 205; Tixier, McDermott, and Salvan, *Tixier's Travels on the Osage Prairies*, 184; "Home Proceedings: Union Mission," *American Missionary Register* 3, no. 1 (July 1822): 13; and George William Featherstonhaugh, *Excursion through the Slave States, from Washington on the Potomac, to the Frontier of Mexico; with Sketches of Popular Manners and Geological Notices* (New York: Harper and Brothers, 1844), 71.

43. Neosho Mission was a branch of the Harmony Mission, commenced in September 1824 as an agricultural settlement for "civilizing" Osage families. It was modeled after Hopefield, a similar agricultural venture and branch of the Union Mission. Neosho Mission was seventy to eighty miles southwest of Harmony along the Neosho River. Tuttle, *Letters on the Chickasaw and Osage Missions*, 107–108; and "Home

Proceedings: Missionary Establishments," *American Missionary Register* 6, no. 1 (January 1825): 19.

44. Jean Dennison, *Colonial Entanglement: Constituting a Twenty-First-Century Osage Nation* (Chapel Hill: University of North Carolina Press, 2012), 54–55; Rollings, *The Osage*, 154–155; and Rollings, *Unaffected by the Gospel*, 72–73, 98–99.

45. William Requa to David Greene, July 3, 1832 (frame 882–887), microfilm reel 779, in "Missions on the American Continents and to the Islands of the Pacific, 1811–1919 (ABC 18–19), 1830–1837," in *American Board of Commissioners for Foreign Missions Archives, 1810–1961* (ABC 1–91) Houghton Library, Harvard University; "Home Proceedings: Journal of the Union Mission," *American Missionary Register* 6, no. 7 (July 1825): 216; "Osages," *Missionary Herald* 27, no. 11 (November 1831): 354; "Osages," *Missionary Herald* 22, no. 4 (April 1826): 118; "Home Proceedings: Union Mission," *American Missionary Register* 5, no. 7 (July 1824): 206–207; "Home Proceedings: Union Mission," *American Missionary Register* 6, no. 8 (August 1825): 244; "Osages: Report of the Station at Union, June 1, 1830," *Missionary Herald* 26, no. 9 (September 1830): 287; and Tuttle, *Letters on the Chickasaw and Osage Missions*, 137–139, 142.

46. "Home Proceedings: Great Osage Mission," *American Missionary Register* 3, no. 6 (December 1822): 212–213; "Home Proceedings: Union Mission," *American Missionary Register* 4, no. 8 (August 1823): 235; "Home Proceedings: Union Mission," *American Missionary Register* 5, no. 3 (March 1824): 78–79; "Home Proceedings: Great Osage Mission," *American Missionary Register* 5, no. 7 (July 1824): 212–213; and "Home Proceedings: Union Mission," *American Missionary Register* 5, no. 7 (July 1824): 206, 208–209. For a similar discussion of wage labor and gender, see Martha C. Knack, "The Dynamics of Southern Paiute Women's Roles," in *Women and Power in Native North America*, ed. Laura F. Klein and Lillian A. Ackerman (Norman: University of Oklahoma Press, 1995), 154–158.

47. Wah-kos-i-toh and Moi-neh Persha (also spelled Moi-reh Per-sha) were the named men who performed agricultural labor at the missions. "Home Proceedings: Union Mission," *American Missionary Register* 4, no. 12 (December 1823): 371; "Home Proceedings: Union Mission," *American Missionary Register* 4, no. 9 (September 1823): 274; Tuttle, *Letters on the Chickasaw and Osage Missions*, 92; Francis La Flesche, "The Osage Tribe: Rite of the Wa-Xo'-Be," *Forty-Fifth Annual Report of the Bureau of American Ethnology (1927–1928)* (1930): 624; "Home Proceedings: Great Osage Mission," *American Missionary Register* 3, no. 6 (December 1822): 212–213; "Home Proceedings: Union Mission," *American Missionary Register* 4, no. 8 (August 1823): 235; and "Home Proceedings: Great Osage Mission," *American Missionary Register* 5, no. 7 (July 1824): 213.

48. Emphasis original; "Home Proceedings: Union Mission," *American Missionary Register* 5, no. 7 (July 1824): 206.

49. "Home Proceedings: Union Mission," *American Missionary Register* 4, no. 12 (December 1823): 369.

50. "Reports of Societies: Great Osage Mission," *American Missionary Register* 4, no. 6 (June 1823): 164.

51. "Home Proceedings: Great Osage Mission," *American Missionary Register* 5, no. 12 (December 1824): 364.

52. La Flesche, "The Osage Tribe: Rite of the Wa-Xo'-Be," 624.

53. "Home Proceedings: Union Mission," *American Missionary Register* 5, no. 3 (March 1824): 79; "Home Proceedings: Union Mission," *American Missionary Register* 5, no. 7 (July 1824): 208.

54. Rollings, *Unaffected by the Gospel*, 52, 56–57.

55. DuVal, *The Native Ground*, 224–226.

56. Claremore is spelled "Clamore" in all of the Protestant missionary records. The Claremore described above was the longtime nineteenth-century leader of the Arkansas Osage (not the eighteenth-century leader of the same name). John Joseph Mathews uses both "Claremore" and "Claremont." According to Mathews, Claremore's formal Osage name was *Gra-Mo'n*, translated as "Arrow-Going-Home," while his personal name was *To-Wo'n Ga-Xe*, translated as "Town Maker." Louis Burns used the names "Claremore II" and "Town Maker," and also provided a detailed description of descent and leadership in the Osage nation at this time. "Home Proceedings: Union Mission," *American Missionary Register* 3, no. 4 (October 1822): 141; Mathews, *The Osages*, 299; and Burns, *A History of the Osage People*, 50–61, 130–131.

57. "Home Proceedings: Union Mission," *American Missionary Register* 4, no. 1 (January 1823): 5.

58. "Home Proceedings: Great Osage Mission," *American Missionary Register* 4, no. 2 (February 1823): 45.

59. "Home Proceedings: Union Mission," *American Missionary Register* 4, no. 6 (June 1823): 176.

60. "Home Proceedings: Union Mission," *American Missionary Register* 5, no. 3 (March 1824), 80.

61. "Home Proceedings: Journal of the Union Mission," *American Missionary Register* 6, no. 7 (July 1825): 215.

62. Rollings, *Unaffected by the Gospel*, 95.

63. "Home Proceedings: Letters from the Superintendent of Indian Trade," *American Missionary Register* 1 (August 1820): 54.

64. William Vaill, "Report of Union Mission for the Year Ending Sept. 30th, 1830" (frame 326–329); William Vaill, "Report of the Union Mission for the Year Ending June 1, 1831" (frame 354–365); William Vaill to David Greene, October 20, 1831 (frame 381–392); William Montgomery to David Greene, August 27, 1832 (frame 579–582),

microfilm reel 779, in "Missions on the American Continents and to the Islands of the Pacific, 1811–1919 (ABC 18–19), 1830–1837," in *American Board of Commissioners for Foreign Missions Archives, 1810–1961* (ABC 1–91) Houghton Library, Harvard University; and Bailey, *Changes in Osage Social Organization*, 109.

65. "Home Proceedings: Great Osage Mission," *American Missionary Register* 4, no. 12 (December 1823): 372.

66. "Home Proceedings: Union Mission," *American Missionary Register* 4, no. 10 (October 1823): 304.

67. See the following for information on boys and girls and their English proficiency: "Reports of Societies: Great Osage Mission," *American Missionary Register* 4, no. 6 (June 1823): 164; "Reports of Societies: Union Mission," *American Missionary Register* 4, no. 6 (June 1823): 162–163; "Home Proceedings: Great Osage Mission," *American Missionary Register* 4, no. 10 (October 1823): 305; "Home Proceedings: Union Mission," *American Missionary Register* 5, no. 3 (March 1824): 77–78; and "Osages," *Missionary Herald* 22, no. 4 (April 1826): 116. For similar discussion of use of schools, see Tracy Neal Leavelle, "'We Will Make It Our Own Place': Agriculture and Adaptation at the Grand Ronde Reservation, 1856–1887," *American Indian Quarterly* 22, no. 4 (Fall 1998): 444.

68. Tuttle, *Letters on the Chickasaw and Osage Missions*, 93; "Home Proceedings: Union Mission," *American Missionary Register* 4, no. 8 (August 1823): 237.

69. "Home Proceedings: Great Osage Mission," *American Missionary Register* 5, no. 6 (June 1824): 179.

70. "Home Proceedings: Union Mission," *American Missionary Register* 4, no. 12 (December 1823): 369.

71. Tixier, McDermott, and Salvan, *Tixier's Travels on the Osage Prairies*, 235–236; "Home Proceedings: Union Mission," *American Missionary Register* 4, no. 2 (February 1823): 41; "Home Proceedings: Union Mission," *American Missionary Register* 4, no. 7 (July 1823): 204; and Betty R. Nett, "Historical Changes in the Osage Kinship System," *Southwestern Journal of Anthropology* 8, no. 2 (1952): 176–179.

72. Rollings, *Unaffected by the Gospel*, 95; and Dennison, *Colonial Entanglement*, 54–55.

73. "Reports of Societies: Great Osage Mission," *American Missionary Register* 4, no. 6 (June 1823): 164.

74. "Home Proceedings: Great Osage Mission," *American Missionary Register* 4, no. 7 (July 1823): 207. For more on Osage female students' yardage completed and days in the kitchen, see "Home Proceedings: Great Osage Mission," *American Missionary Register* 4, no. 9 (September 1823): 275.

75. "Home Proceedings: Great Osage Mission," *American Missionary Register* 5, no. 5 (May 1824): 141.

76. Tuttle, *Letters on the Chickasaw and Osage Missions*, 89.

77. Theda Perdue, *Cherokee Women: Gender and Culture Change, 1700–1835* (Lincoln: University of Nebraska Press, 1998), 186.

78. "Reports of Societies: Great Osage Mission," *American Missionary Register* 4, no. 6 (June 1823): 164.

79. "Home Proceedings: Union Mission," *American Missionary Register* 4, no. 3 (March 1823): 74.

80. "Home Proceedings: Union Mission," *American Missionary Register* 4, no. 6 (June 1823): 177; "Home Proceedings: Union Mission," *American Missionary Register* 4, no. 8 (August 1823): 235; and "Osages: Report of the Station at Union, June 1, 1830," 286.

81. "Home Proceedings: Union Mission," *American Missionary Register* 5, no. 11 (November 1824): 331; and "Home Proceedings: Union Mission," *American Missionary Register* 6, no. 4 (April 1825): 120.

82. There is only one missionary reference to male achievement in agriculture at the school. In the Union mission's annual report, dated October 1, 1822, Reverend Vaill claimed that four Osage boys were "industrious when taken into the field." One of these boys, Tally's son Woh-sis-ter, abandoned the mission on October 23rd. Vaill, six months earlier, described the other three students in his report to Secretary Calhoun as identifying "labour with slavery." "Home Proceedings: Union Mission," *American Missionary Register* 4, no. 3 (March 1823): 74.

83. For examples of students leaving and returning to school, see "Home Proceedings: Great Osage Mission," *American Missionary Register* 3, no. 2 (August 1822): 48; "Home Proceedings: Union Mission," *American Missionary Register* 5, no. 1 (January 1824): 27–28; "Home Proceedings: Union Mission," *American Missionary Register* 5, no. 3 (March 1824): 76; "Home Proceedings: Great Osage Mission," *American Missionary Register* 5, no. 7 (July 1824): 213; "Home Proceedings: Union Mission," *American Missionary Register* 5, no. 8 (August 1824): 232; and "Home Proceedings: Union Mission," *American Missionary Register* 6, no. 3 (March 1825): 87.

84. "Home Proceedings: Union Mission," *American Missionary Register* 3, no. 4 (October 1822): 142–144.

85. "Home Proceedings: Union Mission," *American Missionary Register* 4, no. 1 (January 1823): 4.

86. Ibid., 5.

87. Ibid., 8.

88. "Home Proceedings: Union Mission," *American Missionary Register* 4, no. 5 (May 1823): 136.

89. "Home Proceedings: Union Mission," *American Missionary Register* 4, no. 7 (July 1823): 202.

90. "Home Proceedings: Union Mission," *American Missionary Register* 4, no. 8 (August 1823): 235.

91. Ibid.

92. "Reports of Societies: Great Osage Mission," *American Missionary Register* 2, no. 12 (June 1822): 474.

93. Ibid.

94. "Home Proceedings: Great Osage Mission," 49.

95. Ibid.

96. The Swiss family worked for wages at the Union mission. Abraham Swiss, the child learning the carpenter's trade, along with his twin brothers (Isaac and Jacob) and one sister, repeatedly left the Union mission school. "Home Proceedings: Union Mission," *American Missionary Register* 4, no. 9 (September 1823): 273; "Home Proceedings: Union Mission," *American Missionary Register* 6, no. 4 (April, 1825): 120; and "Home Proceedings: Union Mission," *American Missionary Register* 5, no. 4 (April 1824): 109.

97. "Home Proceedings: Union Mission," *American Missionary Register* 6, no. 3 (March 1825): 87.

98. "Home Proceedings: Union Mission," *American Missionary Register* 6, no. 8 (August 1825): 243.

99. Ibid., 244.

100. "Osages: Report of the Station at Union, June 1, 1830," 286.

101. "Home Proceedings: Union Mission," *American Missionary Register* 5, no. 7 (July 1824): 207; "Osages," *Missionary Herald* 27, no. 11 (November 1831): 354; and Tuttle, *Letters on the Chickasaw and Osage Missions*, 104–105, 118.

102. "Home Proceedings: Union Mission," *American Missionary Register* 6, no. 8 (August 1825): 244.

103. "Home Proceedings: Harmony Mission," *American Missionary Register* 6, no. 5 (May 1825): 147.

104. "Home Proceedings: Union Mission," *American Missionary Register* 4, no. 1 (January 1823): 4; and "Home Proceedings: Union Mission," *American Missionary Register* 3, no. 4 (October 1822): 144.

105. Rollings, *Unaffected by the Gospel*, 80–81.

106. Emphasis original; "Home Proceedings: Great Osage Mission," *American Missionary Register* 5, no. 4 (April 1824): 117.

107. Tuttle, *Letters on the Chickasaw and Osage Missions*, 77; "Osages: Miscellaneous Communications Respecting the Mission," 123–124; and "Home Proceedings: Great Osage Mission," *American Missionary Register* 3, no. 5 (November 1822): 186.

108. "Home Proceedings: Great Osage Mission," *American Missionary Register* 5, no. 9 (September 1824): 272.

109. "Home Proceedings: Union Mission," *American Missionary Register* 2, no. 12 (June 1822): 490.

110. "Home Proceedings: Union Mission," *American Missionary Register* 4, no. 6 (June 1823): 176.

111. "Home Proceedings: Union Mission," *American Missionary Register* 6, no. 2 (February 1825): 48.

112. "Osages: Miscellaneous Communications Respecting the Mission," 123; and "Osages: Extract from a Letter of Mr. Montgomery, Dated Union, Dec. 27, 1831," *Missionary Herald* 28, no. 8 (August 1832): 257.

113. "Home Proceedings: Union Mission," *American Missionary Register* 6, no. 2 (February 1825): 48.

114. N. B. Dodge to David Greene, September 4, 1834 (frame 647–650), microfilm reel 779, in "Missions on the American Continents and to the Islands of the Pacific, 1811–1919 (ABC 18–19), 1830–1837," in *American Board of Commissioners for Foreign Missions Archives, 1810–1961* (ABC 1–91) Houghton Library, Harvard University.

115. Emphasis original; "Home Proceedings: Union Mission," *American Missionary Register* 6, no. 2 (February 1825): 48.

116. Tuttle, *Letters on the Chickasaw and Osage Missions*, 159.

117. "Osages: Extract from a Letter of Mr. Montgomery, Dated Union, Dec. 27, 1831," 258.

118. Ibid.

119. Tuttle, *Letters on the Chickasaw and Osage Missions*, 165.

120. Rollings, *Unaffected by the Gospel*, 6.

121. William Vaill, "Report of the Union Mission for the Year ending June 1, 1831" (frame 354–365), microfilm reel 779, in "Missions on the American Continents and to the Islands of the Pacific, 1811–1919 (ABC 18–19), 1830–1837," in *American Board of Commissioners for Foreign Missions Archives, 1810–1961* (ABC 1–91) Houghton Library, Harvard University; and "Home Proceedings: Great Osage Mission," *American Missionary Register* 3, no. 3 (September 1822): 93.

122. "Osages: Extract from a Letter of Mr. Montgomery, Dated Union, Dec. 27, 1831," 258.

123. "Home Proceedings: Great Osage Mission," *American Missionary Register* 4, no. 7 (July 1823): 205.

124. Ibid.

125. "Home Proceedings: Great Osage Mission," *American Missionary Register* 2, no. 12 (June 1822): 494.

126. "Home Proceedings: Union Mission," *American Missionary Register* 4, no. 7 (July 1823): 201–202.

127. Tuttle, *Letters on the Chickasaw and Osage Missions*, 94.

CHAPTER 4. "THE VEXATIONS THAT THE AMERICAN GOVERNMENT INFLICTED": OSAGE WOMEN AND MEN RESISTING ELIMINATION

1. Emphasis original; Cooke to Arbuckle, January 8, 1839, "Letters Received by the Office of Indian Affairs, 1824–1880: Osage Agency, 1824–1841," National Archives, Record Group 75, M234 (roll 631, frames 734–774); and Brad Agnew, *Fort Gibson: Terminal on the Trail of Tears* (Norman: University of Oklahoma Press, 1980), 173–175.

2. Footnotes in Tixier indicate "Big Soldier" could have been Marcharthitahtoongah, who visited France in 1827, or perhaps Ne-ha-wa-she-tun-ga, who signed the Treaty of 1825. Victor Tixier, John Francis McDermott, and Albert Jacques Salvan, *Tixier's Travels on the Osage Prairies* (Norman: University of Oklahoma Press, 1940), 99–100; and Willard H. Rollings, *The Osage: An Ethnohistorical Study of Hegemony on the Prairie-Plains* (Columbia: University of Missouri Press, 1992), 224.

3. John Mack Faragher, "'More Motley than Mackinaw': From Ethnic Mixing to Ethnic Cleansing on the Frontier of the Lower Missouri, 1783–1833," in *Contact Points: American Frontiers from the Mohawk Valley to the Mississippi, 1750–1830*, ed. Andrew R. L. Cayton and Fredrika J. Teute (Chapel Hill: University of North Carolina Press, 1998), 305; Jack P. Greene, "Colonial History and National History: Reflections on a Continuing Problem," *William and Mary Quarterly* 64, no. 2 (April 2007): 238, 240–241, 246–249; Alan Taylor, "Land and Liberty on the Post-Revolutionary Frontier," in *Devising Liberty: Preserving and Creating Freedom in the New American Republic*, ed. David Thomas Konig (Stanford, CA: Stanford University Press, 1995), 82–87; Stuart Banner, *How the Indians Lost Their Land: Law and Power on the Frontier* (Cambridge, MA: Belknap Press of Harvard University Press, 2005), 124–129; Patrick Wolfe, "Settler Colonialism and the Elimination of the Native," *Journal of Genocide Research* 8, no. 4 (2006): 389–394; and Robert M. Utley, *The Indian Frontier of the American West 1846–1890* (Albuquerque: University of New Mexico Press, 1984), 33, 35–36, 46, 58–59.

4. Banner, *How the Indians Lost Their Land*, 144–148, 198, 227; and Rollings, *The Osage*, 254–256.

5. Rollings, *The Osage*, 262–267, 280–281; Banner, *How the Indians Lost Their Land*, 125–126, 215; and Louis F. Burns, *Osage Indian Customs and Myths* (Tuscaloosa: University of Alabama Press, 1984), 119.

6. John Joseph Mathews, *The Osages: Children of the Middle Waters* (Norman: University of Oklahoma Press, 1961), 529.

7. Louis F. Burns, *A History of the Osage People* (Tuscaloosa: The University of Alabama Press, 2004), 29, 170–171, 487; and Mathews, *The Osages*, 64, 491–493, 498–499, 511, 529–530.

8. The only known epidemic among the Osage prior to the 1820s occurred in 1806 when Zebulon Pike's visit to the Osage was believed to have brought an "unknown fever" that killed an estimated 200 adults and a "large number of children." Zebulon Montgomery Pike and Donald Dean Jackson, *The Journals of Zebulon Montgomery Pike, with Letters and Related Documents*, vol. 2, The American Exploration and Travel Series (Norman: University of Oklahoma Press, 1966), 163; Tai S. Edwards, "Disruption and Disease: The Osage Struggle to Survive in the Nineteenth-Century Trans-Missouri West," *Kansas History: A Journal of the Central Plains* 36, no. 4 (Winter 2013–2014): 219, 222–223; Paul Kelton, *Epidemics and Enslavement: Biological Catastrophe in the Native Southeast, 1492–1715* (Lincoln: University of Nebraska Press, 2007), 1–3, 221–222; Paul Kelton, *Cherokee Medicine, Colonial Germs: An Indigenous Nation's Fight against Smallpox, 1518–1824* (Norman: University of Oklahoma Press, 2015), 7, 9, 19, 173, 214; Catherine M. Cameron, Paul Kelton, and Alan C. Swedlund, "Introduction," in *Beyond Germs: Native Depopulation in North America*, ed. Catherine M. Cameron, Paul Kelton, and Alan C. Swedlund (Tucson: University of Arizona Press, 2015), 6; and Tai S. Edwards and Paul Kelton, "Germs, Genocides, and America's Indigenous Peoples," (forthcoming).

9. Edwards, "Disruption and Disease," 222–223; "Home Proceedings: Great Osage Mission," *American Missionary Register* 4, no. 2 (February 1823): 44; and "Home Proceedings: Great Osage Mission," *American Missionary Register* 5, no. 3 (March 1824): 82.

10. Sarah Tuttle, *Letters on the Chickasaw and Osage Missions*, 2nd ed. (Boston: Massachusetts Sabbath School Society, 1833), 91; Josephine McDonagh, "Infanticide and the Boundaries of Culture from Hume to Arnold," in *Inventing Maternity: Politics, Science, and Literature, 1650–1865*, ed. Susan C. Greenfield and Carol Barash (Lexington: University Press of Kentucky, 1999), 215–216, 220; Theda Perdue, *Cherokee Women: Gender and Culture Change, 1700–1835* (Lincoln: University of Nebraska Press, 1998), 148; Burns, *Osage Indian Customs and Myths,* 81–82; Mathews, *The Osages*, 488–489; Kathleen DuVal, *The Native Ground: Indians and Colonists in the Heart of the Continent* (Philadelphia: University of Pennsylvania Press, 2006), 224; "Home Proceedings: Great Osage Mission," *American Missionary Register* 4, no. 2 (February 1823): 44; "Home Proceedings: Great Osage Mission," *American Missionary Register* 5, no. 3 (March 1824): 81–82; "Osages," *Missionary Herald* 29, no. 2 (February 1833): 62; Francis La Flesche, "The Osage Tribe: Two Versions of the Child-Naming Rite," *Forty-Third Annual Report of the Bureau of American Ethnology (1925–1926)* (1928): 31; "Home Proceedings: Union Mission," *American Missionary Register* 4, no. 7 (July 1823): 203–204; "Home Proceedings: Union Mission," *American Missionary Register* 5, no. 2 (February 1824): 39; "Home Proceedings: Union Mission," *American Missionary Register* 4, no. 12 (December 1823): 371; and "Home Proceedings: Union Mission," *American Missionary Register* 5, no. 8 (August 1824): 230–231.

11. Paul Mary Ponziglione, "The Osages and Father John Schoenmakers," unpublished manuscript, ed. Lowrie J. Daly and Garrick Alan Bailey (St. Louis: Midwest Jesuit Archives), 49, 66.

12. Agnew, Fort Gibson, 174–175; and Edwards, "Disruption and Disease," 224–225.

13. Edwards, "Disruption and Disease," 223.

14. Donna L. Akers, "Removing the Heart of the Choctaw People: Indian Removal from a Native Perspective," *American Indian Culture and Research Journal* 23, no. 3 (1999); Ronald D. Parks, *The Darkest Period: The Kanza Indians and Their Last Homeland, 1846–1873* (Norman: University of Oklahoma Press, 2014), 90; and Edwards, "Disruption and Disease," 227.

15. Willard H. Rollings, *Unaffected by the Gospel: The Osage Resistance to the Christian Invasion (1673–1906): A Cultural Victory* (Albuquerque: University of New Mexico Press, 2004), 123; Ponziglione, "The Osages and Father John Schoenmakers," 49; and Rollings, *The Osage*, 277.

16. Jean Dennison, *Colonial Entanglement: Constituting a Twenty-First-Century Osage Nation* (Chapel Hill: University of North Carolina Press, 2012), 52–55; Tanis C. Thorne, *The Many Hands of My Relations: French and Indians on the Lower Missouri* (Columbia: University of Missouri Press, 1996), 134–137, 141–143; Wolfe, "Settler Colonialism and the Elimination of the Native," 387–388; Rollings, *Unaffected by the Gospel*, 123–124; and Charles J. Kappler, ed. *Indian Affairs: Laws and Treaties, vol. 2 (Treaties)* (Washington, DC: Government Printing Office, 1904), 218–219, 881.

17. ARCIA, 1841, "Report of R. A. Calloway, Sub-Agent for Osages," 94–95; and Ponziglione, "The Osages and Father John Schoenmakers," 112, 200–201.

18. "Osage Indians," *Missionary Herald* 22, no. 9 (September 1826): 267; and Ponziglione, "The Osages and Father John Schoenmakers," 111, 119.

19. Paul Mary Ponziglione, "Kansas. Letter from Fr. P. M. Ponziglione, Dec. 31, 1881," *Woodstock Letters* 11, no. 2 (Woodstock, MD: Woodstock College Press, 1882): 164–165.

20. ARCIA, 1845, "Report of Joel Cruttenden, Sub-Agent for Osages," 98; and Ponziglione, "The Osages and Father John Schoenmakers," 164, 200–201.

21. In 1868, a federal agent claimed that of the 8,000,000 acres on the reservation, 400 were in cultivation by the Osages. Other estimates indicate that in the 1860s and 1870s, the Osage had on average one-third of an acre in cultivation for every person. ARCIA, 1841, "Report of R. A. Calloway, Sub-Agent for Osages," 94–95; ARCIA, 1843, "Report of R. A. Calloway, Sub-Agent for the Osages," 132; ARCIA, 1848, "Report of J. M. Richardson, Sub-Agent for the Osages, and Missionary and School Reports for that Sub-Agency," 156–157; ARCIA, 1850, "Sub-Agent H. Harvey—Osage Sub-Agency," 35; ARCIA, 1868, "Annual Report of T. Murphy, Superintendent," 258; ARCIA, 1871, "Annual Report of J. T. Gibson, Agent Neosho Agency," 483–484;

Thomas Jefferson Farnham, *Part I of Farnham's Travels in the Great Western Prairies, Etc.,* May 21–October 16, 1839, ed. Reuben Gold Thwaites, vol. 28, Early Western Travels, 1748–1846 (Cleveland: A. H. Clark, 1904), 132; Watson Stewart, "Personal Memoirs of Watson Stewart," Manuscript Collections, Miscellaneous Collections: Watson Stewart, Topeka, Kansas State Historical Society, 1904, 46; George F. Will and George E. Hyde, *Corn among the Indians of the Upper Missouri* (Saint Louis: William Harvey Miner, 1917), 107–108; Ponziglione, "The Osages and Father John Schoenmakers," 54, 58, 163–164, 201; and James Edwin Finney, "Reminiscences of a Trader in the Osage Country," *Chronicles of Oklahoma* 33, no. 2 (1955): 150.

22. ARCIA, 1842, "Report of R. A. Calloway, Agent for the Osages," 137; ARCIA, 1867, "Annual Report of George C. Snow, Agent, Neosho Agency," 325; ARCIA, 1871, "Annual Report of J. T. Gibson, Agent Neosho Agency," 483–484; and Eliza J. Wyckoff, "Reminiscences of Early Days in Kansas," Manuscript Collections, Miscellaneous Collections: Jane Baude, Topeka, Kansas State Historical Society, March 1, 1918, 5.

23. ARCIA, 1848, "Report of J. M. Richardson, Sub-Agent for the Osages, and Missionary and School Reports for that Sub-Agency," 158–159.

24. ARCIA, 1845, "Report of Joel Cruttenden, Sub-Agent for Osages," 97–98; ARCIA, 1848, "Report of J. M. Richardson, Sub-Agent for the Osages, and Missionary and School Reports for that Sub-Agency," 156–157; "J. M. Richardson, acting Osage Sub-Agent Annual Report," in *Index to Executive Documents Printed by Order of the Senate of the United States During the First Session of the Thirty-First Congress,* 1849–1850, 1134; ARCIA, 1850, "Sub-Agent H. Harvey—Osage Sub-Agency," 35; ARCIA, 1858, "Report of John Schoenmakers, Superintendent of the Osage Manual Labor School," 139; ARCIA, 1860, "Report of John C. Schoenmakers, Superintendent of the Osage Manual Labor School," 122; ARCIA, 1862, "Report of P. P. Elder, Agent at the Neosho Agency," 145; ARCIA, 1868, "Annual Report of G. C. Snow, Agent Neosho Agency," 272; and Ponziglione, "The Osages and Father John Schoenmakers," 149, 155, 259.

25. ARCIA, 1845, "Report, Joel Cruttenden, Sub-Agent for Osages," 98; ARCIA, 1848, "Report of J. M. Richardson, Sub-Agent for the Osages, and Missionary and School Reports for that Sub-Agency," 158; and Wyckoff, "Reminiscences of Early Days in Kansas," 5.

26. John D. Hunter, *Manners and Customs of Several Indian Tribes Located West of the Mississippi: Including Some Account of the Soil, Climate, and Vegetable Productions, and the Indian Materia Medica: To Which Is Prefixed the History of the Author's Life During a Residence of Several Years among Them* (Philadelphia: J. Maxwell, 1823), 283; and Francis La Flesche, "The Osage Tribe: Rite of the Wa-Xo'-Be," *Forty-Fifth Annual Report of the Bureau of American Ethnology* (1927–1928) (1930): 624.

27. ARCIA, 1848, "Report of J. M. Richardson, Sub-Agent for the Osages, and Missionary and School Reports for that Sub-Agency," 158–159; ARCIA, 1850, "Sub-Agent

H. Harvey—Osage Sub-Agency," 35; and Ponziglione, "The Osages and Father John Schoenmakers," 54.

28. ARCIA, 1848, "Report of J. M. Richardson, Sub-Agent for the Osages, and Missionary and School Reports for that Sub-Agency," 157; ARCIA, 1852, "Report of Agent William J. J. Morrow," 106; ARCIA, 1857, "Report of Andrew J. Dorn, Agent for the Osages, Quapaws, Senecas and Shawnees, and Senecas," 206; and Ponziglione, "The Osages and Father John Schoenmakers," 200–201.

29. ARCIA, 1842, "Report of R. A. Calloway, Agent for the Osages," 137; ARCIA, 1867, "Annual Report of George C. Snow, Agent, Neosho Agency," 325; "March 14, 1870," in "Journal of the Western Missions, vol. 2: January 4, 1869–January 9, 1871," unpublished manuscript, ed. Eugene Grabner (St. Louis: Midwest Jesuit Archives), 28; and Ponziglione, "The Osages and Father John Schoenmakers," 164.

30. ARCIA, 1865, "Annual Report of E. Sells, Superintendent," 258; Tixier, McDermott, and Salvan, Tixier's Travels on the Osage Prairies, 184; and Finney, "Reminiscences of a Trader in the Osage Country," 148–149.

31. Finney, "Reminiscences of a Trader in the Osage Country," 149.

32. ARCIA, 1848, "Report of J. M. Richardson, Sub-Agent for the Osages, and Missionary and School Reports for that Sub-Agency," 161–162.

33. ARCIA, 1848, "Report of J. M. Richardson, Sub-Agent for the Osages, and Missionary and School Reports for that Sub-Agency," 157.

34. Ponziglione, "The Osages and Father John Schoenmakers," 182.

35. "July 1, 1874," in "Journal of the Western Missions, vol. 5: July 1, 1874–December 13, 1876," unpublished manuscript, ed. Eugene Grabner (St. Louis: Midwest Jesuit Archives), 89.

36. ARCIA, 1845, "Report of Joel Cruttenden, Sub-Agent for Osages," 98; ARCIA, 1848, "Report of J. M. Richardson, Sub-Agent for the Osages, and Missionary and School Reports for that Sub-Agency," 159–160; Ponziglione, "The Osages and Father John Schoenmakers," 187–188; Tixier, McDermott, and Salvan, Tixier's Travels on the Osage Prairies, 150–151; and Pekka Hämäläinen, The Comanche Empire (New Haven, CT: Yale University Press, 2008), 154–155.

37. Finney, "Reminiscences of a Trader in the Osage Country," 146.

38. Richardson to Medill, May 18, 1848, "Letters Received by the Office of Indian Affairs, 1824–1880: Osage Agency, 1847–1874," National Archives, Record Group 75, M234 (roll 633, frames 394–396); Richardson to Brown, September 27, 1849, "Letters Received by the Office of Indian Affairs, 1824–1880: Osage Agency, 1847–1874," National Archives, Record Group 75, M234 (roll 633, frames 523–524); ARCIA, 1858, "Report of John Schoenmakers, Superintendent of the Osage Manual Labor School," 139; and ARCIA, 1868, "Annual Report of G. C. Snow, Agent Neosho Agency," 272.

39. ARCIA, 1848, "Report of J. M. Richardson, Sub-Agent for the Osages, and Missionary and School Reports for that Sub-Agency," 158; and ARCIA, 1850, "SubAgent H. Harvey—Osage Sub-Agency," 37.

40. ARCIA, 1863, "Report of P. P. Elder, Agent for the Osages, Etc.," 188.

41. Tixier, McDermott, and Salvan, Tixier's Travels on the Osage Prairies, 167–68; and Ponziglione, "The Osages and Father John Schoenmakers," 63, 201.

42. Tixier, McDermott, and Salvan, Tixier's Travels on the Osage Prairies, 184.

43. Garrick Alan Bailey, Changes in Osage Social Organization: 1673–1906, University of Oregon Anthropological Papers No. 5 (Eugene: University of Oregon Press, 1973), 66–67; and Rollings, The Osage, 271–272.

44. ARCIA, 1858, "Report of Andrew J. Dorn, Agent for the Osages, Quapaws, Senecas and Shawnees, and Senecas," 137; Kappler, ed., Indian Affairs: Laws and Treaties, Vol. 2 (Treaties), 600–602.

45. Rollings, Unaffected by the Gospel, 122–123; and Rollings, The Osage, 268–269, 275–276.

46. Tixier, McDermott, and Salvan, Tixier's Travels on the Osage Prairies, 210–218, 234.

47. Mathews, The Osages, 631; and Tixier, McDermott, and Salvan, Tixier's Travels on the Osage Prairies, 227.

48. Once the Osage removed to Indian Territory and after they finally were allowed access to the proceeds from their Kansas land sales, the tattooing ceremony enjoyed resurgence as people once again had the wealth to have the ceremony performed. The meaning, however, changed to focus on symbolic figures meaning "long life to the individual so tattooed," and it was also a way for an individual to "publicly display his affection toward a relative." Alice C. Fletcher and Francis La Flesche, The Omaha Tribe, vol. 1 (Lincoln: University of Nebraska Press, 1992), 221; Francis La Flesche, "Researches among the Osage," Smithsonian Miscellaneous Collections 70, no. 2 (1919): 112–113; La Flesche, "Ceremonies and Rituals of the Osage," Smithsonian Miscellaneous Collections 63, no. 8 (1914): 66–67; Mathews, The Osages, 325–326; and La Flesche, "The Osage Tribe: Rite of the Wa-Xo'-Be," 531.

49. Tixier, McDermott, and Salvan, Tixier's Travels on the Osage Prairies, 138–139; George Catlin, Letters and Notes on the Manners, Customs, and Condition of the North American Indians, 3rd ed., vol. 2 (New York: Wiley and Putnam, 1844), 41; and "Osage Indians: Account of Their Conditions, Manners, Etc.," Missionary Herald 23, no. 5 (May 1827): 147.

50. This was the wedding of Nivale and Tawagla. Ponziglione, "The Osages and Father John Schoenmakers," 146–147. Reverend Vaill, at Union Mission, witnessed tattooing in 1827, also remarking it designated virtue and honor. "Osage Indians: Account of Their Conditions, Manners, Etc.," Missionary Herald 23, no. 5 (May 1827): 147.

51. Fletcher and La Flesche, The Omaha Tribe, vol. 1, 219–220.

52. U.S. *Statutes at Large*, vol. X (March 3, 1853), 238–239.

53. H. Craig Miner and William E. Unrau, *The End of Indian Kansas: A Study of Cultural Revolution, 1854–1871* (Lawrence: Regents Press of Kansas, 1978), 6–12.

54. Ponziglione, "The Osages and Father John Schoenmakers," 142.

55. ARCIA, 1857, "Report of Andrew J. Dorn, Agent for the Osages, Quapaws, Senecas and Shawnees, and Senecas," 206; and ARCIA, 1871, "Annual Report of J. T. Gibson, Agent Relative to Osages," 491.

56. Chapman to Greenwood, August 26, 1860, "Letters Received by the Office of Indian Affairs, 1824–1880: Neosho Agency, 1859–1861," National Archives, Record Group 75, M234 (roll 532, frames 279–281); and ARCIA, 1859, "Report of Andrew J. Dorn, Agent for the Osages, Quapaws, Senecas and Shawnees, and Senecas," 169–170.

57. Emphasis original. ARCIA, 1868, "Annual Report of G. C. Snow, Agent Neosho Agency," 271–272.

58. ARCIA, 1871, "Annual Report of J. T. Gibson, Agent Neosho Agency," 484–486.

59. Wolfe, "Settler Colonialism and the Elimination of the Native," 388, 393.

60. ARCIA, 1871, "Annual Report of J. T. Gibson, Agent Neosho Agency," 485.

61. ARCIA, 1869, "Annual Report of G. C. Snow, Agent for Osages and Other Tribes," 380–381.

62. ARCIA, 1871, "Annual Report of J. T. Gibson, Agent Neosho Agency," 485; Paul Mary Ponziglione, "Osage Mission, July 1, 1877," *Woodstock Letters* 6, no. 3 (Woodstock, MD: Woodstock College Press, 1877): 195–197; Ponziglione, "The Osages and Father John Schoenmakers," 173, 176; George William Featherstonhaugh, *Excursion through the Slave States, from Washington on the Potomac, to the Frontier of Mexico; with Sketches of Popular Manners and Geological Notices* (New York: Harper and Brothers, 1844), 70–71; Washington Irving, William Peterfield Trent, and George S. Hellman, *The Journals of Washington Irving (Hitherto Unpublished)*, vol. 3 (Boston: The Bibliophile Society, 1919), 126–127; "Osages," *Missionary Herald* 30, no. 1 (January 1834): 24; and Tixier, McDermott, and Salvan, *Tixier's Travels on the Osage Prairies*, 157–158.

63. ARCIA, 1858, "Report of Andrew J. Dorn, Agent for the Osages, Quapaws, Senecas and Shawnees, and Senecas," 137; ARCIA, 1859, "Report of Andrew J. Dorn, Agent for the Osages, Quapaws, Senecas and Shawnees, and Senecas," 169–170; and ARCIA, 1865, "Annual Report of Agent Snow, Neosho Agency," 293.

64. ARCIA, 1867, "Annual Report of George C. Snow, Agent, Neosho Agency," 325.

65. ARCIA, 1871, "Annual Report of J. T. Gibson, Agent Neosho Agency," 484.

66. ARCIA, 1871, "Annual Report of J. T. Gibson, Agent Neosho Agency," 485.

67. Gilbert J. Garraghan, *The Jesuits of the Middle United States*, vol. 2 (New York: America Press, 1938), 493–495.

68. Rollings, *Unaffected by the Gospel*, 11–12.

69. Ponziglione, "The Osages and Father John Schoenmakers," 81.

70. Rollings, *Unaffected by the Gospel*, 146.

71. ARCIA, 1848, "Report of J. M. Richardson, Sub-Agent for the Osages, and Missionary and School Reports for that Sub-Agency," 166.

72. George E. Tinker, *Missionary Conquest: The Gospel and Native American Cultural Genocide* (Minneapolis: Fortress Press, 1993), viii, 4–10; and Wolfe, "Settler Colonialism and the Elimination of the Native," 398–399.

73. "John Bax to Pierre-Jean de Smet, June 10, 1850," in Smet, *Western Missions and Missionaries*, 368.

74. The Jesuits served as a buffer in terms of food provisions as Osage individuals frequently killed mission hogs and cattle for food. ARCIA, 1859, "Report of John C. Schoenmakers, Superintendent of the Osage Manual Labor School," 171.

75. ARCIA, 1854, "School Report of John Schoenmakers," 126.

76. Ponziglione, "The Osages and Father John Schoenmakers," 16.

77. ARCIA, 1845, "Report of Joel Cruttenden, Sub-Agent for Osages," 97–98; Ponziglione, "The Osages and Father John Schoenmakers," 114.

78. Ponziglione, "The Osages and Father John Schoenmakers," 114, 201. Sometimes Ponziglione acknowledged the work of men, "If the old men are allowed to pass their time in 'dolce far niente' it is not so with the young braves, for everyday parties of them starting at day light make short excursions on the plains to get fresh meat for their families and friends." "Dolce far niente" is Italian for "the sweetness of doing nothing."

79. ARCIA, 1853, "Report of Agent A. J. Dorn," 139; ARCIA, 1871, "Annual Report of J. T. Gibson, Agent Neosho Agency," 483; Wyckoff, "Reminiscences of Early Days in Kansas," 7–8, 10; Ponziglione, "The Osages and Father John Schoenmakers," 52, 129, 147, 163–164, 201; Tixier, McDermott, and Salvan, *Tixier's Travels on the Osage Prairies*, 117, 134, 159–160, 170–171; and Stewart, "Personal Memoirs of Watson Stewart," 24.

80. Tixier, McDermott, and Salvan, *Tixier's Travels on the Osage Prairies*, 183.

81. ARCIA, 1854, "School Report of John Schoenmakers," 126; ARCIA, 1856, "Report of Andrew J. Dorn, Agent for the Osages, Senecas, Quapaws, and Senecas and Shawnees," 134; ARCIA, 1871, "Annual Report of J. T. Gibson, Agent Neosho Agency," 488; Paul Mary Ponziglione, "Kansas. Letter from Father Ponziglione, July 2, 1883," *Woodstock Letters* 12, no. 3 (Woodstock, MD: Woodstock College Press, 1883): 292; Ponziglione, "The Osages and Father John Schoenmakers," 169; and Burns, *Osage Indian Customs and Myths*, 73.

82. Tixier, McDermott, and Salvan, *Tixier's Travels on the Osage Prairies*, 182, 184, 258; and Featherstonhaugh, *Excursion through the Slave States*, 71.

83. Ponziglione, "Kansas. Letter from Father Ponziglione, July 2, 1883," 292; and Tixier, McDermott, and Salvan, *Tixier's Travels on the Osage Prairies*, 183. Nevertheless,

in some instances, infidelity and divorce led to domestic violence. Several travelers reported men hitting their wives supposedly because of adultery, and Tixier claimed men could kill their unfaithful wives, though he did not witness this. Tixier also wrote that Majakita, an Osage town chief, abandoned his first wife to marry Vitimé, prompting his first wife to strike Vitimé with a spear. Reverend Pixley observed a similar incident in 1825, where an ex-wife made lacerations on the head of her ex-husband's second wife. Though the second wife's kin attempted to exact revenge, the first wife's determination to fight to the death halted their retaliation. It seems both men and women perpetrated domestic violence. It is unclear if colonization prompted or increased this behavior. Featherstonhaugh, *Excursion through the Slave States*, 71; Tixier, McDermott, and Salvan, *Tixier's Travels on the Osage Prairies*, 182–183, 234; and "Home Proceedings: Journal of Mr. Pixley," *American Missionary Register* 6, no. 7 (July 1825): 217.

84. Kappler, ed., *Indian Affairs: Laws and Treaties*, vol. 2 (*Treaties*), 526.

85. Ponziglione, "The Osages and Father John Schoenmakers," 111.

86. Ibid.

87. ARCIA, 1848, "Report of J. M. Richardson, Sub-Agent for the Osages, and Missionary and School Reports for that Sub-Agency," 162–163, 165–166; ARCIA, 1850, "Teacher Rev. J. Schoenmakers—Osage Sub-Agency," 38–39; and ARCIA, 1853, "School Report of John Schoenmakers," 141.

88. ARCIA, 1854, "School Report of John Schoenmakers," 125, 127.

89. Ponziglione, "The Osages and Father John Schoenmakers," 275.

90. ARCIA, 1848, "Report of J. M. Richardson, Sub-Agent for the Osages, and Missionary and School Reports for that Sub-Agency," 162–163, 165–166; and ARCIA, 1850, "Teacher Rev. J. Schoenmakers—Osage Sub-Agency," 38–39.

91. ARCIA, 1854, "School Report of John Schoenmakers," 126–127.

92. ARCIA, 1856, "Report of John Schoenmakers, Superintendent of the Osage Manual Labor School," 135.

93. ARCIA, 1852, "School Report of Rev. John Schoonmakers [sic]," 109.

94. ARCIA, 1858, "Report of John Schoenmakers, Superintendent of the Osage Manual Labor School," 138.

95. In 1858, Father Schoenmakers noted in his annual report there were forty-seven Osage males and forty-eight Osage female students at the mission. ARCIA, 1858, "Report of John Schoenmakers, Superintendent of the Osage Manual Labor School," 138.

96. ARCIA, 1848, "Report of J. M. Richardson, Sub-Agent for the Osages, and Missionary and School Reports for that Sub-Agency," 162–163, 165; ARCIA, 1850, "Teacher Rev. J. Schoenmakers—Osage Sub-Agency," 39; and ARCIA, 1853, "School Report of John Schoenmakers," 141.

97. ARCIA, 1854, "School Report of John Schoenmakers," 126.

98. ARCIA, 1860, "Report of John C. Schoenmakers, Superintendent of the Osage Manual Labor School," 121; and ARCIA, 1861, "Report of P. P. Elder, Agent for the Indians within the Neosho Agency," 37.

99. ARCIA, 1852, "Report of Agent William J. J. Morrow," 105; ARCIA, 1856, "Report of John Schoenmakers, Superintendent of the Osage Manual Labor School," 136; and ARCIA, 1865, "Annual Report of E. Sells, Superintendent," 257.

100. Ponziglione, "The Osages and Father John Schoenmakers," 115.

101. ARCIA, 1853, "School Report of John Schoenmakers," 141; and ARCIA, 1857, "Report of John Schoenmakers, Superintendent of the Osage Manual Labor School," 207, 209.

102. ARCIA, 1854, "School Report of John Schoenmakers," 125.

103. ARCIA, 1854, "School Report of John Schoenmakers," 127.

104. ARCIA, 1871, "Annual Report of J. T. Gibson, Agent Neosho Agency," 489.

105. "July 27, 1869," in "Journal of the Western Missions, vol. 2: January 4, 1869–January 9, 1871," unpublished manuscript, ed. Eugene Grabner (St. Louis: Midwest Jesuit Archives), 21.

106. "John Bax to Pierre-Jean de Smet, June 10, 1850," in Smet, *Western Missions and Missionaries*, 370.

107. Father Bax also acknowledged the problems he and other priests encountered with the "Catholic" métis Osage, who knew virtually nothing of their "religion" and could not aid in converting and educating their kinfolk. Smet, *Western Missions and Missionaries*, 369. "April 3, 1872," in "Journal of the Western Missions, vol. 3: January 16, 1871–July 1, 1872," unpublished manuscript, ed. Eugene Grabner (St. Louis: Midwest Jesuit Archives), 68.

108. ARCIA, 1855, "Report of the Commissioner of Indian Affairs," 10; ARCIA, 1855, "Report of Andrew J. Dorn, Agent for the Osages, Senecas, Quapaws, and Senecas and Shawnees," 174; and Ponziglione, "The Osages and Father John Schoenmakers," 163.

109. ARCIA, 1860, "Report of Andrew J. Dorn, Agent for the Osages, Quapaws, Senecas and Shawnees, and Senecas," 120; ARCIA, 1860, "Report of John C. Schoenmakers, Superintendent of the Osage Manual Labor School," 122; and Ibid., 194.

110. Ponziglione, "The Osages and Father John Schoenmakers," 194–195.

111. Ibid., 150–151.

112. Ibid., 149–150.

113. ARCIA, 1855, "Report of Andrew J. Dorn, Agent for the Osages, Senecas, Quapaws, and Senecas and Shawnees," 175; Ponziglione, "The Osages and Father John Schoenmakers," 155, 159; and Mathews, *The Osages*, 626.

114. Ponziglione, "The Osages and Father John Schoenmakers," 260; and Wiley

Britton, "The Grasshopper Plague of 1866 in Kansas," *The Scientific Monthly* 25, no. 6 (December 1927): 541–542.

115. Garraghan, *The Jesuits of the Middle United States*, vol. 2, 530; and Ponziglione, "The Osages and Father John Schoenmakers," 117.

116. Ponziglione, "The Osages and Father John Schoenmakers," 118.

117. Ibid., 118–119; La Flesche, "The Osage Tribe: Rite of the Wa-Xo'-Be," 624.

118. Ponziglione, "The Osages and Father John Schoenmakers," 119.

119. ARCIA, 1855, "School Report of J. Schoenmakers," 176.

120. ARCIA, 1856, "Report of John Schoenmakers, Superintendent of the Osage Manual Labor School," 135.

121. Ponziglione, "The Osages and Father John Schoenmakers," 187; and ARCIA, 1867, "Annual Report of John Shoenmaker [sic], Teacher, Neosho Agency," 326.

122. Ponziglione, "The Osages and Father John Schoenmakers," 194–195.

123. Ibid., 220.

124. Ibid.

125. ARCIA, 1864, "Report of J. Schoenmakers, Superintendent of Osage Manual Labor School," 318; and "May 9, 1876," in "Journal of the Western Missions, vol. 5: July 1, 1874–December 13, 1876," unpublished manuscript, ed. Eugene Grabner (St. Louis: Midwest Jesuit Archives), 104.

126. Ponziglione, "The Osages and Father John Schoenmakers," 235–236.

127. ARCIA, 1867, "Annual Report of John Shoenmakers [sic], teacher, Neosho Agency," 326.

128. "March 14, 1870," in "Journal of the Western Missions, vol. 2: January 4, 1869–January 9, 1871," unpublished manuscript, ed. Eugene Grabner (St. Louis: Midwest Jesuit Archives), 28.

129. "December 31, 1872," in "Journal of the Western Missions, vol. 4: December 31, 1872–December 31, 1873," unpublished manuscript, ed. Eugene Grabner (St. Louis: Midwest Jesuit Archives), 78.

130. James Edwin Finney, "The Osages and Their Agency During the Term of Isaac T. Gibson, Quaker Agent," *Chronicles of Oklahoma* 36, no. 4 (1958): 424.

131. Tixier, McDermott, and Salvan, *Tixier's Travels on the Osage Prairies*, 164–166.

132. Mathews, *The Osages*, 583.

133. Ponziglione, "The Osages and Father John Schoenmakers," 15, 112–113.

134. Wyckoff, "Reminiscences of Early Days in Kansas," 7.

135. Rollings, *Unaffected by the Gospel*, 173, 177–178; and Bailey, *Changes in Osage Social Organization*, 93n19.

136. J. Owen Dorsey, "An Account of the War Customs of the Osages," *The American Naturalist* 18, no. 2 (February 1884): 113.

137. Francis La Flesche, "Tribal Rites of Osage Indians," *Smithsonian Miscellaneous Collections* 68, no. 12 (1918): 86–88; and La Flesche, "The Osage Tribe: Rite of the Wa-Xo'-Be," 694–695.

138. Michelene E. Pesantubbee, *Choctaw Women in a Chaotic World: The Clash of Cultures in the Colonial Southeast* (Albuquerque: University of New Mexico Press, 2005), 141–143.

139. One missionary estimated 1,500 were killed in this series of epidemics. *ARCIA, 1852*, "Report of Agent William J. J. Morrow," 106; *ARCIA, 1852*, "School Report of Rev. John Schoonmakers [sic]," 109; Pierre-Jean de Smet, *Western Missions and Missionaries: A Series of Letters* (New York: James B. Kirker, Late Edward Dunigan and Brother, 1863), 383; Edwards, "Disruption and Disease," 226–227; W. W. Graves, *Life and Letters of Fathers Ponziglione, Schoenmakers, and Other Early Jesuits at Osage Mission. Sketch of St. Francis' Church. Life of Mother Bridget* (St. Paul, Kanas: W. W. Graves, 1916), 37–40, 44; and Ponziglione, "The Osages and Father John Schoenmakers," 135–138.

140. *ARCIA, 1855*, "Report of Andrew J. Dorn, Agent for the Osages, Senecas, Quapaws, and Senecas and Shawnees," 174–175; *ARCIA, 1855*, "School Report of J. Schoenmakers," 176; *ARCIA, 1856*, "Report of Andrew J. Dorn, Agent for the Osages, Senecas, Quapaws, and Senecas and Shawnees," 134; and Ponziglione, "The Osages and Father John Schoenmakers," 154–156.

141. Ponziglione, "The Osages and Father John Schoenmakers," 151–152.

142. Tillie Karns Newman, *The Black Dog Trail* (Boston: Christopher Publishing House, 1957), 102; and Valerie Tracy, "The Indian in Transition: The Neosho Agency 1850–1861," *The Chronicles of Oklahoma* 48, no. 2 (1970): 174.

143. *ARCIA, 1862*, "Report of P. P. Elder, Agent at the Neosho Agency," 145; *ARCIA, 1864*, "Report of P. P. Elder, Agent at Neosho Agency," 316; *ARCIA, 1868*, "Annual Report of G. C. Snow, Agent Neosho Agency," 272; and Ponziglione, "The Osages and Father John Schoenmakers," 194–195, 259–260.

144. *ARCIA, 1863*, "Report of P. P. Elder, Agent for the Osages, Etc.," 187; *ARCIA, 1871*, "Annual Report of J. T. Gibson, Agent Neosho Agency," 483; *ARCIA, 1891*, "Report of Osage Agent L. J. Miles," 353; Burns, *A History of the Osage People*, 243–244, 346; and Smet, *Western Missions and Missionaries*, 381.

145. Wolfe, "Settler Colonialism and the Elimination of the Native," 400; and Edwards and Kelton, "Germs, Genocides, and America's Indigenous Peoples" (forthcoming).

146. "Osages: Extracts from the Journal of Mr. Montgomery," *Missionary Herald* 30, no. 1 (January 1834): 23; and Tixier, McDermott, and Salvan, *Tixier's Travels on the Osage Prairies*, 99–100.

147. Edwards, "Disruption and Disease," 227; Mathews, *The Osages*, 632; and Burns, *A History of the Osage People*, 170–171.

148. Ponziglione, "The Osages and Father John Schoenmakers," 221.

149. Ibid., 231.

150. ARCIA, 1861, "Report of P. P. Elder, Agent for the Indians within the Neosho Agency," 37; and Ponziglione, "The Osages and Father John Schoenmakers," 220, 222, 233–235.

151. Ponziglione, "The Osages and Father John Schoenmakers," 235.

152. In 1863, an Osage hunting party led by an Osage man Alexander Biette, with the assistance of warriors sent by the leader of Big Hill Town Joseph Pawnee-no-pah-she (Pa-I'n-No-Pa-She, "Governor Joe," or "Big Hill Joe") killed between twenty and thirty Confederates traveling through their reservation. After this, William G. Coffin, southern superintendent of Indian affairs, distributed nearly $3,000 worth of goods to Osage leaders in return for their "loyalty" to the Union. Ponziglione uses the name "Joseph Watcie-cahikie," which refers to the Osage word Wa-tse-Ki-he-ka, meaning "Star Chief," which likewise referred to "Governor Joe." ARCIA, 1863, "Letter from Superintendent Coffin, Reporting Capture by Osages of a Party of Rebels Passing through Their Country," 207; Ponziglione, "The Osages and Father John Schoenmakers," 236–240; and Burns, A History of the Osage People, 553, 557, 575. For Union service, see ARCIA, 1865, "Annual Report of Agent Snow, Neosho Agency," 293; and Ponziglione, "The Osages and Father John Schoenmakers," 221, 254. For Confederate service, see ARCIA, 1861, "Report of P. P. Elder, Agent for the Indians within the Neosho Agency," 37; and ARCIA, 1864, "Report of W. G. Coffin, Superintendent," 306.

153. Rollings, Unaffected by the Gospel, 164–166.

154. White Hair to Snow, February 23, 1866, "Letters Received by the Office of Indian Affairs, 1824–1880: Neosho Agency, 1866–1867," National Archives, Record Group 75, M234 (roll 534, frame 186).

155. ARCIA, 1867, "Annual Report of George C. Snow, Agent, Neosho Agency," 325.

156. ARCIA, 1867, "Annual Report of George C. Snow, Agent, Neosho Agency," 325.

157. ARCIA, 1869, "Annual Report of G. C. Snow, Agent for Osages and Other Tribes," 380–381.

158. ARCIA, 1868, "Report of the Commissioner of Indian Affairs," 5; ARCIA, 1868, "Letter of Secretary of the Interior, Transmitting to Congress Report of A. R. Banks, Special Agent, Dated April 3, 1868," 54; ARCIA, 1868, "Letter of Secretary of the Interior, Transmitting to Congress One from Commissioner of Indian Affairs to Secretary of the Interior, June 24, 1868, with Enclosed Letter of T. Murphy, Superintendent, June 23, 1868," 60; ARCIA, 1868, "Annual Report of G. C. Snow, Agent Neosho Agency," 271; Rollings, Unaffected by the Gospel, 166–168; and James R. Christianson, "A Study of Osage History Prior to 1876" (PhD diss., University of Kansas, 1968), 239–255, 265–266, 275–276.

159. Wolfe, "Settler Colonialism and the Elimination of the Native," 393, 399.

160. Cooke to Arbuckle, January 8, 1839, "Letters Received by the Office of Indian Affairs, 1824–1880: Osage Agency, 1824–1841," National Archives, Record Group 75, M234 (roll 631, frames 734–774); and Agnew, *Fort Gibson: Terminal on the Trail of Tears*, 173–175.

161. Francis La Flesche, "The Osage Tribe: The Rite of Vigil," *Thirty-Ninth Annual Report of the Bureau of American Ethnology* (1917–1918) (1925): 364.

CONCLUSION: RECOVERING THE FEMININE
IN THE OSAGE EMPIRE AND BEYOND

1. Alice C. Fletcher and Francis La Flesche, *The Omaha Tribe*, vol. 1 (Lincoln: University of Nebraska Press, 1992), 141; Francis La Flesche, "The Osage Tribe: Two Versions of the Child-Naming Rite," *Forty-Third Annual Report of the Bureau of American Ethnology* (1925–1926) (1928): 29–30; Francis La Flesche, "The Osage Tribe: Rite of the Chiefs; Sayings of the Ancient Men," *Thirty-Sixth Annual Report of the Bureau of American Ethnology* (1914–1915) (1921): 48–49, 59; and Francis La Flesche, "The Osage Tribe: Rite of the Wa-Xo'-Be," *Forty-Fifth Annual Report of the Bureau of American Ethnology* (1927–1928) (1930): 681–682.

2. La Flesche, "The Osage Tribe: Two Versions of the Child-Naming Rite," 48; Louis F. Burns, *A History of the Osage People* (Tuscaloosa: The University of Alabama Press, 2004), 10, 23–29; Willard H. Rollings, *The Osage: An Ethnohistorical Study of Hegemony on the Prairie-Plains* (Columbia: University of Missouri Press, 1992), 67–69; and Francis La Flesche, "The Osage Tribe: The Rite of Vigil," *Thirty-Ninth Annual Report of the Bureau of American Ethnology* (1917–1918) (1925): 364.

3. John Joseph Mathews, *The Osages: Children of the Middle Waters* (Norman: University of Oklahoma Press, 1961), 156; La Flesche, "The Osage Tribe: The Rite of Vigil," 302; and La Flesche, "The Osage Tribe: Rite of the Wa-Xo'-Be," 681–683.

4. Louis F. Burns, *Osage Indian Customs and Myths* (Tuscaloosa: University of Alabama Press, 1984), 97–98; J. Frederick Fausz, "Becoming 'a Nation of Quakers': The Removal of the Osage Indians from Missouri," *Gateway Heritage: Quarterly Journal of the Missouri Historical Society* 21 (2000): 30–31; J. Frederick Fausz, *Founding St. Louis: First City of the New West* (Charleston, SC: The History Press, 2011), 150–151; La Flesche, "The Osage Tribe: Rite of the Chiefs; Sayings of the Ancient Men," 185–191; and Patrick Wolfe, "Settler Colonialism and the Elimination of the Native," *Journal of Genocide Research* 8, no. 4 (2006): 388–389.

5. Wolfe, "Settler Colonialism and the Elimination of the Native," 388–389, 399–400; Paula Gunn Allen, *The Sacred Hoop: Recovering the Feminine in American Indian Traditions* (Boston: Beacon Press, 1986); Stuart Banner, *How the Indians Lost Their Land: Law*

and *Power on the Frontier* (Cambridge, MA: Belknap Press of Harvard University Press, 2005), 124–126, 139, 144–148; and Burns, *A History of the Osage People*, 243, 292–299.

6. Willard H. Rollings, *Unaffected by the Gospel: The Osage Resistance to the Christian Invasion (1673–1906): A Cultural Victory* (Albuquerque: University of New Mexico Press, 2004), 174; Garrick Alan Bailey, *Changes in Osage Social Organization: 1673–1906*, University of Oregon Anthropological Papers No. 5 (Eugene: University of Oregon Press, 1973), 79–80, 82.

7. Bailey, *Changes in Osage Social Organization*, 85–86.

8. Rollings, *Unaffected by the Gospel*, 182–183.

9. Ibid., 185; La Flesche, "The Osage Tribe: Rite of the Wa-Xo'-Be," 529, 532; Garrick Alan Bailey and Daniel C. Swan, *Art of the Osage* (Seattle: St. Louis Art Museum in association with University of Washington Press, 2004), 138.

10. Jean Dennison, *Colonial Entanglement: Constituting a Twenty-First-Century Osage Nation* (Chapel Hill: University of North Carolina Press, 2012), 95–96.

11. Rollings, *Unaffected by the Gospel*, 174–175; Tai S. Edwards, "Disruption and Disease: The Osage Struggle to Survive in the Nineteenth-Century Trans-Missouri West," *Kansas History: A Journal of the Central Plains* 36, no. 4 (Winter 2013–2014): 233; Dennison, *Colonial Entanglement*, 21–22; and Bailey, *Changes in Osage Social Organization*, 80–83.

12. Rollings, *Unaffected by the Gospel*, 181–182; Terry P. Wilson, "Osage Indian Women During a Century of Change, 1870–1980," *Prologue* 14 (1982): 196.

13. Bailey and Swan, *Art of the Osage*, 138; Burns, *A History of the Osage People*, 405; and Terry P. Wilson, *The Underground Reservation: Osage Oil* (Lincoln: University of Nebraska Press, 1985), 92, 97.

14. Rollings, *Unaffected by the Gospel*, 173; and Wilson, *The Underground Reservation*, 77–82.

15. Bailey and Swan, *Art of the Osage*, 143, 146, 148.

16. Ibid., 143, 148, 157–158, 161; Alice Anne Callahan, *The Osage Ceremonial Dance I'n-Lon-Schka* (Norman: University of Oklahoma Press, 1990), 19–21, 29, 127, 129, 139; Jami C. Powell, "Osage Ribbon Work and the Expression of Osage Nationalism: Re-Imagining Approaches to Material Culture and Nationhood" (MA thesis, University of North Carolina at Chapel Hill, 2014), 37–38, 47–50; and Dennison, *Colonial Entanglement*, 83, 96.

17. Dennison, *Colonial Entanglement*, 7; Garrick Alan Bailey, ed. *The Osage and the Invisible World: From the Works of Francis La Flesche* (Norman: University of Oklahoma Press, 1995), 26; Jean Dennison, "Stitching Osage Governance into the Future," *American Indian Culture and Research Journal* 37, no. 2 (2013): 117; and Powell, "Osage Ribbon Work and the Expression of Osage Nationalism," 7–8, 12–13, 18–20.

18. "Paying for the Drum," *Osage News: The Official Newspaper of the Osage Nation* 5, issue 7 (July 2009): 1, 11–13, accessed July 21, 2017, http://static.osagenews.org.s3 .amazonaws.com/cms_page_media/43/2009_07_OsageNews.pdf; Callahan, *The Osage Ceremonial Dance I'n-Lon-Schka*, 64–65, 115–117; Daniel C. Swan and Jim Cooley, "Chiefs, Brides, and Drum Keepers: Material Culture, Ceremonial Exchange, and Osage Community Life," in *Material Vernaculars: Objects, Images, and Their Social Worlds*, ed. Jason Baird Jackson (Bloomington: Indiana University Press, 2016), 166–168, 170, 173, 175–176, 180–182; Burns, *Osage Indian Customs and Myths*, 151; Mathews, *The Osages*, 356–357; and Wilson, "Osage Indian Women During a Century of Change, 1870–1980," 193. See also the forthcoming Daniel C. Swan and Jim Cooley, *A Giving Heritage: Wedding Clothes and the Osage Community* (Bloomington: University of Indiana Press, tentatively 2018).

19. Dennison, "Stitching Osage Governance into the Future," 117; Swan and Cooley, "Chiefs, Brides, and Drum Keepers," 185–187.

20. Powell, "Osage Ribbon Work and the Expression of Osage Nationalism," 7–8, 19–20, 46–47, 49–50; Dennison, *Colonial Entanglement*, 7; Dennison, "Stitching Osage Governance into the Future," 117; and Nancy Shoemaker, ed., *Negotiators of Change: Historical Perspectives on Native American Women* (New York: Routledge, 1995), 20.

BIBLIOGRAPHY

Ackerman, Lillian A. "Complementary but Equal: Gender Status in the Plateau." In *Women and Power in Native North America*, edited by Laura F. Klein and Lillian A. Ackerman, 75–100. Norman: University of Oklahoma Press, 1995.

———. *A Necessary Balance: Gender and Power among Indians of the Columbia Plateau.* Norman: University of Oklahoma Press, 2003.

Agnew, Brad. *Fort Gibson: Terminal on the Trail of Tears.* Norman: University of Oklahoma Press, 1980.

Akers, Donna L. "Removing the Heart of the Choctaw People: Indian Removal from a Native Perspective." *American Indian Culture and Research Journal* 23, no. 3 (1999): 63–76.

Allen, Paula Gunn. *The Sacred Hoop: Recovering the Feminine in American Indian Traditions.* Boston: Beacon Press, 1986.

Anderson, Gary Clayton. "The Native Peoples of the American West: Genocide or Ethnic Cleansing?" *Western Historical Quarterly* 47, no. 4 (Winter 2016): 407–433.

Annual Reports of the Commissioner of Indian Affairs (ARCIA), 1841–1891. Washington, DC, 1841–1891.

Axtell, James. "Ethnohistory: An Historian's Viewpoint." *Ethnohistory* 26, no. 1 (Winter 1979): 1–13.

———. *The Rise and Fall of the Powhatan Empire: Indians in Seventeenth-Century Virginia.* Williamsburg, VA: Colonial Williamsburg Foundation, 1995.

Bailey, Garrick Alan. *Changes in Osage Social Organization: 1673–1906.* University of Oregon Anthropological Papers No. 5. Eugene: University of Oregon Press, 1973.

Bailey, Garrick, ed. *The Osage and the Invisible World: From the Works of Francis La Flesche,* Civilization of the American Indian series, vol. 217. Norman: University of Oklahoma Press, 1995.j

———, ed. *Traditions of the Osage: Stories Collected and Translated by Francis La Flesche.* Albuquerque: University of New Mexico Press, 2010.

Bailey, Garrick Alan, and Daniel C. Swan. *Art of the Osage.* Seattle: St. Louis Art Museum in association with University of Washington Press, 2004.

Banner, Stuart. *How the Indians Lost Their Land: Law and Power on the Frontier.* Cambridge, MA: Belknap Press of Harvard University Press, 2005.

Barr, Juliana. *Peace Came in the Form of a Woman: Indians and Spaniards in the Texas Borderlands.* Chapel Hill: University of North Carolina Press, 2007.

Barrett, S. M. *Shinkah: The Osage Indian*. Oklahoma City: Harlow Publishing, 1916.

Berry, Brewton, Carl Chapman, and John Mack. "Archaeological Remains of the Osage." *American Antiquity* 10, no. 1 (1944): 1–11.

Blackwood, Evelyn. "Sexuality and Gender in Certain Native American Tribes: The Case of Cross-Gender Females." *Signs* 10, no. 1 (Autumn, 1984): 27–42.

Brackenridge, H. M. *Views of Louisiana: Together with a Journal of a Voyage up the Missouri River, in 1811*. [in English] Nineteenth Century American Literature, Series A: The Ohio Valley. Pittsburgh: Cramer, Spear, and Eichbaum, 1814.

Bradbury, John. *Travels in the Interior of America, in the Years 1809, 1810, and 1811: Including a Description of Upper Louisiana, Together with the States of Ohio, Kentucky, Indiana, and Tennessee, with the Illinois and Western Territories, and Containing Remarks and Observations Useful to Persons Emigrating to Those Countries*. Liverpool: Printed for the author, by Smith and Galway, and published by Sherwood, Neely, and Jones, London, 1817.

Braund, Kathryn E. Holland. *Deerskins and Duffels: The Creek Indian Trade with Anglo-America, 1685–1815*. Lincoln: University of Nebraska Press, 1993.

Bringier, L. "L. Bringier, Esq. On the Region of the Mississippi, Etc." *American Journal of Science and Arts* 3 (1821): 15–46.

Britton, Wiley. "The Grasshopper Plague of 1866 in Kansas." *The Scientific Monthly* 25, no. 6 (December 1927): 540–545.

Brooks, George R. "George C. Sibley's Journal of a Trip to the Salines in 1811." *Missouri Historical Society Bulletin* 21 (April 1965): 167–207.

Burns, Louis F. *A History of the Osage People*. Tuscaloosa: The University of Alabama Press, 2004.

———. *Osage Indian Customs and Myths*. Tuscaloosa: University of Alabama Press, 1984.

Callahan, Alice Anne. *The Osage Ceremonial Dance I'n-Lon-Schka*. Norman: University of Oklahoma Press, 1990.

Cameron, Catherine M. "The Effects of Warfare and Captive-Taking on Indigenous Mortality in Postcontact North America." In *Beyond Germs: Native Depopulation in North America*. Edited by Catherine M. Cameron, Paul Kelton, and Alan C. Swedlund, 174–197. Tucson: University of Arizona Press, 2015.

Cameron, Catherine M., Paul Kelton, and Alan C. Swedlund. "Introduction," In *Beyond Germs: Native Depopulation in North America*. Edited by Catherine M. Cameron, Paul Kelton, and Alan C. Swedlund, 3–15. Tucson: University of Arizona Press, 2015.

Carter, Clarence Edwin, ed. *The Territorial Papers of the United States*, vol. 15. Washington, DC: Government Printing Office, 1951.

Catlin, George. *Letters and Notes on the Manners, Customs, and Condition of the North American Indians*. 3rd ed., vol. 2, New York: Wiley and Putnam, 1844.

Chapman, Carl. "The Indomitable Osage in Spanish Illinois (Upper Louisiana), 1763–1804." In *The Spanish in the Mississippi Valley, 1762–1804*, edited by John Francis McDermott, 286–308. Urbana: University of Illinois Press, 1974.

———. "The Little Osage and Missouri Indian Village Sites, Ca. 1727–1777 A.D." *The Missouri Archaeologist* 21 (December 1959): 1–67.

Chapman, Carl Haley. "Journey to the Land of the Osages, 1835–1836, by Louis Cortambert." *Missouri Historical Society Bulletin* 19 (April 1963): 199–229.

———. "The Origin of the Osage Indian Tribe: An Ethnographical, Historical and Archaeological Study." University of Michigan, 1959.

Chapman, Carl Haley, and Eleanor F. Chapman. *Indians and Archaeology of Missouri*. Missouri Handbook, No 6. Columbia: University of Missouri Press 1964.

Christianson, James R. "A Study of Osage History Prior to 1876." PhD diss., University of Kansas, 1968.

Croffut, W. A., ed. *Fifty Years in Camp and Field: Diary of Major-General Ethan Allen Hitchcock, U.S.A.* New York: G. P. Putnam's Sons, 1909.

D'Altroy, Terence N. "Empires in a Wider World." In *Empires: Perspectives from Archaeology and History*, edited by Susan E. Alcock et al., 125–127. New York: Cambridge University Press, 2001.

Dennison, Jean. *Colonial Entanglement: Constituting a Twenty-First-Century Osage Nation*. Chapel Hill: University of North Carolina Press, 2012.

———. "Stitching Osage Governance into the Future." *American Indian Culture and Research Journal* 37, no. 2 (2013): 115–127.

Devens, Carol. *Countering Colonization: Native American Women and Great Lakes Missions, 1630–1900*. Berkeley: University of California Press, 1992.

Din, Gilbert C., and Abraham Phineas Nasatir. *The Imperial Osages: Spanish-Indian Diplomacy in the Mississippi Valley*. Norman: University of Oklahoma Press, 1983.

Dorsey, James Owen. "An Account of the War Customs of the Osages." *The American Naturalist* 18, no. 2 (February 1884): 113–133.

———. "A Study of Siouan Cults." *Eleventh Annual Report of the Bureau of Ethnology to the Secretary of the Smithsonian Institution, 1889–90* (1894).

DuVal, Kathleen. "'A Good Relationship, & Commerce': The Native Political Economy of the Arkansas River Valley." *Early American Studies* 1, no. 1 (Spring 2003): 61–89.

———. "Indian Intermarriage and Metissage in Colonial Louisiana." *William and Mary Quarterly* 65, no. 2 (April 2008): 267–304.

———. *The Native Ground: Indians and Colonists in the Heart of the Continent*. Philadelphia: University of Pennsylvania Press, 2006.

Eccles, W. J. "The Fur Trade and Eighteenth-Century Imperialism." *William and Mary Quarterly* 40, no. 3 (July 1983): 342–362.

Edwards, Tai S. "Disruption and Disease: The Osage Struggle to Survive in the Nineteenth-Century Trans-Missouri West." *Kansas History: A Journal of the Central Plains* 36, no. 4 (Winter 2013–2014): 218–233.

Edwards, Tai S., and Paul Kelton. "Germs, Genocides, and America's Indigenous Peoples." Forthcoming.

Faragher, John Mack. "'More Motley than Mackinaw': From Ethnic Mixing to Ethnic Cleansing on the Frontier of the Lower Missouri, 1783-1833." In *Contact Points: American Frontiers from the Mohawk Valley to the Mississippi, 1750–1830*, edited by Andrew R. L. Cayton and Fredrika J. Teute, 304–326. Chapel Hill: University of North Carolina Press, 1998.

Farnham, Thomas Jefferson. *Part I of Farnham's Travels in the Great Western Prairies, Etc.*, May 21–October 16, 1839. Early Western Travels, 1748–1846. Edited by Reuben Gold Thwaites. Vol. 28. Cleveland: A. H. Clark, 1904.

Fausz, J. Frederick. "Becoming 'a Nation of Quakers': The Removal of the Osage Indians from Missouri." *Gateway Heritage: Quarterly Journal of the Missouri Historical Society* 21 (Summer 2000): 28–39.

———. *Founding St. Louis: First City of the New West.* Charleston, SC: The History Press, 2011.

Featherstonhaugh, George William. *Excursion through the Slave States, from Washington on the Potomac, to the Frontier of Mexico; with Sketches of Popular Manners and Geological Notices.* New York: Harper and Brothers, 1844.

Fenton, William N. "Indian and White Relations in Eastern North America: A Common Ground for History and Ethnology." In *American Indian and White Relations to 1830: Needs and Opportunities for Study*, 3–27. Chapel Hill: University of North Carolina Press, 1957.

Finley, Chris. "Decolonizing the Queer Native Body (and Recovering the Native Bull-Dyke): Bringing 'Sexy Back' And Out of Natives Studies' Closet." In *Queer Indigenous Studies: Critical Interventions in Theory, Politics, and Literature*, edited by Qwo-Li Driskill, Chris Finley, Brian Joseph Gilley, and Scott Lauria Morgensen, 31–42. Tucson: University of Arizona Press, 2011.

Finney, James Edwin. "The Osages and Their Agency During the Term of Isaac T. Gibson, Quaker Agent." *Chronicles of Oklahoma* 36, no. 4 (1958): 416–428.

———. "Reminiscences of a Trader in the Osage Country." *Chronicles of Oklahoma* 33, no. 2 (1955): 145–158.

Fletcher, Alice C., and Francis La Flesche. *The Omaha Tribe.* Vols. 1–2. Lincoln: University of Nebraska Press, 1992.

Foley, William E., and C. David Rice. *The First Chouteaus: River Barons of Early St. Louis.* Urbana: University of Illinois Press, 1983.

Foreman, Grant. "Our Indian Ambassadors to Europe." *Missouri Historical Society Collections* 5 (February 1928): 108–128.

Fowler, Loretta. *Wives and Husbands: Gender and Age in Southern Arapaho History.* Norman: University of Oklahoma Press, 2010.

Fur, Gunlög. *A Nation of Women: Gender and Colonial Encounters among the Delaware Indians.* Early American Studies. Philadelphia: University of Pennsylvania Press, 2009.

———. "'Some Women Are Wiser Than Some Men': Gender and Native American History." In *Clearing a Path: Theorizing the Past in Native American Studies,* edited by Nancy Shoemaker, 75–103. New York: Routledge, 2002.

Garraghan, Gilbert J. *Chapters in Frontier History: Research Studies in the Making of the West.* Milwaukee: Bruce Publishing, 1934.

———. *The Jesuits of the Middle United States.* Vol. 2. New York: America Press, 1938.

Graves, W. W. *Life and Letters of Fathers Ponziglione, Schoenmakers, and Other Early Jesuits at Osage Mission. Sketch of St. Francis' Church. Life of Mother Bridget.* [in English] St. Paul, KS: W. W. Graves, 1916.

Greene, Jack P. "Colonial History and National History: Reflections on a Continuing Problem." *William and Mary Quarterly* 64, no. 2 (April 2007): 235–250.

Gregg, Josiah. Part 2 of *Gregg's Commerce of the Prairies, 1831–1839.* Early Western Travels, 1748–1846. Edited by Reuben Gold Thwaites. Vol. 20. Cleveland: A. H. Clark, 1904.

Gregg, Josiah, and Max L. Moorhead, eds. *Commerce of the Prairies.* Norman: University of Oklahoma Press, 1954.

Hämäläinen, Pekka. *The Comanche Empire.* New Haven, CT: Yale University Press, 2008.

Hennepin, Louis, and Reuben Gold Thwaites, eds. *A New Discovery of a Vast Country in America.* Vol. 1. [in English] Chicago: A. C. McClurg, 1903.

Herdt, Gilbert. "The Dilemmas of Desire: From 'Berdache' To Two-Spirit." In *Two-Spirit People: Native American Gender Identity, Sexuality, and Spirituality,* edited by Sue-Ellen Jacobs, Wesley Thomas, and Sabine Lang, 276–283. Urbana: University of Illinois Press, 1997.

Hixson, Walter L. *American Settler Colonialism: A History.* New York: Palgrave Macmillan, 2013.

Hoig, Stan. *The Chouteaus: First Family of the Fur Trade.* Albuquerque: University of New Mexico Press, 2008.

"Home Proceedings: Great Osage Mission." *American Missionary Register* 2, no. 11 (May 1822): 433–437.

"Home Proceedings: Great Osage Mission." *American Missionary Register* 2, no. 12 (June 1822): 491–498.

"Home Proceedings: Great Osage Mission." *American Missionary Register* 3, no. 2 (August 1822): 47–50.

"Home Proceedings: Great Osage Mission." *American Missionary Register* 3, no. 3 (September 1822): 90–95.

"Home Proceedings: Great Osage Mission." *American Missionary Register* 3, no. 4 (October 1822): 144–148.

"Home Proceedings: Great Osage Mission." *American Missionary Register* 3, no. 5 (November 1822): 185–188.

"Home Proceedings: Great Osage Mission." *American Missionary Register* 3, no. 6 (December 1822): 211–214.

"Home Proceedings: Great Osage Mission." *American Missionary Register* 4, no. 2 (February 1823): 43–45.

"Home Proceedings: Great Osage Mission." *American Missionary Register* 4, no. 7 (July 1823): 204–207.

"Home Proceedings: Great Osage Mission." *American Missionary Register* 4, no. 9 (September 1823): 275–276.

"Home Proceedings: Great Osage Mission." *American Missionary Register* 4, no. 10 (October 1823): 305–307.

"Home Proceedings: Great Osage Mission." *American Missionary Register* 4, no. 12 (December 1823): 372–373.

"Home Proceedings: Great Osage Mission." *American Missionary Register* 5, no. 2 (February 1824): 39–49.

"Home Proceedings: Great Osage Mission." *American Missionary Register* 5, no. 3 (March 1824): 81–82.

"Home Proceedings: Great Osage Mission." *American Missionary Register* 5, no. 4 (April 1824): 110–117.

"Home Proceedings: Great Osage Mission." *American Missionary Register* 5, no. 5 (May 1824): 140–144.

"Home Proceedings: Great Osage Mission." *American Missionary Register* 5, no. 6 (June 1824): 179–180.

"Home Proceedings: Great Osage Mission." *American Missionary Register* 5, no. 7 (July 1824): 211–213.

"Home Proceedings: Great Osage Mission." *American Missionary Register* 5, no. 9 (September 1824): 271–277.

"Home Proceedings: Great Osage Mission." *American Missionary Register* 5, no. 12 (December 1824): 364–366.

"Home Proceedings: Harmony Mission." *American Missionary Register* 6, no. 5 (May 1825): 146–147.

"Home Proceedings: Journal of Mr. Pixley." *American Missionary Register* 6, no. 7 (July 1825): 217–218.

"Home Proceedings: Journal of the Union Mission." *American Missionary Register* 6, no. 7 (July 1825): 214–217.

"Home Proceedings: Letters from the Superintendent of Indian Trade." *American Missionary Register* 1 (August 1820): 53–57.

"Home Proceedings: Missionary Establishments." *American Missionary Register* 6, no. 1 (January 1825): 18–20.

"Home Proceedings: Union Mission." *American Missionary Register* 2, no. 2 (August 1821): 58–59.

"Home Proceedings: Union Mission." *American Missionary Register* 2, no. 3 (September 1821): 106–116.

"Home Proceedings: Union Mission." *American Missionary Register* 2, no. 5 (November 1821): 181–185.

"Home Proceedings: Union Mission." *American Missionary Register* 2, no. 6 (December 1821): 221–224.

"Home Proceedings: Union Mission." *American Missionary Register* 2, no. 12 (June 1822): 488–491.

"Home Proceedings: Union Mission." *American Missionary Register* 3, no. 1 (July 1822): 9–17.

"Home Proceedings: Union Mission." *American Missionary Register* 3, no. 4 (October 1822): 138–144.

"Home Proceedings: Union Mission." *American Missionary Register* 3, no. 5 (November 1822): 180–185.

"Home Proceedings: Union Mission." *American Missionary Register* 4, no. 1 (January 1823): 3–8.

"Home Proceedings: Union Mission." *American Missionary Register* 4, no. 2 (Februray 1823): 39–43.

"Home Proceedings: Union Mission." *American Missionary Register* 4, no. 3 (March 1823): 73–75.

"Home Proceedings: Union Mission." *American Missionary Register* 4, no. 5 (May 1823): 135–139.

"Home Proceedings: Union Mission." *American Missionary Register* 4, no. 6 (June 1823): 176–178.

"Home Proceedings: Union Mission." *American Missionary Register* 4, no. 7 (July 1823): 201–204.

"Home Proceedings: Union Mission." *American Missionary Register* 4, no. 8 (August 1823): 234–237.

"Home Proceedings: Union Mission." *American Missionary Register* 4, no. 9 (September 1823): 271–274.

"Home Proceedings: Union Mission." *American Missionary Register* 4, no. 10 (October 1823): 303–305.

"Home Proceedings: Union Mission." *American Missionary Register* 4, no. 12 (December 1823): 368–372.

"Home Proceedings: Union Mission." *American Missionary Register* 5, no. 1 (January 1824): 20–28.

"Home Proceedings: Union Mission." *American Missionary Register* 5, no. 2 (February 1824): 36–39.

"Home Proceedings: Union Mission." *American Missionary Register* 5, no. 3 (March 1824): 75–81.

"Home Proceedings: Union Mission." *American Missionary Register* 5, no. 4 (April 1824): 109–110.

"Home Proceedings: Union Mission." *American Missionary Register* 5, no. 7 (July 1824): 206–211.

"Home Proceedings: Union Mission." *American Missionary Register* 5, no. 8 (August 1824): 230–232.

"Home Proceedings: Union Mission." *American Missionary Register* 5, no. 11 (November 1824): 330–333.

"Home Proceedings: Union Mission." *American Missionary Register* 5, no. 12 (December 1824): 362–364.

"Home Proceedings: Union Mission." *American Missionary Register* 6, no. 2 (February 1825): 45–49.

"Home Proceedings: Union Mission." *American Missionary Register* 6, no. 3 (March 1825): 87–89.

"Home Proceedings: Union Mission." *American Missionary Register* 6, no. 4 (April 1825): 119–120.

"Home Proceedings: Union Mission." *American Missionary Register* 6, no. 8 (August 1825): 242–244.

"Home Proceedings: Union Mission." *American Missionary Register* 6, no. 9 (September 1825): 271–272.

Houck, Louis, ed. *The Spanish Regime in Missouri.* Vol. 1. Chicago: R. R. Donnelley & Sons, 1909.

Hunter, Andrea A. "An Ethnoarchaeological Analysis of the Women's Role in Osage Society." MA thesis, University of Missouri, 1985.

Hunter, John D. *Manners and Customs of Several Indian Tribes Located West of the Mississippi: Including Some Account of the Soil, Climate, and Vegetable Productions, and* the *Indian Materia Medica: To Which Is Prefixed the History of the Author's Life During a Residence of Several Years among Them.* Philadelphia: J. Maxwell, 1823.

Hurtado, Albert L. "Sex, Gender, Culture, and a Great Event: The California Gold Rush." *Pacific Historical Review* 68, no. 1 (1999): 1–19.

"Indian Mode of Life in Missouri and Kansas: George C. Sibley to Thomas L. Mckenney, October 1, 1820." *Missouri Historical Review* 9 (1914): 43–49.

"Introduction." In *Queer Indigenous Studies: Critical Interventions in Theory, Politics, and Literature*, edited by Qwo-Li Driskill, Chris Finley, Brian Joseph Gilley, and Scott Lauria Morgensen, 1–28. Tucson: University of Arizona Press, 2011.

Irving, Washington. *A Tour on the Prairies.* Paris: A. and W. Galignani 1835.

Irving, Washington, William Peterfield Trent, and George S. Hellman. *The Journals of Washington Irving (Hitherto Unpublished).* Vol. 3. Boston: The Bibliophile Society, 1919.

Isern, Thomas D. "Exploration and Diplomacy: George Champlin Sibley's Report to William Clark, 1811." *Missouri Historical Review* 73 (October 1978): 85–102.

Jacobs, Sue-Ellen, Wesley Thomas, and Sabine Lang. "Introduction." In *Two-Spirit People: Native American Gender Identity, Sexuality, and Spirituality*, edited by Sue-Ellen Jacobs, Wesley Thomas and Sabine Lang, 1–18. Urbana: University of Illinois Press, 1997.

James, Edwin. *Part 2 of James's Account of S. H. Long's Expedition, 1819–1820.* Early Western Travels, 1748–1846. Edited by Reuben Gold Thwaites. Vol. 15. Cleveland: A. H. Clark, 1905.

———. *Part 3 of James's Account of S. H. Long's Expedition, 1819–1820.* Early Western Travels, 1748–1846. Edited by Reuben Gold Thwaites. Vol. 16. Cleveland: A. H. Clark, 1905.

Jesuits, and Reuben Gold Thwaites. *The Jesuit Relations and Allied Documents: Travels and Explorations of the Jesuit Missionaries in New France, 1610–1791.* Vol. 64. New York: Pageant Book, 1959.

Jeter, Marvin D. "From Prehistory through Protohistory to Ethnohistory in and near the Northern Lower Mississippi Valley." In *The Transformation of the Southeastern Indians, 1540–1760*, edited by Robbie Franklyn Ethridge and Charles M. Hudson, 177–223. Jackson: University Press of Mississippi, 2002.

"Journal of the Western Missions, vol. 2: January 4, 1869–January 9, 1871." Edited by Eugene Grabner. St. Louis: Midwest Jesuit Archives, Unpublished Manuscript.

"Journal of the Western Missions, vol. 3: January 16, 1871–July 1, 1872." Edited by Eugene Grabner. St. Louis: Midwest Jesuit Archives, Unpublished Manuscript.

"Journal of the Western Missions, vol. 4: December 31, 1872–December 31, 1873." Edited by Eugene Grabner. St. Louis: Midwest Jesuit Archives, Unpublished Manuscript.

"Journal of the Western Missions, vol. 5: July 1, 1874–December 13, 1876." Edited by Eugene Grabner. St. Louis: Midwest Jesuit Archives, Unpublished Manuscript.

Kappler, Charles J., ed. *Indian Affairs: Laws and Treaties, vol. 2 (Treaties)*. Washington, DC: Government Printing Office, 1904.

Kehoe, Alice B. "Blackfoot Persons." In *Women and Power in Native North America*, edited by Laura F. Klein and Lillian A. Ackerman, 113–125. Norman: University of Oklahoma Press, 1995.

———. "Osage Texts and Cahokia Data." In *Ancient Objects and Sacred Realms: Interpretations of Mississippian Iconography*, edited by F. Kent Reilly and James Garber, 246–261. Austin: University of Texas Press, 2007.

———. "The Shackles of Tradition." In *The Hidden Half: Studies of Plains Indian Women*, edited by Patricia Albers and Beatrice Medicine, 53–73. Lanham, MD: University Press of America, 1983.

Kelton, Paul. *Cherokee Medicine, Colonial Germs: An Indigenous Nation's Fight against Smallpox, 1518–1824*. Norman: University of Oklahoma Press, 2015.

———. *Epidemics and Enslavement: Biological Catastrophe in the Native Southeast, 1492–1715*. Lincoln: University of Nebraska Press, 2007.

Kidwell, Clara Sue. "Indian Women as Cultural Mediators." *Ethnohistory* 39, no. 2 (Spring 1992): 97–107.

Kinnaird, Lawrence, ed. *Spain in the Mississippi Valley, 1765–1794: Part 1, the Revolutionary Period, 1765–1781*, Annual Report of the American Historical Association for the Year 1945. Washington, DC: US Government Printing Office, 1949.

———, ed. *Spain in the Mississippi Valley, 1765–1794: Part 3, Problems of Frontier Defense, 1792–1794*, Annual Report of the American Historical Association for the Year 1945. Washington, DC: US Government. Printing Office, 1946.

Klein, Laura F., and Lillian A. Ackerman. "Introduction." In *Women and Power in Native North America*, edited by Laura F. Klein and Lillian A. Ackerman, 3–16. Norman: University of Oklahoma Press, 1995.

Knack, Martha C. "The Dynamics of Southern Paiute Women's Roles." In *Women and Power in Native North America*, edited by Laura F. Klein and Lillian A. Ackerman, 146–158. Norman: University of Oklahoma Press, 1995.

Kohn, Margaret. "Colonialism." In *The Stanford Encyclopedia of Philosophy*, edited by Edward N. Zalta. Accessed May 11, 2017. https://plato.stanford.edu/archives /spr2014/entries/colonialism/.

La Flesche, Francis. "Ceremonies and Rituals of the Osage." *Smithsonian Miscellaneous Collections* 63, no. 8 (1914): 66–69.

———. "A Dictionary of the Osage Language." [In English] Smithsonian Institution.

Bureau of American Ethnology. Bulletin 109. Washington, DC: Government Printing Office, 1932.

———. "Ethnology of the Osage Indians." *Smithsonian Miscellaneous Collections* 76, no. 10 (1924): 104–107.

———. "Osage Marriage Customs." *American Anthropologist* 14, no. 1 (January–March 1912): 127–130.

———. "The Osage Tribe: Rite of the Chiefs; Sayings of the Ancient Men." [In English] *Thirty-Sixth Annual Report of the Bureau of American Ethnology (1914–1915)* (1921): 37–604.

———. "The Osage Tribe: Rite of the Wa-Xo'-Be." *Forty-Fifth Annual Report of the Bureau of American Ethnology (1927–1928)* (1930): 529–833.

———. "The Osage Tribe: The Rite of Vigil." *Thirty-Ninth Annual Report of the Bureau of American Ethnology (1917–1918)* (1925): 37–630.

———. "The Osage Tribe: Two Versions of the Child-Naming Rite." *Forty-Third Annual Report of the Bureau of American Ethnology (1925–1926)* (1928): 29–164.

———. "Researches among the Osage." *Smithsonian Miscellaneous Collections* 70, no. 2 (1919): 110–113.

———. "Right and Left in Osage Ceremonies." In *Holmes Anniversary Volume: Anthropological Essays,* 278–287. Washington, DC: J. W. Bryan Press, 1916.

———. "The Symbolic Man of the Osage Tribe." *Art and Archaeology* 9 (February 1920): 68–72.

———. "Tribal Rites of Osage Indians." *Smithsonian Miscellaneous Collections* 68, no. 12 (1918): 84–90.

———. "War Ceremony and Peace Ceremony of the Osage Indians." *Bureau of American Ethnology Bulletin,* No. 101. Washington, DC: Government Printing Office, 1939.

Lang, Sabine. *Men as Women, Women as Men: Changing Gender in Native American Cultures.* Translated by John L. Vantine. Austin: University of Texas Press, 1998.

Lansing, Michael. "Plains Indian Women and Interracial Marriage in the Upper Missouri Trade, 1804–1868." *Western Historical Quarterly* 31, no. 4 (Winter 2000): 413–433.

La Vere, David. *Contrary Neighbors: Southern Plains and Removed Indians in Indian Territory.* Norman: University of Oklahoma Press, 2000.

Leavelle, Tracy Neal. "'We Will Make It Our Own Place': Agriculture and Adaptation at the Grand Ronde Reservation, 1856–1887." *American Indian Quarterly* 22, no. 4 (Fall 1998): 433–456.

"Letter Book of the Arkansas Trading House, 1805–1810." *Records of the Office of Indian Trade.* National Archives, Record Group 75.

"Letters Received by the Office of Indian Affairs, 1824–1880: Osage Agency, 1824–1841." National Archives, Record Group 75.

Lewis, Anna. "Du Tisne's Expedition into Oklahoma." *Chronicles of Oklahoma* 3, no. 4 (December 1925): 319–323.

Maltz, Daniel, and JoAllyn Archambault. "Gender and Power in Native North America: Concluding Remarks." In *Women and Power in Native North America*, edited by Laura F. Klein and Lillian A. Ackerman, 230–249. Norman: University of Oklahoma Press, 1995.

Mathews, John Joseph. *The Osages: Children of the Middle Waters*. Norman: University of Oklahoma Press, 1961.

McCoy, Isaac. *History of Baptist Indian Missions: Embracing Aboriginal Tribes; Their Settlement within the Indian Territory, and Their Future Prospects*. Washington, DC: William M. Morrison, 1840.

McDonagh, Josephine. "Infanticide and the Boundaries of Culture from Hume to Arnold." In *Inventing Maternity: Politics, Science, and Literature, 1650–1865*, edited by Susan C. Greenfield and Carol Barash, 215–237. Lexington: University Press of Kentucky, 1999.

McHugh, Tom. *The Time of the Buffalo*. New York: Alfred A. Knopf, 1972.

Medicine, Beatrice. "'Warrior Women'—Sex Role Alternatives for Plains Indian Women." In *The Hidden Half: Studies of Plains Indian Women*, edited by Patricia Albers and Beatrice Medicine, 267–280. Lanham, MD: University Press of America, 1983.

Merrell, James H. "Second Thoughts on Colonial Historians and American Indians." *William and Mary Quarterly* 69, 3 (July 2012): 451–512.

Miller, Robert J. *Native America, Discovered and Conquered: Thomas Jefferson, Lewis & Clark, and Manifest Destiny*. Westport, CT: Praeger, 2006.

Miller, Susan A. "Native Historians Write Back: The Indigenous Paradigm in American Indian Historiography." In *Native Historians Write Back: Decolonizing American Indian History*, edited by Susan A. Miller and James Riding In, 25–40. Lubbock: Texas Tech University Press, 2011.

Miner, H. Craig, and William E. Unrau. *The End of Indian Kansas: A Study of Cultural Revolution, 1854–1871*. Lawrence: Regents Press of Kansas, 1978.

"Miscellanies: The Arkansas Territory." *American Missionary Register* 1, no. 7 (1821): 286–287.

"Missions on the American Continents and to the Islands of the Pacific, 1811–1919 (ABC 18–19), 1830–1837." In *American Board of Commissioners for Foreign Missions Archives, 1810–1961 (ABC 1–91)*. Houghton Library, Harvard University, Microfilm.

Morrison, T. F. "Mission Neosho: The First Kansas Mission." *Kansas Historical Quarterly* 4, no. 3 (August 1935): 227–234.

Morse, Jedidiah. *A Report to the Secretary of War of the United States, on Indian Affairs, Comprising a Narrative of a Tour Performed in the Summer of 1820.* [in English] New Haven, CT: Converse, 1822.

Mun, Jules Louis Renâe de, Nettie Harney Beauregard, Thomas Maitland Marshall, and Pierre Alexandre de Mun. *Journals of Jules De Mun.* St. Louis, 1928.

Nasatir, Abraham Phineas, ed. *Before Lewis and Clark: Documents Illustrating the History of the Missouri, 1785–1804.* Vols. 1–2. St. Louis: St. Louis Historical Documents Foundation, 1952.

Nett, Betty R. "Historical Changes in the Osage Kinship System." *Southwestern Journal of Anthropology* 8, no. 2 (1952): 164–181.

Newman, Tillie Karns. *The Black Dog Trail.* Boston: Christopher Publishing House, 1957.

Nuttall, Thomas. *A Journal of Travels into the Arkansa Territory During the Year 1819. With Occasional Observations on the Manners of the Aborigines.* Philadelphia: Thos. H. Palmer, 1821.

"Osage Indians." *Missionary Herald* 22, no. 9 (September 1826): 267–271.

"Osage Indians: Account of Their Conditions, Manners, Etc." *Missionary Herald* 23, no. 5 (May 1827): 146–150.

"Osages." *Missionary Herald* 22, no. 4 (April 1826): 116–118.

"Osages." *Missionary Herald* 27, no. 11 (November 1831): 354–355.

"Osages." *Missionary Herald* 29, no. 2 (February 1833): 61–62.

"Osages." *Missionary Herald* 30, no. 1 (January 1834): 22–24.

"Osages: Extract from a Letter of Mr. Montgomery, Dated Union, Dec. 27, 1831." *Missionary Herald* 28, no. 8 (August 1832): 257–259.

"Osages: Extracts from the Journal of Mr. Montgomery." *Missionary Herald* 30, no. 1 (January 1834): 22–24.

"Osages: Journal of Mr. Vaill, During a Preaching Tour." *Missionary Herald* 29, no. 10 (October 1833): 366–371.

"Osages: Miscellaneous Communications Respecting the Mission." *Missionary Herald* 25, no. 4 (April 1829): 123–126.

"Osages: Report of the Station at Union, June 1, 1830." *Missionary Herald* 26, no. 9 (September 1830): 285–288.

"Osages: Their Character, Manners, and Condition." *Missionary Herald* 24, no. 3 (March 1828): 78–81.

Parks, Ronald D. *The Darkest Period: The Kanza Indians and Their Last Homeland, 1846–1873.* Norman: University of Oklahoma Press, 2014.

Patterson, Victoria D. "Evolving Gender Roles in Pomo Society." In *Women and Power in Native North America,* edited by Laura F. Klein and Lillian A. Ackerman, 126–145. Norman: University of Oklahoma Press, 1995.

"Paying for the Drum." *Osage News: The Official Newspaper of the Osage Nation* 5, issue 7 (July 2009): 1, 11–13. Accessed July 21, 2017. http://static.osagenews.org.s3 .amazonaws.com/cms_page_media/43/2009_07_OsageNews.pdf.

Pease, Theodore Calvin, and Ernestine Jenison. Illinois on the Eve of the Seven Years' War, 1747–1755, Collections of the Illinois State Historical Library. [in English] Vol. 29. Springfield, IL. Trustees of the State Historical Library, 1940.

Perdue, Theda. *Cherokee Women: Gender and Culture Change, 1700–1835*. Lincoln: University of Nebraska Press, 1998.

Perdue, Theda, and Michael D. Green. *The Cherokee Removal: A Brief History with Documents*. 2nd ed. Boston/New York: Bedford/St. Martin's, 2005.

———. *North American Indians: A Very Short Introduction*. New York: Oxford University Press, 2010.

Pesantubbee, Michelene E. *Choctaw Women in a Chaotic World: The Clash of Cultures in the Colonial Southeast*. Albuquerque: University of New Mexico Press, 2005.

Pike, Zebulon Montgomery. *The Expeditions of Zebulon Montgomery Pike, to Headwaters of the Mississippi River, through Louisiana Territory, and in New Spain, During the Years 1805–6–7*. Edited by Elliott Coues. Vol. 2. New York: F. P. Harper, 1895.

Pike, Zebulon Montgomery, and Donald Dean Jackson. *The Journals of Zebulon Montgomery Pike, with Letters and Related Documents*. The American Exploration and Travel Series, vols. 1–2, Norman: University of Oklahoma Press, 1966.

Ponziglione, Paul Mary. "The Osages and Father John Schoenmakers." Edited by J. Daly Lowrie and Garrick Alan Bailey. St. Louis: Midwest Jesuit Archives, Unpublished Manuscript.

Post, Susan. "Species Spotlight: American Lotus." *Illinois Natural History Survey Report* (July–August 1997).

Powell, Jami C. "Osage Ribbon Work and the Expression of Osage Nationalism: Re-Imagining Approaches to Material Culture and Nationhood." MA thesis, University of North Carolina at Chapel Hill, 2014.

"Reports of Societies: Great Osage Mission." *American Missionary Register* 2, no. 12 (June 1822): 470–475.

"Reports of Societies: Great Osage Mission." *American Missionary Register* 4, no. 6 (June 1823): 163–165.

"Reports of Societies: Third Report of the United Foreign Missionary Society." *American Missionary Register* 1 (July 1820): 14–22.

"Reports of Societies: Union Mission." *American Missionary Register* 2, no. 12 (June 1822): 465–470.

"Reports of Societies: Union Mission." *American Missionary Register* 4, no. 6 (June 1823): 161–163.

Rollings, Willard Hughes. *The Osage: An Ethnohistorical Study of Hegemony on the Prairie-Plains.* Columbia: University of Missouri Press, 1992.

———. "Prairie Hegemony: An Ethnohistorical Study of the Osage, from Early Times to 1840." PhD diss., Texas Tech University, 1983.

———. *Unaffected by the Gospel: The Osage Resistance to the Christian Invasion (1673–1906): A Cultural Victory.* Albuquerque: University of New Mexico Press, 2004.

Rosaldo, Michelle Zimbalist, and Louise Lamphere, eds. *Woman, Culture, and Society.* Stanford, CA: Stanford University Press, 1974.

Roscoe, Will. *Changing Ones: Third and Fourth Genders in Native North America.* 1st ed. New York: St. Martin's Press, 1998.

Rushforth, Brett. *Bonds of Alliance: Indigenous and Atlantic Slaveries in New France.* Chapel Hill: Unveristy of North Carolina Press, 2012.

———. "'A Little Flesh We Offer You': The Origins of Indian Slavery in New France." *William and Mary Quarterly* 60, no. 4 (2003): 777–808.

Scott, Joan W. "Gender: A Useful Category of Historical Analysis." *American Historical Review* 91, no. 5 (December 1986): 1053–1075.

Sharp, Henry S. "Asymmetric Equals: Women and Men among the Chipewyan." In *Women and Power in Native North America*, edited by Laura F. Klein and Lillian A. Ackerman, 46–74. Norman: University of Oklahoma Press, 1995.

Sheehan, Bernard W. *Seeds of Extinction: Jeffersonian Philanthropy and the American Indian.* Chapel Hill: University of North Carolina Press, 1973.

Shoemaker, Nancy, ed. *Negotiators of Change: Historical Perspectives on Native American Women.* New York: Routledge, 1995.

Sibley, Major George C. "Extracts from the Diary of Major Sibley." *Chronicles of Oklahoma* 5, no. 2 (June 1927): 196–218.

Smet, Pierre-Jean de. *Western Missions and Missionaries: A Series of Letters.* New York: James B. Kirker, Late Edward Dunigan and Brother, 1863.

Smith, Andrea. "Queer Theory and Native Studies: The Heteronormativity of Settler Colonialism." In *Queer Indigenous Studies: Critical Interventions in Theory, Politics, and Literature*, edited by Qwo-Li Driskill, Chris Finley, Brian Joseph Gilley and Scott Lauria Morgensen, 43–65. Tucson: University of Arizona Press, 2011.

Smith, Linda Tuhiwai. *Decolonizing Methodologies: Research and Indigenous Peoples.* New York: Zed Books, 1999.

Smith, Thomas Edward. "Who We Were, Is Not Who We Are: Wa.Zha.Zhe Representations, 1960–2010." MA thesis, University of Kansas, 2013.

Spector, Janet D. "Male/Female Task Differentiation among the Hidatsa: Toward the Development of an Archeological Approach to the Study of Gender." In *The Hidden Half: Studies of Plains Indian Women*, edited by Patricia Albers and Beatrice Medicine, 77–99. Lanham, MD: University Press of America, 1983.

Stewart, Watson. *Personal Memoirs of Watson Stewart*. Manuscript Collections, Miscellaneous Collections: Watson Stewart. Topeka, KS. Kansas State Historical Society, 1904.

Sundstrom, Linea. "Steel Awls for Stone Age Plainswomen: Rock Art, Religion, and the Hide Trade on the Northern Plains." *Plains Anthropologist* 47, no. 181 (May 2002): 99–119.

Surrey, Nancy Maria Miller. *The Commerce of Louisiana During the French Régime, 1699–1763*. New York: Columbia University Press, 1916.

Swan, Daniel C., and Jim Cooley, "Chiefs, Brides, and Drum Keepers: Material Culture, Ceremonial Exchange, and Osage Community Life." In *Material Vernaculars: Objects, Images, and Their Social Worlds*, edited by Jason Baird Jackson, 160–193. Bloomington: Indiana University Press, 2016.

Taylor, Alan. "Land and Liberty on the Post-Revolutionary Frontier." In *Devising Liberty: Preserving and Creating Freedom in the New American Republic*, edited by David Thomas Konig, 81–108. Stanford, CA: Stanford University Press, 1995.

Thorne, Tanis C. "The Chouteau Family and the Osage Trade: A Generational Study." *Rendezvous: Selected Papers of the Fourth North American Fur Trade Conference*, 1981, edited by Thomas C. Buckley (1984): 109–119.

———. *The Many Hands of My Relations: French and Indians on the Lower Missouri*. Columbia: University of Missouri Press, 1996.

Tinker, George E. *Missionary Conquest: The Gospel and Native American Cultural Genocide*. Minneapolis: Fortress Press, 1993.

Tixier, Victor, John Francis McDermott, and Albert Jacques Salvan. *Tixier's Travels on the Osage Prairies*. Norman: University of Oklahoma Press, 1940.

Tracy, Valerie. "The Indian in Transition: The Neosho Agency 1850–1861." *The Chronicles of Oklahoma* 48, no. 2 (1970): 164–183.

Tuttle, Sarah. *Letters on the Chickasaw and Osage Missions*. [in English] 2nd ed. Boston: Massachusetts Sabbath School Society, 1833.

United Nations. "Convention on the Prevention and Punishment of the Crime of Genocide." Accessed July 17, 2017. www.un.org/en/genocideprevention /documents/atrocity-crimes/Doc.1_Convention on the Prevention and Punishment of the Crime of Genocide.pdf.

Usner, Daniel H., Jr. *Indians, Settlers & Slaves in a Frontier Exchange Economy: The Lower Mississippi Valley before 1783*. Chapel Hill: University of North Carolina Press, 1992.

Utley, Robert M. *The Indian Frontier of the American West, 1846–1890*. Albuquerque: University of New Mexico Press, 1984.

Van Kirk, Sylvia. *Many Tender Ties: Women in Fur-Trade Society, 1670–1870*. Norman: University of Oklahoma Press, 1983.

Wallace, Anthony F. C. *Jefferson and the Indians: The Tragic Fate of the First Americans.* Cambridge, MA: Belknap Press of Harvard University Press, 1999.

Warrior, Robert Allen. *Tribal Secrets: Recovering American Indian Intellectual Traditions.* Minneapolis: University of Minnesota Press, 1995.

W. B. Royall to R. Jones, June 21, 1848. Manuscript Collections, Miscellaneous Collections: W. B. Royall. Topeka, KS. Kansas State Historical Society.

Wedel, Mildred Mott. "Claude-Charles Dutisne: A Review of His 1719 Journeys (Parts 1 and 2)." *Great Plains Journal* 12, no. 1–2 (Fall 1972–Spring 1973): 5–25, 147–173.

White, Richard. *The Middle Ground: Indians, Empires, and Republics in the Great Lakes Region, 1650–1815.* Cambridge: Cambridge University Press, 1991.

———. "The Winning of the West: The Expansion of the Western Sioux in the Eighteenth and Nineteenth Centuries." *Journal of American History* 65, no. 2 (September 1978): 319–343.

Wiegers, Robert P. "A Proposal for Indian Slave Trading in the Mississippi Valley and Its Impact on the Osage." *Plains Anthropologist* 33, no. 120 (May 1988): 187–202.

Will, George F., and George E. Hyde. *Corn among the Indians of the Upper Missouri.* St. Louis: William Harvey Miner, 1917.

Williams, Walter L. *The Spirit and the Flesh: Sexual Diversity in American Indian Culture.* Boston: Beacon Press, 1986.

Williams, W. D., and Louis Bringier. "Louis Bringier and His Description of Arkansas in 1812." *The Arkansas Historical Quarterly* 48, no. 2 (1989): 108–136.

Wilson, Terry P. "Osage Indian Women During a Century of Change, 1870–1980." *Prologue* 14 (1982): 184–201.

———. *The Underground Reservation: Osage Oil.* Lincoln: University of Nebraska Press, 1985.

Wishart, David. "The Roles and Status of Men and Women in Nineteenth Century Omaha and Pawnee Societies: Postmodernist Uncertainties and Empirical Evidence." *American Indian Quarterly* 19, no. 4 (Autumn 1995): 509–518.

Wolfe, Patrick. "Settler Colonialism and the Elimination of the Native." *Journal of Genocide Research* 8, no. 4 (2006): 387–409.

The Woodstock Letters: A Record of Current Events and Historical Notes Connected with the Colleges and Missions of the Society of Jesus. Vols. 1–18. Woodstock, MD: Woodstock College Press, 1872–1889.

Wyckoff, Eliza J. *Reminiscences of Early Days in Kansas.* Manuscript Collections, Miscellaneous Collections: Jane Baude. Topeka, KS. Kansas State Historical Society, March 1, 1918.

mission schools and, 84–85, 115
multiple genders, 4, 18–21
and resistance to colonization, 132
value of analysis centered on, 3
women adopting men's roles, 19–20,
    33, 104, 127
See also men's roles in Osage culture;
    women's roles in Osage culture
Gibson, Isaac, 108–109
graves, Osage, settlers' pillaging of, 109
Great Elk, 15
Great Osage
    homeland, 39, 41, 66, 66
    Little Osage rejoining of, 66
    removal to Kansas, 92, 98
    territory in Kansas, 94, 99
    and trade in furs and hides, 46
    and Treaty of 1808, 64
"Green-Corn Dance," 27–28, 43
Gregg, Josiah, 68

"half-breeds." See mixed-bloods
Hämäläinen, Pekka, 5, 102–103,
    135n13
Harmony Mission, 73, 80, 84, 86–87,
    160n43
Harrison, William Henry, 63–64,
    156n9
Hearing of the Sayings of the Ancient
    Men (Ni'-ki Non-k'-on), 21, 22
Hon-be'-do-ka (Wakon'dahionbe), 10,
    22–23, 31
Hon'-ga moiety, 17, 21–22
Hopefield agricultural settlement, 78,
    83–84, 87–88, 160n43
horses
    acquisition through raids, 48
    arrival in Osage empire, 42
    biannual buffalo hunts and, 46–47
    breeding of, Osage gender
        construction and, 48, 60

limited use in warfare, 48
and marriage gift exchange, 56
as measure of wealth, 47–48, 103, 110,
    121–122
number owned by Osage
    (1830s–1840s), 103
Osage care for, 103
Osage word for, 42, 147n13
settlers' theft of, from Kansas
    reservation, 109–110
as trade item, 47, 60, 103, 121–122
hospitality
    and food sharing, 75
    meals for guests, women's role in, 29,
        36
    and older men as hosts, 75–77
Hunter, Andrea, 9, 45
Hunter, John, 43, 48–49, 50, 52, 54, 55,
    56, 153n71
hunting
    clans as basis of parties for, 53–54
    game sought in, 28, 29, 44
    hunting territory, 39, 44
    in Kansas, methods of, 100
    by men living in agricultural
        settlements, 78
    missionaries' efforts to turn men
        from, 74
    rituals surrounding, 24, 25, 27, 71,
        127
    weapons used in, 28
    women's ritual participation in, 7, 25,
        127
    See also buffalo hunt; commercial
        hunting, by Osage

imperialism, Euro-American. See settler
    colonialism
imperialism, Indigenous, characteristics
    of, 4–6, 41
Indian Removal Act of 1830, 95